Just Load The Wagon Publishing
PO Box 2093
Kirkland, WA 98083

Cover photo courtesy of Melissa Gregg-Cabral.
All other photos from the Harvey family collection.

More information at www.AuthorTomHarvey.com.
Email the author at AuthorTomHarvey@gmail.com.

LIBRARY OF CONGRESS CATALOGING-IN-PUBLICATION DATA
has been applied for.

Library of Congress Control Number: 2010910509
Just Load The Wagon Publishing, Kirkland, WA

ISBN 10, paperback: 0-9828742-0-0
ISBN 13, paperback: 978-09828-7420-2
ISBN 13, e-format: 978-09828-7422-6

PRINTED IN THE UNITED STATES OF AMERICA
10 9 8 7 6 5 4 3 2 1 12 13 14 15

The year, 1985.

Singing the Monache High School alma mater . . . on helium . . . dressed in girls' cheerleading uniforms. Later that day, I was reprimanded by our Student Council advisor for being "disrespectful to the sacred institution that is our alma mater."

Gimme a break.

This book is dedicated to the guys who wore parachute pants and "Members Only" jackets and to those pretty girls who wore tight Jordache jeans and leg-warmers. You know who you are and it's OK to admit to your kids that you *were* cool back in the day.

Speaking of cool . . .

I bought my niece, Chloe, an AC/DC denim jacket with sequins and asked if she was "cool enough to wear it." She said she was *not* cool ("Constipated, Overweight, Out-Of-Style Loser") but that she was hoping her first boyfriend would be a real nerd ("Never Ending Radical Dude").

Despite the dramatic difference in semantics, I think Chloe *is* cool (per my definition) because she can sing the Scorpions' *Rock You Like A Hurricane* with as much enthusiasm as Justin Bieber's *One Less Lonely Girl*.

Not bad for a twelve-year-old.

The author proudly supports the Christopher and Dana Reeve Foundation, dedicated to curing spinal cord injury by funding innovative research and improving the quality of life for people living with paralysis through grants, information, and advocacy.

The Christopher and Dana Reeve Foundation is a registered 501©(3) nonprofit organization designated by the Internal Revenue Code. All contributions made to it are fully tax-deductible. Gifts may be sent to Reeve Foundation, 636 Morris Turnpike, Suite 3A, Short Hills, NJ 07078.

More information at christopherreeve.org.

In loving memory of . . .

My mother, Patricia Ann Harvey.

My uncle, Harold Jean Newton.

My friend, Odie Dewayne Miller.

My father-in-law, Jerry Watkins.

Dictionary.com defines "bitchen" as

—adjective *Slang*
marvelous; wonderful

That's too sterile.

"Bitchen" is like chicken stock—it can be used effectively in a variety of settings, such as:

"See you on the cruise tonight?"
"Bitchen."
Translation: Yes.

"I flunked my Algebra 2 quiz."
"Bitchen."
Translation: Bummer.

The first time I heard the word was in the sixth grade, circa 1980, in the form of a guy's name: Bob Bitchen.

It went something like this:
"Hey, how do you like my new bike?"
"Bob Bitchen, man!"

The word is a derivative of "bitch" and bitch, despite what the American Kennel Club says, is a "bad" word. As a twelve-year-old, I found it easier to use the word in mainstream conversation if it was a guy's name. Somewhere along the way we dropped the Bob part of it. An infinite improvement.

If you don't care for the word "bitchen," feel free to try out some other eighties words like "radical," "awesome," or "gnarly." I'm partial to "bitchen" so that's what I'm going with.

TABLE OF CONTENTS

PROLOGUE

I started this book in March 2010 with tears blurring my vision. The world felt solid again after spending three nearly-sleepless, bumpy nights on the Amtrak from Seattle to Raleigh, NC. A huge fan of the 1976 movie *Silver Streak*, I've always wanted to take the train across country. At least now I can say that I have.

Reeling from the deaths of my mother, my uncle, and my best friend in a thirteen month period, I gazed out of our cabin on Hyco Lake, NC. With ten days of solitude, the plan was to finish writing the life story of my recently departed friend, Odie. While reading what he and I had down on paper over a two year period, the familiar feeling of grief washed over me. The flashing cursor on the blank page of my laptop offered no comfort. I turned the stereo on, put my Ipod on shuffle, and went to the upstairs balcony with tears in my eyes. Another good cry was on the way.

And then . . .

Loverboy's *Turn Me Loose* filtered up to where I sat, followed by Men Without Hats' *Safety Dance*, followed by The Tubes' *She's a Beauty*. I was in 1980s shuffle heaven.

My mind raced.

Amidst the tears, I ran downstairs and resumed my place in front of the open laptop. My fingers flew across the keyboard. Eight hours and thirty single-spaced pages later, this book was born.

• • •

For me, there are sights, there are sounds, there are *smells* unique to the eighties. On a daily basis, something–a song, a movie, a random thought, walking through an airport duty-free store–takes me back to my teenage years.

Where have the decades gone?

Friends from high school are now parents–hell, some are *grandparents*.

Blink and ten years get behind you. Blink twice and it's twenty years. No one told me when to run. I missed the starting gun.

I look in the mirror and *sort of* recognize the guy staring back. He's put on twenty pounds, has a receding hairline that's picking up steam, his vision has degraded, and he can't get through the night without at least one trip to the bathroom. But just behind those middle-aged brown eyes is a glimmer–a spark–some days when I'm lucky, I can see that mischievous kid from the eighties staring back, if only for a second. God I love that guy.

• • •

For the majority of the decade, I was the *other* Harvey–the younger, less-perfect version of my brother, David. Following two years behind him in the same classrooms with the same teachers, I heard with alarming regularity, "Why aren't you more like your brother?" Every time those words were spoken, I silently vowed to find *more* ways to step outside his shadow.

David was a better student and I'm OK with that. I relished being the rebel, the class clown, the guy who had to be moved because he disrupted the girls around him.

In the absence of our father, he became more than just my older brother. In many ways, I looked up to him like a father. This allowed me to break out of my shy and conservative mold. He became the studious one so I didn't have to.

I wasn't a total screw-off, but I stopped to smell a lot more roses.

Drank a lot more beer.

Kissed a lot more girls.

Settled for a B instead of stretching for the A.

I entered my teens with a license to enjoy myself. It was a liberating realization at the time.

Before we go any further, I have the following disclaimer:

I would be doing a disservice not to acknowledge events that had a major impact on society during the decade. In terms of global events, Mount St. Helens blew her stack, the Berlin Wall fell, Chernobyl melted down, and a drunk asshole spilled millions of gallons of oil in Prince William Sound–the list goes on.

America endured Michael Milken's junk-bond fiasco, a disastrous Wall Street crash in 1987 where the Dow dropped nearly 23% in one day, the death of the Andy's (Kaufman and Warhol), and the rise of cocaine as the street drug of choice.

In professional football, the decade belonged to Joe Montana and the San Francisco 49ers with four Super Bowl wins (counting the pinnacle of the 1989 season played in January 1990).

In the NBA, it was Magic versus Bird with the Los Angeles Lakers taking five NBA titles; the Boston Celtics three. A kid from the University of North Carolina, Michael Jordan, redefined the term *super star* and enthralled us with his tongue-wagging super-aerial feats. Nike did well to latch onto him as his star rose.

In baseball, ailing Kirk Gibson's homerun in the 1988 World Series was the quintessential baseball moment of the decade–perhaps, of all-time.

In boxing, a young slab of solid steel named Mike Tyson pummeled anyone who dared stand in the ring opposite him–Tyson wasn't a boxer, he was an annihilator. He was also a biter but that came later.

I mention these events here, not to lessen their importance in anyway, but to say that you won't find them in the pages to come. This isn't a chronological history book, nor is it a book full of lists and trivia (though you'll get a smattering of both and a whole lot more).

This book is *my* experience growing up in, to borrow an album title from Motley Crue, the Decade of Decadence.

Dictionary.com defines decadence as 1) the act or process of falling into an inferior condition or state; deterioration; decay: 2) moral degeneration or decay; turpitude, 3) unrestrained or excessive self-indulgence.

Was it really a time of self-indulgence and *decay?* You're entitled to your own opinion.

Names–not all, but *many,* including girls and teachers–have been changed. However, everything in the book happened exactly as I remember it. I've not take any creative liberties to "liven" up the story. I've not blended fiction with fact.

According to recent US Census data (check it out at factfinder2.census.gov), over twenty three percent of the American population–nearly seventy million people–can claim at least one teenage year in the eighties decade. If you're a Generation Xer, I have one word: Congrats! I spent my entire teenage span within the decade and embrace this fact with pride.

Your comments are appreciated and you can email me at AuthorTomHarvey@ gmail.com.

Also, please visit AuthorTomHarvey.com and my Facebook community page at facebook.com/86kicks. As in, *"We've got spirit that really kicks 'cause we're the Class of '86!"*

Now, let's get on with some bitchen recollection.

INTRODUCTION

I came into the world black, blue, and yellow all over (jaundiced), on February 8, 1968. I'd like to thank my parents for their enthusiasm in May 1967 and the manufacturers of the defective spermicidal foam.

Mom always said I was a good swimmer.

• • •

As the seventies gave way to the eighties, I was just shy of my twelfth birthday and it's clear to me that my growing up years–if you define "growing up" via milestones like smoking your first joint, losing your virginity, and becoming a licensed driver (in that order)–did, indeed, occur in the decade.

Before we get nostalgic, let's take a peek at the adolescent years.

My mom, Patricia, God rest her soul, had four children. I am the youngest of the boys but not the youngest in the family: Lorne is the oldest; David follows two years behind him and I follow two years behind David. The lone girl, Tricia, is seven years younger than I am.

My brothers and I share the same father, God rest *his* soul, a blue-collar guy named Thomas C. Harvey, Jr. That marriage didn't last and, upon remarrying a guy named Metro, Mom and he conceived my little sister.

Metro is pronounced MEE-TRO–not the way Terri Nunn of Berlin sings it. Look at that, we're already into eighties references and I'm not even trying.

Mom always wanted a girl, so at least MEE-TRO got that one right. Behind his back, the stepsons called him "Meatball," but I guess there's no relevance to that. The guy was a real douche bag–as deadbeat ex-step-fathers go–but I'll spare you that digression.

Our stepdad was in the Coast Guard, so we did our share of relocating: Oakland, CA; Mystic, CT; Honolulu, HI. For our third move in less than four years, we had a choice between Oakland again and Honolulu. Meatball took a family poll and it was unanimous. Where the hell would *you* live given the choice?

The Harvey brothers in Hawaii:
David, Lorne, and the author

We arrived in Honolulu in 1976, the year after my sister was born. Meatball brought his son, Brian, to the mix so we had quite the family dynamic: three boys from one marriage, one boy from another marriage, and one new baby–a half-sister to all four boys. Brian had the unfortunate luck of being twenty days younger than me, and, hey, twenty days is twenty days. He was in fourth position on the totem pole as far as the Harvey brothers were concerned.

Note to self: Find Brian and apologize. Profusely.

Life in Hawaii was exotic and full of adventure. The military housing on Red Hill sat next to an extensive tract of undeveloped jungle. And Red Hill *was* (and is, for that matter) a hill. We lived on Kukui Drive, the last cul-de-sac at the bottom of a long and winding road. It was a great skateboarding hill, and I left massive amounts of skin and blood on the gravelly road–the speed-bumps were hell, let me tell you. If I wasn't actively bleeding from somewhere (knees, palms, elbows, big toe, forehead), I wasn't keeping up with the bro's.

Not three hundred yards from our house, beyond the chain-link fence (as if that was going to stop us) was a waterfall in dense jungle. Had Mom known how close to death we put ourselves in on a daily basis, she would have surely banished us from the forest. (And don't call me Shirley.) The waterfall was fifty feet wide with a hundred foot drop. We'd climb down the rocky perimeter to hold meetings in the concave.

Agenda items included who hated stuffed bell peppers the most (that would be me), a status update on cute girls at Moana Loa Intermediate School (Lorne's contribution), and what we thought would happen on the next episode of Himitsu Sentai Goranger (group discussion).[1] It was our own private paradise, complete with bright-red, foot long centipedes and brown-spotted, green geckos. When the water was calm, we gingerly walked on moss-covered rocks to the edge and peered over the precipice. One slip and it would have been one less kid in this year's ukulele recital. Seriously.

In an effort to keep us safe, we made a sacrificial offering to the jungle gods in the form of our mascot: a red, rusted tricycle named Kawasaki Junior. David launched Junior over the falls–the thing exploded upon impact–and I shed a tear at what we'd done. Oh, the guilt.

A few miles into the jungle, we discovered a vast, unfinished stretch of freeway. Known today as the western most section of the H-1 interstate highway, all we knew was that there were miles of white, unexplored concrete. Elevated a hundred feet above the jungle floor, the thing just abruptly ended, connecting to absolutely nothing. One crazy sailor two units over (his name was John and he looked just like Jerry Lee Lewis) found the entrance to the construction area. He'd borrow our ugly brown station wagon and all the neighborhood kids piled in for the biggest thrill of our young lives: driving the H-1. Yes, ladies and gentlemen, John drove a carload of kids to this abandoned stretch of freeway and turned us loose behind the wheel. It's a miracle no one plummeted that crappy old Ford right off the edge. Scratch half a dozen kids from the next ukulele recital.

In the cool, overgrown jungle, we also discovered bunkers. We're talking real-life, World War II anti-aircraft bunkers. Red Hill was well-fortified some thirty years ago. The abandoned bunkers were dark and damp. We explored the spooky web of underground tunnels with flashlights and listened to our voices reverberate into the dark unknown. It was scary and dangerous. We loved every minute of it.

In the evenings *we were* the Five Rangers, masquerading around in the dark, karate chopping each other and anyone unfortunate enough to be out walking. David was our ring-leader, the red guy (weapon: bullwhip). I was the blue guy in the number two position (weapon: crossbow). John Jr. (son of the crazy neighbor) was the yellow guy (weapon: staff). Maxine, our pretty blonde next door neighbor (the girl who *swore to God* she wasn't moving the planchette as it flew across the Ouija Board the moment she

---

1   Himitsu Sentai Goranger was a Japanese show with English sub-titles. It was a classic Good vs. Evil struggle between five superheroes and any number of preposterous villains from the Black Cross Army. We called them the Five Rangers. They morphed into the Power Rangers in the States.

touched it–she also cheated at Monopoly) was the pink girl (weapon: uh, see below).[2] Brian was the green guy (weapon: boomerang). Even in superhero fantasyland, poor Brian was relegated to last.

Our overactive imaginations were our only weapons.

Life in Hawaii wasn't dull: we were explorers, we idolized Japanese superheroes (especially the fourth Goranger), and we gobbled up treats unknown on the mainland: li hing mui, manapua, and rock salt plum. We drove abandoned stretches of unfinished Hawaiian freeway and hunted crayfish, centipedes and geckos. We swam with sharks and stingrays off Barbers Point (pre-*Jaws*, so, in our ignorance, we were fearless). We picked bananas from a tree in our backyard.

One Saturday morning, David arranged my marriage to the homeliest girl in the neighborhood. At high noon, there she stood on the small sidewalk in front of her four-plex. In her Coke bottle glasses and best muumuu (a nice floral pattern), she wore flowers in her hair and patiently waited for the groom-to-be. A dozen kids stood around waiting for something to happen–girls beamed, boys looked bored. *Tiny Bubbles* (the tune, not the soapy concoction) drifted out of her upstairs bedroom window. Her little brother wore a suit and held a Bible.

Quite the organizer, my brother.

We rode our bikes through the ceremony without so much as a backward glance. The jilted bride burst into tears as the boys cheered. Kids can be so damn cruel.

For a two story four-plex, the units were surprisingly spacious with four bedrooms and two and a half baths. Lorne and David had their own rooms, Brian and I shared a room, and Trish slept in a crib in the master bedroom. This worked out well enough except that I slept on the top bunk and one morning awoke on the cold linoleum floor. How a kid falls five feet and crashes to the floor without waking up is still a mystery to me–but it gave me an idea. Twenty minutes before it was time to get up for school, I climbed down the ladder careful not to wake my step-brother. Mom walked in, found me "asleep" on the floor, and checked for broken bones. Claiming *pain all over*, I stayed home from school. Unfortunately, this only worked a few times before Mother's Intuition kicked in and she was on to my scam. Why didn't I like Red Hill Elementary School? Two words: Gino Tolleto.

Gino was the bully of the second grade. Six inches taller than me–with the afro, twelve inches taller–and he did not like "howlies." For those unfamiliar with the

---

2   The fourth Goranger was the only female in the group. Her earrings were mini-grenades and she shot bullets from her molded breastplate nipples (you have to see it to believe it). How could an eight-year-old boy not love this woman?

Hawaiian caste system, a howlie is a non-Hawaiian-native. I think Gino was mulatto (not that I knew that word in 1976) because he was white and had an afro. I had enough sense not to question his heritage. Why piss him off further?

Gino picked on me constantly. He reveled in Kill Howlie Day, a supposed Hawaiian holiday where locals had a one day pass to beat the crap out of their non-native brethren. Not one to pass on tradition, Gino embraced *every day* as Kill Howlie Day. Lucky me.

He specialized in picking me up by the collar while pinning me against the wall–as my feet dangled six inches off the ground. This made the girls giggle. It didn't matter that I had an older brother that could've kicked Gino's ass. Gino claimed to have an older brother of his own.

So I endured the second grade and won the award for "Most Days Missed." I am not making this up. Everyone won something and that's the only thing they could come up with for me. I accepted the recognition with mixed feelings.

Third grade wasn't much different since the two grades were combined and taught concurrently by the same trio of teachers: Mrs. Carr, Mrs. Kanishiro, and Mrs. Matsuda. One day, Mrs. Matsuda sent me home with a progress note that read: "Tommy does have periods when he tends to become absentminded and I have tried many ways to help him overcome it. I have found that he is capable and that he can remember most things when he wants to."

Hmpf. Clearly *she* didn't have Gino picking *her* up by the collar.

I wasn't a shy kid–which may have partly explained Gino's hostility–and jumped at the chance to enter the school's 1977 talent show. Trouble was, I didn't have a talent so I created one.

Dressed in metallic purple pants, a shiny purple shirt, and a black fedora borrowed from a black neighbor, I lip-synced *Car Wash* by Rose Royce. David huffed and reminded me that "a chick sings that song." I was OK with it. A girl named Becky won with her rendition of *I'm Being Swallowed By A Boa Constrictor*. As she sang, she slowly lifted a green sleeping bag up her body. C'mon people, it was a sleeping bag!

The best thing to happen that year was my Cub Scout troupes' Pine Wood Derby. John, the crazy neighbor two doors down, helped me pour liquefied lead into three holes drilled into the little block of wood. The guy got the weight right (not enough and the car was too light, too much and the car would be disqualified) and I was shocked that my plain red car went undefeated. We have a silent 8mm movie of the trophy presentation where I practically fall down in surprise. David's car, carved into

5

a shark and painted gray, won Most Original. The red paint splattered all over its open mouth put him over the top. Poor Brian didn't win jack.

The marriage to Meatball didn't work out and a divorce in Hawaii, at least in 1977, was not something that happened overnight. So we were shipped out: Lorne to Washington State to live with our dad and David and I to our grandparents in Terra Bella, California. I'll never forget my carryon luggage for the flight from Honolulu to Los Angeles: a suitcase full of Richie Rich comic books. In the event of a plane crash, I was going down clutching my most prized possession.

Terra Bella lies in Central California, population 3,000 in 1977 (population Not Much More in 2012). Downtown consisted of a one-room library, a tiny post office, a Circle K convenience store, a row of boarded-up abandoned single story buildings, and a laundry mat. The day I ventured into the small library in search of Richie Rich comics, the blue-haired librarian just about hit the floor in ecstasy (either that or she was asleep in her chair). She gave me the rock star treatment–she had a bona fide customer! The library didn't have Richie Rich, so I read all the Boxcar Children books making me a repeat customer much to the delight of the bored old hoot.

Terra Bella, California 1978, in our church duds.
David with the thumbs up–he really did think he was the Fonz.

Grandma was an English teacher at Steve Garvey Junior High (they loved the Dodger so much that they named a school after him) in Lindsay, California, fifteen miles down the road. Her husband, our step-grandpa Adam, owned a junk yard. Surrounded by agriculture (oranges, olives, and pomegranates) and dirt, we led a frugal existence. For entertainment, we threw fruit at each other–the pomegranates were particularly effective in staining school clothes. Hey, we had to occupy ourselves someway and no longer had bunkers, and jungle, and a pink superhero who used her breasts as lethal weapons.

The most excitement revolved around the frequency in which the Circle K was robbed at gunpoint–nearly every Saturday night between 10 p.m. and 2 a.m. Our house was one street over from the main drag, and David and I used to sit in the dark watching the convenience store in anticipation. To get in on the action, we walked in one day and pointed our Colt .45 BB guns at the clerk. "Stick 'em up!" we said with a smile. Back then, toy guns weren't plastic and bright-orange like they are today. Our BB guns looked and felt like the real thing. It's a wonder we didn't get our faces blown off by the paranoid clerk or arrested for armed robbery.

Another form of entertainment was finding tiny body parts scattered in our yard. We lived on two large lots surrounded by a tall chain-link fence. We loved Grandpa's two guard dogs fiercely: John the black Greyhound ("undefeated on the track during his prime" Grandpa gushed), and Killer, the red Doberman. Killer was one bad hombre, too, since, as a puppy, he survived Grandma's meat cleaver to the tail and scissors to the ears. Pay a vet to do it? Not my Grandma. Without proper treatment, he scratched his ears so that they healed looking like two pieces of red cauliflower stuck on either side of his head. When he grinned on command for Grandpa, the poor dog looked like a reject from The Muppet Show.

No one came into our yard with these two brutes on twenty four hour patrol. No human, that is. On a regular basis, we found evidence that a cat had *tried* its luck running the gauntlet–the draw of the chicken coop too much for the damned–but you don't see that many two or three-legged cats so we assumed the rest went down the hatch. Occasionally, we found saliva-soaked kitty heads, much to our morbid fascination.

I spent the fourth and fifth grades at Terra Bella Elementary School. The coolest thing about that first year was being the youngest kid in the A band. (The school had a B band, comprised mostly of fifth and sixth graders still learning music.) There I was, in the A band *as a 4th grader* pounding away on the sole bass drum. I realize now that I got the job because I was the only kid willing to play the thing. David, a sixth grader,

7

not to be outdone by his little brother, picked up the French horn like he knew what he was doing and made the A band as well. We wore red and white polyester uniforms (white shoes and a white beret finished the look) at the annual band review in Selma. Mr. Vangsness, our clever bandleader, had his six-year-old daughter, Kirsten, pull the drum on a cart as I marched behind it. As the little girl labored in front of me, huffing and puffing in the 102 degree heat, we played the theme from *Rocky* and won absolutely nothing.[3]

My favorite girl (you can't have a girlfriend as a ten-year-old, can you?), a little blonde with a button nose and glasses named Pam, made Mrs. Ward's class bearable in the stifling heat. The poor girl got busted trying to pass a note one day and suffered the consequences.

Mrs. Ward: "Pam, if you're going to pass notes, why not share it with the entire class?" It was more of a command, not a question.

Pam stood up, unfolded the note, and mumbled under her breath.

Mrs. Ward: "Speak up Pam!"

Pam: "Thomas. Baby face."

The class erupted into chaos as Pam sat down in misery and I buried my face in my hands. Thank God the nickname didn't stick.

• • •

February 8, 1978 was a Wednesday–my tenth birthday. The phone rang at 9:30 p.m., but David and I were already in our bunk bed for the night. We were awake–talking about the birthday party invitations we'd pass out the next day. Since our birthdays are three days apart, the party was scheduled for Saturday the 11th, David's twelfth birthday. In hushed tones, we heard our grandparents on the phone. When they told us the news the next day, we didn't pass out the invitations. The party was cancelled.

• • •

When Mom joined us in the waning months of 1978–and it wasn't soon enough for this Mama's Boy–we spent another year under my grandparents roof.

---

3   Kirsten Vangsness sound familiar? Yep, she's the actress who plays the character of Penelope Garcia on the TV series "Criminal Minds."

Fifth grade passed uneventfully with the exception of the appearance of the new kid, Tracey. Dressed in plaid skirts with ribbons in her curled brown hair, Tracey made my heart beat a little faster in Mrs. Taylor's class. The girl had some serious mojo and came to school, everyday, looking like she was dressed for church. She also wore glasses which made her look really smart. As my classmates openly wept at Mrs. Taylor's reading of *Where The Red Fern Grows*, I tried to suck it up and look stoic for Tracey. It didn't work. I cried like a baby with everyone else. Visiting Tracey at her house had two distinct benefits: 1) fifth grade romance in the air (consisting of holding hands of the sweaty variety) and 2) her dad's Playboy centerfolds pinned-up all over the garage. Inspirational on both accounts.

I tired of the bass drum so tried the trombone, then the baritone, but failed on both accounts. Brass instruments took a lot more skill than banging a big drum and I lost my spot in the A band. Live and learn.

It was a simple existence.

Grandma lined us up with the migrant farm workers for free blocks of cheese ("welfare cheese" we called it—one block per person!) every time the County gave it away. We ate bread from the Day Old Wonderbread Store (only ten cents a loaf!), collected eggs from a heavily-fortified henhouse in the corner of the yard, and, occasionally, killed the chickens for dinner.

We watched Charlie's Angels, Fantasy Island, The Love Boat, The Dukes of Hazzard and my favorite, BJ & the Bear, on the thirteen-inch black-and-white TV setup in the corner of the kitchen.

We played Russian Rummy (the card game, not anything involving a loaded revolver) on Saturday nights and it was hell to pay during Sunday's white glove bedroom inspection if Grandma didn't win. Uh, I'm not kidding.

For Christmas that year we asked for a dirt bike (a Yamaha YZ80 to be exact). The adults sprung for a 50cc moped—the thing lasted a couple months before every spoke snapped from too many jumps on our homemade dirt track down the road.

Six people in the small three-bedroom, one-bath house wore on Mom so we moved six miles north to Porterville. With thirty thousand people, Porterville was ten times the size of Terra Bella—thank God for that.

It was mid-1979 and I was in the sixth grade.

That's how we ended up an hour and a half south of Fresno and an hour north of Bakersfield—not exactly the center of the cultural world, but I'm not complaining.

1980 Fun Fact #1:

Mattel releases the Intellivision video game console. Our video game addiction began with the likes of "Baseball," "Football," and "Night Stalker."

CHAPTER 1

Not quite 1980 but close.

We moved to Porterville the second week of the new school year making me, officially, the new kid in Mrs. Alexander's sixth grade class.

The girls took notice of my long hair and peach fuzz upper lip. (The picture to the right is the "school picture haircut" look.) Unfortunately, so did the guys. By the end of the *first day*, one guy–Ryan Bernasconi–decided I needed an ass kicking. Images of Gino rushed in my mind. Here we go again!

Kids are creative and Ryan was clever enough to enunciate my name Tom-Ass.

As in: "Your name is Tom-Ass, huh? Tom-Ass, whatta name! Is that what we call you, Tom-Ass?"

I countered: "Your last name is Bernasconi? What kind of dumb name is that? Sounds like cheap pasta to me, pal."

Our insults were mild by today's standards. Nobody's mother was brought into the discussion, but my retort was all Ryan needed.

"Meet me after school!" he growled.

A group of guys (and you know who you are Todd Bailey, Billy Pritchett, and Lenny Manson) stood around hoping for the best. I was still a stranger and junior high fist fights can be so much fun.

I replied flatly, "I take the bus after school."

And that's exactly what I did since, without a doubt, Ryan would have kicked my ass. He was bigger than me. Before I say another word, let me be clear that Ryan and I became good friends and after that initial week of posturing, I never had a problem with anyone at Burton Junior High.

Mom rented a three-bedroom, two-bath apartment on West Olive Avenue and the Wildwood Apartments became home for the next six years. David and I initially shared a room and, once again, I occupied the top bunk. Lorne stayed in Washington, so David became the de facto "man of the apartment."

I called Tracey that first week in the new digs with the intent of lamenting how our six mile distance felt like six hundred miles. I never got the chance. As soon as I said "Hi," David snatched the phone away and growled, "Put Tracey on the phone right now!" I grabbed the phone just in time to hear her dad snap, "I outta come over there and ring yer scrawny little neck! Don't you *ever* call back!"

Click.

As fast as that, images of a long distance relationship evaporated. I never saw Tracey again. *Thanks bro!*

Aside from squelching his little brother's love interest, one thing David and I had in common was a love of music. Our combination record player/8-track saw a lot of action. The baddest LP in our small collection was AC/DC's Highway To Hell. Just the name was cool since "hell" was (and is), technically, a cuss word and it felt rebellious just to say the album title out loud. Throw in the fact that the album cover displays Bon Scott wearing a pentagram necklace and Angus Young sporting horns and a spiked tail–all evil signs–and you've got yourself a real rebellion of an album cover. The music could have been total crap and we would have still bought it for the album cover alone.

One example of just how old we pre-teen AC/DC listeners have become, consider this: Alanis Morissette was *five years old* when Highway To Hell was released. Years later, she released the best-selling debut album by a female artist in the U.S. and the highest selling debut album worldwide. (Oh, yes, I'm a big fan.) I seriously doubt that little Alanis listened to these hard-rocking Aussies on her plastic pink record player as a five-year-old (but it's fun to imagine).

When we weren't listening to albums, we watched the coolest thing since Checkers and Pogo[4]: Home Box Office (HBO). In the beginning, God made HBO and it was *good*.

HBO in the eighties was quite a bit different from what it is today. For starters, there was only one channel. It had "Short and Special" featurettes in between movies. (Who can forget Hardware Wars? If you haven't seen it, you have to YouTube it. I

---

4   Another Hawaiian TV show where one lucky kid in the audience crammed his hand in a jar
     of pennies and got to keep what he pulled out. What would that have been, all of fifty cents?

mean it. If you haven't seen it, put this book down and go watch it. Now! I mean it.) "Short and Specials" were just that–usually a few minutes long and always entertaining. Sometimes they were cartoons just a few seconds long (*Godzilla vs. Bambi*– Bambi peacefully grazing, Godzilla's foot crashes down, The End) and sometimes they were funny skits with characters made of clay. One episode featured fans of Elvis Presley. My jaw hit the floor as a woman gushed on about a ring Elvis had given her–and the kid standing next to her was *me!* We had gone to an Elvis convention in San Jose a few months earlier–who would've known I'd end up on HBO?

Those early HBO movies really stuck with me too. *American Gigolo, Who Is Killing The Great Chefs of Europe?, A Little Romance, How To Beat The High Cost of Living*, and *Flash Gordon*. Young minds are impressionable, that much I know. After watching the Chuck Norris classic, *Good Guys Wear Black*, countless times, I became enamored with Porsches. Who can forget the black Porsche 911 with obnoxious whale tail? My love of the matte-black Porsche was forever cemented after watching the 1983 classic, *The Big Chill*, with my weed-smoking-friend, Don, at the Porter Theater.

HBO also had a show called *Not Necessarily The News*–a family favorite–even my little sister watched it, and she was only five. This show satired recent news of the day. The one scene I remember is the Pope stepping off a plane and kissing the ground. At just the right moment, the camera cuts to a close-up of the pontiff's hands while he slips a discarded cigar into his white sleeve. The Pope–the real one–stands up and waves to the crowd. It was preposterous and perfect.

With all the forms of entertainment these days–from the internet to video games to hundreds of TV channels–it's almost impossible to convey how special something as simple as HBO was.

When I told Ryan I took the bus after school, that was a true statement at the time. But it only took that first week at the new junior high to realize that I wasn't a bus person for the simple reason that I wasn't a morning person. I was more than willing to trade an extra half hour of sleep for riding my bike the mile and a half to school. It was also great exercise for the sport we soon discovered: bicycle motocross ("BMX").

As soon as I started riding my bike to school, I learned from a classmate, Martin Szoke, that he raced BMX in Ivanhoe, a small town thirty miles to the north. With directions in hand, we piled in our 1978 Chevy Monza–Mom, David, Trish, and I–and on one Sunday in the early part of 1980, drove out for a look.

Getting to the track in Ivanhoe was a trick because it was, literally, built in the middle of an orange grove. And there were thousands of acres of orange groves in the area. We did find the track and after watching that first race, we wanted in on the action.

The following Sunday, I signed up with the twelve-year-old novices; David, with the fourteen-year-old novices. Wearing blue jeans and my Burton flag football shirt, David in gold corduroys and a long-sleeve Yamaha shirt, we promptly got smoked.[5] Big time.

As the Sundays rolled by, we didn't get discouraged and, in a couple months, we were qualifying for our respective Main Events with equal consistency. Trophying, however, was a different matter since only the top three finishers received a trophy; fourth through sixth received a small ribbon; seventh and eighth received nothing. David earned the first ribbon (a pink one at that) and taped it, facing outward, to our small, living-room window. Kids walking by began to notice the growing number of pink, blue, and yellow ribbons accumulating on the glass.

In less than a year, our bikes underwent major modifications, and we ditched the jeans for actual racing uniforms: colorful polyester jerseys and nylon racing pants. We were on our way. Ribbons came down. Gold plastic trophies went up.

Life in Mrs. Alexander's class cruised along and my new friends realized that I was a serious student (either that or a royal kiss ass) after I couldn't stop giving book reports in front of the class. Everyone had to do one but I did half a dozen, (I specifically remember Clive Cussler's *Night Probe!*) much to Mrs. Alexander's delight.

1979 gave way to 1980 and February 20, 1980, will forever be a day to remember. Having just finished my homework at the kitchen table, I walked into the bedroom David and I shared. Mom's arm was draped around his shoulder and his eyes were red.

"Are you . . ."

I looked closer.

". . . *crying?*"

"No," he lied, "but Bon Scott is dead!"

He held out the Highway To Hell album as if to affirm this. I looked at the picture of Angus in shock.

He went on. "He died of alcohol poisoning yesterday. I just heard it on the radio." Mom left the room with a sigh, turning the comforting responsibility over to me, the little brother.

With that, I hopped up on the top bunk and gazed at the album cover as he played the entire record from start to finish.

---

5   I define "smoked" as getting our butts handed to us–as in, dead last.

I'm embarrassed to say that I mistakenly thought Bon was Angus Young since the guy in the middle of the picture is always the lead singer, right? Bon had to be the guy with the horns, pitch-fork tail, and sneer, right? Remember that we didn't have the internet information superhighway and MTV wasn't yet born so, for at least the next ten years, when I thought of Bon my mind's eye pictured Angus.[6]

One distraction from Bon's untimely death was the ongoing Winter Olympics and, specifically, the U.S. vs. Soviet Union hockey game. What happened on February 22, 1980, is now known as The Miracle on Ice.

What made it so miraculous?

The Soviets masqueraded as amateurs but, by all reasonable definitions, were professionals.

The American team consisted of college athletes since most of the professionals that played on American NHL teams were Canadian.

In the same matchup a few weeks earlier, the Soviets beat us 10-3.

The Soviets didn't know how to lose. They were the defending gold medalists for the last four Olympic games.

I wish I could say we watched the shocking upset live but that wouldn't be the truth. Most of the country heard the outcome on the radio then watched it on tape delay—which is what we did. Even though we *thought* we knew the outcome, it was nail biting to watch the Soviets take the early lead, then have the Americans tie it—back and forth three times in this manner. With exactly ten minutes left in the third period, Team USA took the lead for good, 4-3.

The last ten minutes were amazing. The Soviets went on a tear, firing up shot after shot after shot. Even though we were *pretty sure* the news accounts were accurate, every one of the Soviet near misses built up the intensity. Every save by our goalie, incredible. Even on tape delay, the game was electric for a couple of Central California kids who didn't know the difference between a hockey stick and a pogo stick.

What is sometimes overlooked is that The Miracle On Ice wasn't even the gold-medal game. Team USA went on to defeat Finland a few days later in another come-from-behind victory to claim the gold.

Hockey, at least for a few days, took our minds off of Bon Scott. Miracle or not, though, Bon Scott was just as dead after the game as he was before it. As we mourned

---

6   MTV's first broadcast was August 1, 1981.

the loss and wondered if he was *literally* burning in hell thanks to Highway To Hell, (no stop signs or speed limit, damn!) another album spent time under the needle, the self-titled-debut, Loverboy. Released in the summer of 1980, the band from Calgary quickly became one of our all-time favorites.

It wasn't all AC/DC and Loverboy on the music scene that year. We enjoyed live music in the sixth grade courtesy of Mr. Matsuda and his acoustic guitar.

Mr. Matsuda was a small Asian guy with thick glasses and a thick Asian accent. A couple of times a year, he'd sit on a stool in front of the class and take requests–just him and his beat-up guitar. This was officially considered "music class."

A few girls closest to him quietly sang under their breath out of empathy and unfortunate proximity. Most of us either rolled our eyes or outright laughed at him. Being a back-of-the-class dweller, I was guilty of both. I do give Mr. Matsuda credit for busting out my two favorites, *Greensleeves* and *Streets of Laredo*. One time, after my usual request, he turned to the class in exasperation. "Does *anyone* have any other request than *Greensleeves*?" No one did.

It was about this time that Pac-Man made its appearance in the local Pizza Hut. The first time I saw the upright video game, a dozen excited kids surrounded it. Though we didn't know it at the time, Pac-Man would become a cultural phenom and spawned a whole line of related video games, merchandise, and even a hit song (who can forget *Pac-Man Fever*?). No one played it like my friend, Arthur Cowley. Every time I'd drop into Pizza Hut–not for the pizza, for the game–he was in the far corner twisting and jerking the joystick enthusiastically. Wonka, wonka, wonka, wonka . . .

The location of the game was advantageous–as far away from the entrance/cash register/salad bar as possible. I suppose the management thought keeping the rowdy kids away from the eating patrons was a good thing–and it was a good thing, *for the Pac-Man players*. Arthur had the touch when it came to playing the game *for free*. He knew just where to smack it with his open palm to register a credit. With a lookout or two, he'd rack up ten to twenty credits in a rapid-fire exchange between his palm and the sensor inside the game. I smacked it once and scrambled the circuitry causing it to reset–losing all the credits in the process. The manager figured something was up when he went to unload the treasure chest full of quarters–after hours and hours of dedicated playtime–only to find a few dollars worth. They eventually caught Arthur red palmed and red faced and threw us out.

Banned from Pizza Hut. Does it get any worse than that?

Pac-Man was the beginning of our video game craze and we spent countless hours–and quarters–playing Donkey Kong, Dig Dug, Robotron, and Defender. Some of my favorites were the lesser-known Scramble, Kangaroo, Popeye, and Make Trax (a Pac-Man knock-off). God bless Mom for feeding the cookie jar with money—our only source of revenue—as there were always a few bucks to feed the video game addiction.

Speaking of video games, David spent twelve hours playing Asteriods one day much to the chagrin of the local Mini-Mart owner. Twelve hours on one quarter didn't even cover the electricity to run the game. For every ten thousand in points, my brother earned an extra spaceship and had them stretched all the way across the top of the black and white screen. I stood in during his quick bathroom breaks (through the stock room, past the cases of cheap vodka, first door on the left). He'd hurry back to a few less spaceships and, wired on microwave burritos and thirty-two oz. sodas, resume the monotonous assault against asteroids and agitated alien spacecraft. They kicked us out at midnight.

• • •

Burton was both an elementary and a junior high school. Kindergarten through fifth grade sat on one corner of the large square lot, sixth through eighth on the other; the playgrounds separated by a four-foot white picket fence. One day at recess, just after losing at Four-Square (I was good, but not as good as Chris Moore or "Paulie" Moreno—they both cheated), I noticed a group of kids waving from the other side of the fence. Looking closer, it was my sister and all her girlfriends. I walked over and chatted with her, bringing giggles from all the little girls peering up through the fence. The image of Trish's shining face and short blonde hair still makes me smile.

I didn't graduate out of the sixth grade—there wasn't a ceremony like some schools have—but I do remember the last day of school. As David and I walked past the junior high lockers, I spread out my arms, pressed my face against one, and hugged a row of them. "Next year, one of you will be mine."

David replied, "Uh, those are the girls' lockers, dummy."

17

1980 Fun Fact #2:

"Star Wars Episode V: The Empire Strikes Back" is released in theaters. Darth Vader is one bad dude.

CHAPTER 2

THE SUMMER OF 1980

Our step grandpa owned a junkyard in Lindsay. I'm not sure if junkyard is politically correct nowadays, but that's what it was: a big automobile graveyard. In his small, non-air-conditioned grungy office, he wheeled and dealed with the best of them. In the summer of 1980, he announced a road trip in his newest prized-possession: a worn-out, orange and lime green Winnebago. I don't know what he traded for it, but I bet it wasn't much.

Destination: Walla Walla, Washington. The adults had some making up to do with the brothers.

The reason that we didn't have a birthday party in 1978 was because our dad died on the night of my tenth birthday. That mysterious call was *the news* delivered by our brother, Lorne.

Dad was a rough-and-tumble guy who lived in his small hometown in southeastern Washington State. He was an auto mechanic, a welder, a roadpaver–a bluecollar jack-of-all trades, really. He was also an outdoorsman and loved to hunt. To give you an idea how badass Dad was, he and his younger brother, Bart, killed a bear during one trip into the woods. No big deal? They got lost and had to sleep *inside the warm, bloody bear carcass* to keep from freezing overnight. If that's not badass, I don't know what is. The next day they walked out of the forest with a story for the ages.

He drowned the sorrows of his unhappy second marriage at The Green Lantern over cold Olympia and shots of Crown Royal. This only made home life worse.

On the night of February 8, 1978, he came home from the bar and an argument ensued with our stepmother. Behind the closed door of their bedroom, the shouting abruptly ended when his .357 magnum revolver went off with a deafening explosion. Lorne scrambled in to find Dad on the floor with a single gunshot wound to the chest. The bullet ripped through his heart and, despite a herculean effort by a local ER physician (who, ten minutes after the injury, fearlessly ripped open Dad's chest, jammed his finger in the hole, and manually squeezed his failing heart), the damage was done.[7]

Thomas C. Harvey, Jr., dead at 34. Cause of death: accidental gunshot wound.

For years, the demons whispered that his death was *my* fault. *They argued because he was out celebrating your birthday. You're his namesake. It's your fault he's dead.*

Which brings us back to the summer of 1980 and the reason for our trip to Walla Walla—David and I never got the chance to say goodbye.

Grandpa loaded up the small RV and away we went—Grandpa, Grandma, Mom, David, Trish, and me. A thousand miles down the road lay our destination.

The clunky RV was not much more than a box on wheels. It didn't have a bed. It didn't have a bathroom. It didn't have air conditioning. It was loud and reeked of gas fumes and dried sweat. Grandpa loved it.

He had a favorite saying: "We were so poor we didn't have a pot to piss in or a place to throw it!" He lived through the whole Oklahoma Dust Bowl thing, and, after reading *The Grapes of Wrath*, I sort of understood his meaning.

Not to be delayed with the biological mechanics of five human bladders operating on different clocks, he brought a pot when nature called. You could say he wasn't as poor as he used to be.

Not an hour into the trip, Grandma announced she was going to use the pot—*"eyes forward!"*—and we plugged our ears to block out the sound of spattering urine not ten feet behind us. We had nothing to drown out the noise—Mom couldn't afford to buy us a first generation Walkman cassette player and the RV didn't have a radio. David and I exchanged looks of disgust while Mom patted us on the back in good cheer. We were stuck in RV Hell and she knew it.

When Grandma's deed was done, I pondered the important questions.

How do we keep the pot from spilling?

Is that the same pot we cook spaghetti in?

How many bladders could the pot hold?

Anyone have asparagus in the last 24 hours? (All right, I didn't think that as a twelve-year-old, but I'd think it now.)

My five-year-old sister could probably get by with a styrofoam cup.

---

7   I obtained the ER records when I was in my early twenties. They are impressive and tragic to read.

These thoughts raced through my mind as Grandma settled back into the passenger seat, pot-in-question firmly fixed in her hands.

David and I sat at the small dinette table staring at each other glumly.

Without warning, Grandma gave the pot a quick jerk out the open window thereby ejecting the contents into the great-wide-open. Repulsed, I whispered to David, "I guess we've got a pot to piss in." Without hesitation, he replied "and a place to throw it." A light blue Datsun B210 passed us on the right, windshield wipers at full-speed even though there wasn't a cloud in the sky.

When we finally arrived in Walla Walla, it was the only time I saw both of my grandmothers in the same room. No one seemed anxious to visit the cemetery and this confused me. Wasn't that the purpose of the trip?

"Aren't we going to the cemetery?" I asked Mom.

"We'll go," she said quietly.

For three days I asked this question. By the time we drove into Mountain View Cemetery, I was excited. Finally!

Cypress 33.

When I think of my dad, I think of Cypress 33. His grave is located at the intersection of Lilac and Cypress–third row from the intersection, third marker to the right.

Cypress 33.

We piled out of the RV and made the short walk.

All the excitement and anticipation vanished as I approached the marker for the first time. There, on the ground, was *my* name–not once, but twice. Two Thomas Harveys, father and son, dead at 44 and 34, lung cancer and trauma, respectively.

No one said a word. Birds chirped in a far off galaxy.

The word I attribute to that moment is *permanence.*

Mom stood between her two youngest sons, her hands firmly clasped around our shoulders. Tears dropped from her eyes onto the dirty brass marker.

I fought back the urge to vomit.

This wasn't *fun.* Dad was never coming back. He wasn't gone on a trip. He wasn't going to surprise us with a knock at the door. He was contained in a box six feet below my feet. This was . . . *permanent.*

David knelt down and pulled away grass that had grown over the edges of the concrete perimeter, wiping away tears with the back of his hands as he worked. When he was done, he stood up and drew in a long breath. With red eyes, he turned to Mom and asked, "Do you have a new penny?"

It was an odd question.

"Probably. Why?"

"I'd like to leave a 1980 penny to remind us of the year we were here."

She produced one and, after carefully wedging the shiny coin in the ground, David turned and walked back to the RV in silence. Mom followed.

But I wasn't ready to go.

I looked at the freshly-pulled grass and the shiny drops of tears dotting the marker.

I thought the tears would come. They didn't.

What came instead was anger.

My eyes went back and forth across the letters and numbers on the ground.

This was all wrong.

Dads weren't supposed to be gone forever. Dads were supposed to be around when twelve-year-old boys needed them.

What was *wrong* with him? *Why* did he leave?

A breeze rustled through the trees. Birds chirped but this wasn't a happy place. My hands clenched into fists so tight my fingernails drew blood. I felt like pounding my fists on the marker. I wanted to scream, *Why? Why did you leave us? This is all wrong!*

Dad was so close.

No, my demons whispered, *Dad isn't here. Dad is gone. Dad left in a fit of rage and confusion and frustration. You'll never, ever see him again. And guess what, Sport? It's . . . all . . . your . . . fault.*

I was dizzy.

Confused.

Angry.

Sad.

Empty.

Mom's hand gently found my shoulder.

"Let's go, baby," she whispered.

We turned and walked back to the RV as tears streamed down my face.

It took until my mid-twenties to fight the voices in my brain: *It wasn't my fault. His emotion–his temper–got the best of him. No one was to blame but himself.*

• • •

Back in Porterville, David burst through the front door holding the album in front of him. His eyes were wide with excitement and sweat dripped off his face.

"What's that?" I asked.

"It's the new AC/DC album. It just came out today!"

"You rode your bike all the way to Midnite Records and back for some lame recording without Bon Scott?" I scoffed. "No Bon Scott, no AC/DC."

"There was a line out the door for this," he countered. "I got the last one!"

Not one to totally blow off my brother who had gone to the trouble of a four-mile trek in the sweltering heat of that July evening, I followed him to our room where he put needle to record.

Bong.

Bong.

Bong.

Bong.

The intro to *Hells Bells* played and for the next forty-three minutes, time stood still—the only interruption when he flipped the record over after the first five songs.

We looked at each other in amazement.

"No Bon Scott, no AC/DC, huh?" David grinned.

"Play the first song again! The one with the bell!"

Never has there been a purer moment of appreciation for something initially regarded with such skepticism.

After playing the album for the second time through, David gushed, "This album kicks ass!"

Even at twelve, I got it. The album was both a tribute to Bon and a take-no-prisoners introduction of new lead singer, Brian Johnson. There was no way of knowing at the time that Back In Black would become the second highest selling album of all time, second only to Michael Jackson's not-yet-released Thriller. All we knew was that AC/DC didn't miss a beat after the sudden death of Bon Scott and we loved the band *with and without* Bon.

Nowadays, you're likely to hear the trademark gonging of *Hells Bells* at major sporting events. It's become an institution alongside Ozzy Osbourne's *Crazy Train* and Queen's *We Are The Champions*. Every time I hear the bells while watching Monday Night Football (usually to start the third quarter), I instinctively jump up, point to the TV, and exclaim to my wife, "Listen! AC/DC in the house! An eighties *classic!*" She humors me.

"Raiders of the Lost Ark" is the top grossing film of the year, raking in over $384 million at the box office. Oh, and some guy named Tom Cruise makes his big screen debut in "Endless Love" and "Taps."

CHAPTER 3

Unlike the sixth grade, where Mrs. Alexander taught every subject in the same classroom, seventh grade meant a homeroom, multiple teachers, multiple classrooms, and lockers. Most of us turned thirteen in the seventh grade, meaning we were, by definition, *teen*agers.

Paul "Skip" Sonksen was my homeroom teacher and my first male teacher (not counting the guitar-toter from the previous year). He was a likable guy, always smiling and interested in his students. His bushy moustache and glasses later reminded me of Richard Dreyfuss' character in the 1995 drama *Mr. Holland's Opus*.

I tried out for basketball and made the B team. We didn't practice much, but I remember a few games. Our coach, social science teacher, Bruce Lankford, would throw us our "uniform" after school–a frayed, no-longer-white, yellowing tanktop with a B on the front and a number on the back. I played with the jeans I wore to school that day, complete with Goody-brand plastic comb in the back pocket. (Hey, you gotta look good for the ladies at *all* times.)

I sucked at basketball–I know it now and I knew it then–and the guys only passed me the ball when they absolutely had to. We had five offensive and five defensive formations. Coach Lankford would yell out a number, "Four! Four! Four!" and,

25

more times than not, I'd stand there confused while my teammates scrambled into position.

One cold afternoon, we traveled to Pioneer Junior High–a milestone, traveling across town to another school for a sanctioned sporting event. Getting on and off a bus *in uniform–parents take note, these are big moments in your kids' lives.*

As I brought the ball down court, a defender rushed me at the top of the key. I turned my back and head-faked to the left. The kid jumped back. I head-faked to the right. The kid jumped back again. *Hell, I'm a player*, I thought. Then I realized that it wasn't my athletic prowess at work, it was my runny nose. With each head-fake, a long string of clear, warm snot flew to the left, then to the right. I turned and fired off an uncontested shot.

Woosh.

Nothing but air.

I did make a basket one time, though it was a different game. I put up the shot. *Swish!* I was so busy celebrating at our basket that the other team inbounded the ball, ran down the court, and made an easy layup. Coach Lankford threw up his hands and yelled, "It's called *defense!* You should try it sometime, Tom!"

I wasn't cut out to be a basketball player so I tried something else: Drama.

Drama is one of those polarizing things–kids either get it or they don't. I took a lot of flak for being in drama, but my fellow thespians–David Fine, Todd Bailey, Stacy Roberts, Shelley Furr, Gina Pitigliano, Josh Byrd, and Anthony Gibson–were cool in their own right, so it equaled out. We were our own little support group.

Ms. Jane Smith was our drama teacher.

Ms.

Jane.

Smith.

Not Mrs.

Not Miss.

Ms.

Pronounced "*Miz.*"

Ms. Smith decided that we'd do James Brock's *The Prince Who Wouldn't Talk* and cast me in the title role. Despite the title, the prince had a lot to say, and I struggled trying to memorize the lengthy script.

As costumes were made (a green tunic, green felt hat, and white pants for me) and props prepared (my horse had a cardboard head, stick body, and yarn tail), I announced I wasn't ready. The play would have to be postponed.

"Well, you better get ready! The play's a week away!" Ms. Smith snapped.

The big day came and I was terrified.

Looking out at a couple of hundred faces, my sister one of them, teachers standing up and down the aisles, it could have easily been a crowd of ten thousand.

I had the first twenty minutes of the play down pretty good, but after that required massive intervention. David Fine, the narrator (lucky freaking guy) sat on a stool, on-stage, with the entire script in front of him. He didn't have to memorize a damn thing! As the rest of us struggled with our lines—with long, excruciating pauses—David whispered the dialogue to the person closest to him, that person whispered it to the next person, and so on. We must have looked pathetic. No, *we were pathetic*.

As we struggled along, Ms. Smith stood off to the side, hands wringed together, white knuckles gleaming. All she could offer was moral support: the exaggerated head nod, the plastered-on smile. She was a bit quirky—she never wore make-up, she was pale and thin and her shoulder-length brown hair was never curled—in a word, she was plain. Some kids called her Plain Jane. Plain or not, I didn't want to let her down. I didn't want to embarrass her. The jury's still out on that one.

There's a point in the play where I ask: "What did it look like?"

The response: "A tail."

Then I say, excitedly, "A tail?"

The prince is looking to slay a dragon, but there are no dragons around, so the townsfolk make a fake dragon's tail which makes its appearance in several scenes. (This is the interactive part of the play, at least with the elementary school kids, where 200 squealed in unison, *"There it is! There it is!"* Naturally, the prince is oblivious—hey, oblivious I had down pat.)

We were beyond the "tail" scene by ten minutes when I blurted out:

"What did it look like?"

Response: "A tail!"

We circled back to that scene and performed everything from that point forward not once, but *twice*. As it unfolded in front of us, in real time onstage, we knew it was wrong. I looked at my classmates with wide eyes. They looked back not knowing how far along the path we should go. The inflection in our voices turned monotone. No one knew how to put us back on course. Do we improvise?

Sweat poured down my face. I felt like I was on fire. I glanced down at Ms. Smith and she kept nodding that exaggerated nod. She mouthed, *"Keep going!"*

If hell exists, my version of it would be stuck in this moment—on stage, completely lost, making a fool of myself and dragging my classmates into the fire with me.

Despite the rough debut, we were instant celebrities with the elementary school kids. We took a two week break to *learn the damn lines* for the junior-high presentation.

Drama is cool, don't let anyone convince you otherwise. Thanks to *The Prince Who Wouldn't Talk*, I found a girlfriend. Better said, she found me.

After our second performance, an eighth grader named Patty asked me if I had a girlfriend. She did it right in front of a bunch of kids during recess. It was a bold question and, suddenly, everyone within earshot stopped talking. All eyes turned to me.

"Well, no," I said.

"Good," she smiled, nodded, turned, and walked off.

All I could think was, *Wow, an older woman*.

Our relationship–if you can call it that–only existed within the confines of the school grounds. We hung out during recess. We met up at a school dance and danced to all the slow Air Supply songs. (They were all slow, weren't they?) She was a pretty brunette, but my interest in her was lukewarm at best–to this day, I'm not sure why.

Our romance peaked and suffered the deathblow at the same moment. Patty, impatient with my lack of action, took the initiative after school one day. I pushed my bike as we walked together. At the far corner we said our goodbye, so she knew her limited window of opportunity.

It happened fast.

She pivoted in front of me and went in with her eyes closed.

It was very . . .

Wet.

I wiped my mouth with the back of my hand.

There are a lot of defining moments in a guy's life and having a girl jam her tongue in your mouth for the first time ranks right up there.

We continued our walk in awkward silence. I couldn't wait to jump on my bike and pedal home to report the news to David–the whole thing was weird.

I don't remember the actual break-up–not that there really was one–but it was clear that our love was on the rocks. Ain't no big surprise.

• • •

On December 8, 1980, the Patriots and Dolphins were bashing each other on Monday Night Football.

Mom was in the kitchen.

A message, in ticker-tape form, scrolled across the bottom of the screen.

"Who's John Lennon?" I yelled.

She yelled back, "One of the Beatles. You know, (she began singing) *'she loves you, yeah, yeah, yeah . . .'*"

"He's just been shot dead according to Monday Night Football."

"*. . . she loves you . . .*"

Her singing stopped.

She walked out of the kitchen in disbelief staring at the TV. The dishtowel in her hand dropped to the floor.

• • •

On Monday, March 30, 1981, I stayed home from school after suffering a sunburn from a weekend Walk-A-Thon. As I sat in front of our 19" TV–HBO wouldn't be on until noon–President Reagan walked out of the DC Hilton. He waved. He smiled. He exuded confidence.

Pop! Pop! Pop! Pop! Pop!

Chaos erupted on live TV.

The world soon learned that John Hinkley wasn't a very good shot. The bullet that hit the president ricocheted off the presidential limo; the bullet that did the most damage hit Press Secretary James Brady in the head. I fretted in silence throughout the day since I was the only one home. By the time school was out and Mom was home from work, it was apparent the president was going to make it. James Brady, on the other hand, was dead–at least according to the initial news reports. Turns out that Mr. Brady *wasn't* dead, but he was in dire straits. I went to bed that night praying for Mr. Brady (prior to that I'd only prayed for myself and my family)–no one thought he'd survive the night. He survived but was permanently paralyzed.

As a result of Hinkley's brazen attack, handgun control became a major political agenda item and one only need look at our wheelchair-bound Press Secretary to see the ravaging effect a handgun could have in the hands of a lunatic. The Brady Bill, requiring federal background checks for handgun purchasers, eventually became law.

It's shocking that the leader of the free world damn near died according to Del Quentin Wilber's brilliant account of that day (*Rawhide Down: The Near Assassination of Ronald Reagan*). How little we knew at the time.

President Reagan gained a cool nickname–the "Teflon President"–and enjoyed an unprecedented level of popularity from adoring Democrats and Republicans, alike.

• • •

A coworker of Mom's at Montgomery Ward (she worked there part-time while going to nursing school at Porterville Junior College), a thin guy with a huge red beard named Don, offered to take us to our first BMX National. David and I loaded up his van and we drove two and a half hours south to Northridge, home to a sprawling track called Devonshire Downs. It was on Devonshire Boulevard, hence the name.

We camped at the track, along with hundreds of other kids, anticipating the crack of dawn and two full days of racing. That night I said to Don, "Hey, you should buy us some beer!"

Don, a likable guy in his twenties with the hots for our thirty seven-year-old mother, looked at me skeptically. "You sure you want to do that since you're racing tomorrow?" He would have done it, for sure.

David answered, "Not a good idea."

That was that.

Forty-eight thirteen-year-old novices made up my class. The task at hand was to whittle that down to eight for the Main. This was accomplished via motos, semis, and heats with six gates worth of competitors–and that was *just* the thirteen-year-old novices. To my surprise, I advanced through each round easily.

David, on the other hand, raced the fifteen-year-old *experts* and had his hands full with kids that were factory-sponsored. That is, kids who were members of organized racing teams from major manufacturers such as SE Racing, GT, Redline, Schwinn, and Diamond Back. These kids traveled all over the country nearly every weekend, racing at all the big events. In David's age group, Diamond Back-sponsored "Pistol Pete" Loncarevich, was virtually unbeatable along with Robinson-sponsored Gary Ellis. David needed a moto win to advance and finished second all three times. While disappointed, we agreed his showing was impressive (beating future hall-of-famer Gary Ellis two out of three races).

We were too excited to sleep on Saturday. Sunday rolled around and the thirteen-novice main approached. I was exhausted, mentally and physically, before the day began.

Picking poker chips out of a coffee can to determine gate position, my heart sank when I pulled the number one. The track swept around to the right meaning all seven guys would be to my left. It would take a monster holeshot to have a chance at leading the pack through the banked first turn.

My body trembled as the demons awoke. *You're the only racer not wearing an expensive full face helmet. Your Redline outfit doesn't match your PK Ripper bike. You don't belong here, dummy.*

I looked over my left shoulder and studied Diamond-Back-sponsored twelve expert Doug Davis. He was relaxed and smiling. A picture of total confidence. His silver and black uniform matched his gleaming chrome bike. *What a stud. He knows he's going to win. There isn't a doubt in his mind.* (He actually took third that day.)

My heart pounded.

Relax, you can do this. We've come this far.

The starting cadence began: *Riders ready!*

Balanced on my pedals, the seconds ticked off in super-slow-motion.

Boom, boom, boom. The sound of my heartbeat, deafening in my head.

I shifted my weight back then forward. *Bam!* My front wheel hit the gate. The gate dropped a split-second later and seven guys lurched forward as I stood with my feet on the ground.

A second passed.

My mind screamed, *You are blowing it! Get on your pedals you idiot!* I gave chase down the thirty yard sloped straightaway.

And then the funniest thing happened.

Like falling dominoes, five riders vying for the inside line came together and crashed in front of me. I swerved to the inside narrowly avoiding the bodies and bikes on the ground. Time slowed to a standstill in my mind.

The two racers out of gates seven and eight flew by on the outside and I shot straight up into the banked turn behind them. They had the momentum and stretched out into the lead, a two-man race for the win. I pedaled with all my might, the adrenalin surging through my body, my mind yelling, *You're in third place! Your name's going to be in Bicycle Motocross magazine! Don't crash now! Don't get passed!*

I pedaled around the winding track with no one within forty yards of me. Crossing the finish-line, I skidded to a stop earning the third place trophy–at three feet tall, the tallest one I'd ever received.

Later that night, Mom couldn't believe it. Don got a kiss on the cheek for all his trouble.

1981 Fun Fact #2:

The first, and only, stainless steel car, the DeLorean DMC-12, rolls off the production line. Four years later, it became Marty McFly's time machine in the hit movie, "Back to the Future."

CHAPTER 4

My brother, Lorne, graduated from Walla Walla High School in 1981. Unfortunately for Mom, she was the only licensed driver (David was fifteen, I was thirteen, and Trish was six) but that didn't discourage her.

In early June, we hit the road in our 1978 two-door brown Chevy Monza. A few years earlier, the salesman *assured us* the Monza would replace the Camaro in popularity and style. He also said the 8-track would never be replaced with the cassette tape and we believed him.

After a few hours on the road, our music selection wore thin: the only two 8-tracks we owned were Elvis Today and Elton John's Greatest Hits Volume II. There's only so much *Philadelphia Freedom* and *Levon* a kid can take. Even Elvis gets old after awhile, if you can believe that.

After twelve hours on the road (with six to go), Mom said things like, "Keep talking to me!" and "Tell me another story!" Despite the insistence from the fifteen-year-old that he was more than capable of driving (he was, after all, just two months from his learner's permit), Mom pressed on, her small five-foot, two-inch, 105-pound frame hunched behind the wheel.

All I remember of that trip was one graduate's contribution to the ceremony. Dressed in his royal blue cap and gown, the guy plugged an electric guitar into an amplifier and started strumming.

Then he started jamming.

David and I looked at each other, the tune familiar.

"That's . . ." I started to say.

"*Eruption* by Van Halen!" David finished.

Sure enough, the Wa-High graduating class of 1981 had a guy that learned the guitar solo from Van Halen's self-titled, debut album. And he nailed it. (I learned just recently that the guy's name is Dane Rinehart and he still busts out *Eruption* upon request! Dane . . . now there's a cool name!)

I thought, *High school is going to be cool.*

We left a shiny new penny at Dad's grave.

• • •

A few weeks later, Mom beamed, "I found you two a job!"

"Swell! Doing what?" I asked.

"Working on a farm. You start tomorrow!"

"Cool! What time?" David asked.

"6 a.m."

It was all downhill from there.

At the butt-crack of dawn, Mom delivered the mostly-asleep, reluctant day laborers that were the Harvey brothers to a farm outside of town. We were tired, cold, and hungry–not the best way to make a first impression.

The first thing the farmer had us do was plug all the gopher holes dotting his manicured fields of orange tree saplings. He thrust a heavy shovel in my hand and pointed off in the distance. "Over there!"

"I don't . . . (yawn) . . . see any holes."

"When I irrigate the field, you'll see the holes when the water pours down the hole."

Yawn. "What if I see a gopher?"

"Kill the little bastard!"

"Kill it with what?"

"Kill it with your shovel!"

David and I plugged holes as the sun steadily rose.

A few hours into this first task while watching a stream of water pour into a hole, out popped the live incarnation of everyone's favorite *Caddyshack* character. The gopher shook a blob of mud off its furry head looking surprised and pissed-off at the same time (if I can be so bold as to interpret a gopher's expression). I smiled down at it apologetically. *How cute!* It scampered off. The farmer, standing two rows over from me, witnessed the whole thing. He let out a large gasp and threw his shovel at the rodent.

"Why didn't you smash that little sumbitch?"

"Oh, is *that* what a gopher looks like? I'll get him next time for sure."

The farmer huffed off.

It went from freezing cold to blazing heat in the course of six hours. At high noon, the farmer's wife brought out sandwiches and iced tea.

"I guess we should talk about money, huh?" the farmer asked.

I looked at my older brother hoping to deflect the negotiation. He looked back, expressionless, careful not to make eye contact with the farmer. *Thanks bro!* Meanwhile, the farmer's steely gaze never left my face.

"OK," I said slowly, "how much do you pay?"

"How much do you want?"

I looked at David again. *Absolutely no help coming from the fifteen-year-old.*

"How about five dollars an hour?" I asked meekly. It was worth a shot. (Note this was well above the minimum wage at the time.)

The farmer studied me for a long time—ten seconds that felt like ten minutes—before finally saying, "OK."

David broke into a grin. *Freaking, no-help-brother!*

After lunch, the farmer had a different job for us.

"See that?" he asked, pointing to a massive, twenty-foot pile next to a large aluminum building.

"Yeah."

"Follow me."

He pulled back the building's sliding door to reveal thousands of baby chickens that began chirping in unison.

"You guys need to spread this pile of feed across the entire floor of this chicken house in an equal distribution," he said over the drone of cheep-cheep-cheep-chirp-chirp-chirp. "By the time you're done, you'll be two feet deep in feed."

"Spread it with what?" I asked incredulously.

With that, he thrust heavy steel shovels at us, the likes of which we had never seen before (they were basically snow shovels with extremely large, flat heads). *Holy crap* they weighed a ton.

David whispered, "This is gonna take forever."

There were so many bright yellow chicks that we couldn't even see the floor and the building must have been a hundred feet long and thirty feet wide.

With my brother suddenly deaf and mute, I asked, "How are we supposed to spread this feed with all these chicks in here? We can't even walk without stepping on one."

David shot me a quick nod of approval.

"You guys start in the far corner and *this* is how you walk in here!" The farmer marched through the sea of gold, kicking up baby chicks with his knee-high rubber boots. "If you happen to step on one . . ."

Crunch!

"... just kick it aside and keep going!"

I gasped at the crumpled carcass of one very dead baby chicken. A dozen chicks instantly devoured it. David whispered, "That dead chick is your fault. Look at those little cannibals!"

"You guys will need some help so my boy's gonna help you." He yelled out his kid's name, Jeb or Jed or some damn thing. A young, stocky blonde kid with broad shoulders appeared with a gleaming shovel. He looked about as excited as we were. "Now, you kid's get to work!"

Jeb or Jed or whatever-the-hell his name was lasted about an hour before disappearing back in the house–coinciding exactly with the time his dad headed into town. The kid was a few years younger than I was but he wasn't a dummy.

David and I huffed and puffed, back and forth, between the massive pile of bird feed and the far end of the building.

Cheep-cheep-cheep. Chirp-chirp-chirp.

CHEEP-CHEEP-CHEEP. CHIRP-CHIRP-CHIRP.

We took small steps to avoid any more fatalities. Jeb (or was it Jed?) left his shovel behind and, after about an hour, I picked it up.

"Hey, check this out!" I called to David and threw him the shovel.

"This shovel's aluminum!" David scoffed. "That little bastard!"

At that moment, the sound of the farmer's approaching truck caught our attention and Jeb (or was it Jed?) flew out the side door and grabbed the nearest shovel–David's heavy, steel one–and fell back in line. We glared at him but said nothing.

The day wore on in the sauna-like building as the pile slowly dwindled.

Cheep-cheep-cheep. Chirp-chirp-chirp. CHEEP-CHEEP-CHEEP. CHIRP-CHIRP-CHIRP.

The drone, maddening.

Cheep-cheep-cheep. Chirp-chirp-chirp. CHEEP-CHEEP-CHEEP. CHIRP-CHIRP-CHIRP.

The heat, unbearable.

Cheep-cheep-cheep. Chirp-chirp-chirp. CHEEP-CHEEP-CHEEP. CHIRP-CHIRP-CHIRP.

I never got a turn with the aluminum shovel.

Finally, the farmer came out of the house and said, "My wife tells me that your mom is going to pick you guys up at four."

"What time is it?" I asked wearily, wiping sweat and dirt off my face.

"3:30. Put down those shovels. I have one more thing I need today."

I dropped my steel shovel–*crunch!*–and didn't even bother looking down. Another chick bites the dust.

The farmer led us to a foul-smelling pig pen. "I'm gonna pull my truck up to this here pen. I have a ramp, and I need to get this big hog up the ramp and into the back of my pickup."

"Where you taking him?" I asked.

"This here sumbitch's pea brain has a date with a .22 bullet," the farmer replied. "You know where bacon comes from, right, boy?" He cackled a high pitched laugh.

David whispered, "Quit pissing him off, will ya?"

The farmer pulled his truck into position and set up the narrow ramp leading up to the rear of his truck. The bed had tall wooden siding so the hog was to transfer from one pen to the other.

"When I open the pen, I want you guys to stand on either side of the ramp and push this hog up it."

I looked at David, grinned, and shook my head slightly. *No way* a couple of kids were going to manhandle a four hundred pound hog.

We took our places and the farmer looped a piece of rope around the hog's thick neck.

"OK, go!" the farmer yelled. He opened the pen and pulled on the rope, intending to back up the ramp with the hog in tow. "Push! Push! PUUSSHHHH!"

The hog snorted and squealed. Thick strands of frothy saliva flew from its mouth. He wasn't going *anywhere*. The farmer pulled with all his might. The hog sat down.

"COME ON YOU SUMBITCH! Help me boys! Help me!"

David and I and Jeb/Jed stood by with our arms crossed. We had no idea what to do.

Mom's car approached down the dirt road. *Sweet! We're going to get out of this crappy job.*

As if reading my mind, the farmer said, "You guys are *not* leaving until I get this damn hog up this damn ramp!"

He handed my brother the rope.

"You pull and everyone else push!"

David backed up the narrow ramp, pulled the rope tight and leaned back. I grabbed the hog's hind leg, but it jerked its head over in protest. I jumped back as its frothy mouth snapped at me. David let the rope go, narrowly avoiding a rope burn.

"GET UP YOU SUMBITCH!" the farmer screamed and grabbed the hog by its curly, hairless tail. The hog squealed in protest but didn't move.

"STAND UP YOU SUMBITCH!" The farmer's face turned redder and redder, spit flew from his mouth, and his eyes bulged. The massive hog didn't budge.

"I'VE GOT JUST THE THING FOR YOU, YOU SUMBITCH!" the farmer yelled, oblivious to the fact that both Mom and the farmer's wife had joined the group of wide-eyed spectators. The farmer picked up a branch and started whipping the poor creature.

"GET!

UP!

THAT!

RAMP!

YOU!

STU!

PID!

SUM!

BITCH!"

With every syllable, the farmer smacked the hog's rear end. Blood flowed from welts on the hog's hips.

The hog stood up and the farmer lashed harder and faster. David took a hold of the rope again and backed up the ramp. The farmer dropped to his knees and put his shoulder into the butt of the bleeding hog. The animal skidded an inch forward in the dirt, shrieking and squealing in panic and pain.

Still, the big hog refused to budge.

Out of breath, the farmer collapsed in the dirt, cursing to himself. A clump of pigshit clung to his sweaty blue work shirt.

No one said a word. The hog snorted twice then laid down.

"You boys can go now," the farmer gasped. "See you back here tomorrow at six?"

We couldn't scramble in the car fast enough.

We spent one more dreadful day on the farm spreading the rest of the chicken-feed. I felt sorry for the hog and told him he was a "good boy" when I saw it lounging in its pen the next day. Hell, for all I know, he's still there today.

• • •

I stayed up the night of August 1, 1981–a Friday–to watch the midnight debut of Music Television. Rob Sheffield in his book, *Talking to Girls About Duran Duran: One Young Man's Quest for True Love and a Cooler Haircut* aptly notes that, even at that time, we knew MTV was special. Rob points out that if you didn't like the current video, another one would soon follow. How very true.

It's well known that the Buggles' *Video Killed The Radio Star* has the honor of being the first video broadcast by MTV. Most of us at the time took this to be Christopher Cross' theme song. Famous for his ballads *Sailing, Ride Like The Wind*, and *Arthur's Theme (Best That You Can Do)*, Mr. Cross could sing but he wasn't going to win any beauty contests. With the advent of MTV, his career went straight down the crapper. Video killed the radio star, indeed!

The first music video I remember was Loverboy's *Turn Me Loose*, a video compilation of black and white silent picture scenes depicting damsels smacking the crap out of well-dressed gentlemen. I was mesmerized. *This was worth staying up for.*

It's a memorable year for the self-proclaimed "Prince of Darkness." Ozzy Osbourne makes headlines by biting the head off a live bat, getting arrested for whizzing on The Alamo, losing Randy Rhodes to a freak accident, and marrying his manager, Sharon. And that just took him through July!

CHAPTER 5

Ms. Smith had three plays that year, the first a reverse-super-hero plot, *Flimsy Kid*. A muscular guy (myself) says the magic phrase and transforms into a weakling (played by the petite Stacy Roberts). After momentarily turning off the lights, Stacy appeared in her home made superhero costume as I ducked out of sight.

In one scene, I sat on the beach with my girlfriend; two bullies come along and kick imaginary sand at us. (Props consisted of three foot cardboard waves and a beach umbrella.) I say the magic words, "*Aw shucks!*," the lights go out, and I drop behind the waves. Stacy takes my place as the scene continues.

We're in the middle of the beach scene–pre-bullies–and Anthony Gibson, hiding behind the waves not two feet behind me, starts laughing.

I start to snicker which makes him giggle harder. The tragedy was that I was the only one who could hear him. The audience only saw *me* laughing out loud. Ms. Smith's smile turned to a frown. Oh, the humiliation. Anthony, that's one I owe you.

The second play was about Abraham Lincoln. For a change, I didn't have the lead role. I was young Abe's father. The narrator explains that Abe's mother has died, and my line was:

"Abe, it hurts . . ."

Like one evil organism, the room exploded into laughter. "HAHAHAHAHA-HAHAHAHA!"

I waited for this unanticipated reaction from the packed lunchroom to subside. Waiting is akin to a visiting quarterback calling timeout to quiet a hostile home crowd–it only makes it worse.

I started again.

"Abe, it hurts . . ."

"HAHAHAHAHAHAHAHAHA!"

Teachers joined in the wall of noise. Three hundred people in the room–slapping each other on the back doubled over. The cafeteria shook with laughter.

"HAHAHAHAHAHAHAHAHA!"

All eyes were on me.

I plowed ahead–*to hell with everyone*–and we defiantly rushed through the lines. "Abe it hurts, but we can't stop living."

Afterward, Paul Moreno said, "That was the funniest thing I've ever seen."

I replied, "Thanks, jackass! That was a serious play."

I was given the prince role, once again, for our third play. On the day before the play, Ms. Smith presented me with a black pair of tights.

"I am not wearing panty hose," I snarled.

She calmly responded, "If you do not wear the *required costume*, I will announce on the school wide intercom that the play has been cancelled based on *your* decision not to cooperate."

"I. Am. Not. Wearing. Panty. Hose."

Undeterred, Ms. Smith held it out to me, and I stuffed it in my jacket.

I took the costume home that night and David laughed at my predicament. "Do you have any idea what this is going to do to your reputation? You are so screwed."

Under protest, I took the stage in the tights–with a pair of black Oakland Raiders shorts over them. Maybe no one would notice.

When it came time to sing, still defiant over my mandated costume, I sang the slow, melodic tune at triple-speed. I knew it was botched when Mr. Caulk, my Civics teacher, looked up at me with a confused frown on his face, his bushy eyebrows deeply furrowed.

Afterward, the *only* topic of conversation was my costume. It only slightly helped that my girlfriend, Ellen, was very pretty.

Still, my sexuality was in question and the exchanges went like this:

"Are you gay, man?"

"No."

"But, you wore tights."

"No shit, Sherlock. That doesn't make me gay."

"But, you wore tights!"

• • •

Ms. Smith kept a small metal box on her desk that contained notes on all the kids in class. The day she called in sick was the day I made my move.

Substitute teachers are so gullible.

"What are you doing?" the substitute, Mr. Facio, asked.

"Oh, this is the box that holds our drama cards. Ms. Smith has scenes written on cards and we're supposed to improvise lines. It's good for our confidence."

My classmates stared in hushed reverence.

I slid the metal tab to open the hinge.

Locked.

"Why is it locked then?" Mr. Facio asked, his eyes narrowing in suspicion.

My mind raced for an explanation.

Before I could answer, he opened the desk drawer, produced a small key and said, "Try this."

The key opened the lock and everyone sighed in relief. I flipped to the H's.

I read my card aloud: "Tom Harvey. Makes farting noises in class."

That was it. No more, no less.

I erupted into laughter and passed the box on. After everyone read Ms. Smith's notes to herself, we locked the box, put it back on the desk, and returned the key to Mr. Facio.

"What about your lines?" he asked.

"Obviously that was the wrong box."

• • •

She took a few of us to a play at Porterville College. It's funny that I can't remember the play, but I remember we went to Baskin Robbins afterward. I had a single scoop of coconut ice cream and felt guilty that she paid for it. She ate her ice cream in silence and her eyes sparkled. At that moment she was suddenly very pretty.

• • •

A couple times a year, Burton published a junior high newsletter that included song dedications. Someone had the idea that by only publishing initials there would be anonymity. Nothing could be further from the truth. There were four dedications of Foreigner's *Waiting For a Girl Like You*, one dedication of Air Supply's *Lost In Love*, and mine: "TH to EM–*When It's Over* by Loverboy." Since there was only one TH and one EM, there wasn't any mystery to it at all. I passed Ellen in the walkway that day clutching the newsletter. She was blushing. Loverboy–both the band and the tights-wearing guy–strikes again!

Unlike Patty the year before, I spent time with Ellen away from school. Most of our time we spent kissing in her darkened driveway.

I came over one afternoon and her mom invited me in the house–a first. At that moment, Ellen was in the shower. Thinking I was smarter than the average mother, I wandered outside with a specific objective in mind. Walking around the side of the house, I tapped on the bathroom window and waited for Ellen to emerge through the curtains.

C'mon full-frontal, dripping wet, eighth grade nudity!

Ellen's shocked, wet *face* emerged at the same moment her mom tapped me on the shoulder.

Smooth move Ex-lax. I never pulled *that* stunt again.

We didn't make it through the eighth grade before the relationship ended. I don't specifically remember the break-up–and that surprises me–but we both moved on.

I took interest in a popular girl, Debbie. Now an experienced kisser, I pulled a familiar move.

As we walked together after school, I turned to her.

I closed my eyes and moved in.

Our lips gently touched.

Nice.

When I stepped back and opened my eyes, a glop of snot shone on her left cheek.

Damn runny nose.

Wiping her cheek without looking at her hand, she said, "We shouldn't date anymore." To this day I'm not even sure she knew what happened.

"What?"

"We're about to start high school and we shouldn't be tied down."

The girl was wise beyond her years but, *oh the pain!*

• • •

It was a monumental day when my brother turned sixteen in February thereby doubling the number of licensed drivers in the household. We were excited to receive his birthday present: a car from our wheeling and dealing grandpa. Over the years, we witnessed Grandpa trade for all kinds of cool vehicles: Trans Ams, Camaros, Mustangs, a TT-500 dirt bike with chrome gas tank–oh, this was going to be good.

At the first knock of the door, we flew out of the apartment and scanned the parking lot.

No Trans Am.

No Camaro.

No Mustang.

We walked back in the apartment, confused.

"Well, Son, what do you think?" Grandpa beamed.

David looked back in silence, not sure what to say.

We walked back out with Grandpa and he pointed at a car.

"There it is! What do you think?"

David said nothing. I choked back laughter.

The Volkswagen Baja Bug was a dirty yellow–dented, rusted, with huge rear tires. Both sets of wheels angled inward. The thing looked *bow-legged*.

Grandpa handed David a set of keys. At least the key chain was cool: Wile E. Coyote held a dead roadrunner by the throat with the caption, *Beep Beep Your Ass!*

We piled in the car and sputtered away as Grandpa looked on.

As we bounced along, David became . . . *angry*.

We came to a four-way stop at the busy intersection of Morton and Newcomb. Wanting another look at the key chain, I reached over and inadvertently turned the key to the left. The engine shut off.

"What are you doing?" David screamed.

Before I could answer, he turned the ignition key to restart the motor.

Glug, glug, glug.

Nothing.

He tried again, glaring at me.

Glug, glug, glug.

Nothing.

There we sat at the intersection in his dead bloated yellow tick of a birthday present.

The car behind us honked. Others followed suit.

"Get out and push!" he yelled.

I jumped out and ran around to the back. Because the hot engine was in the rear and exposed, I was only able to push against the flared rear fender–and that wasn't working.

"I need help!" I yelled.

David flung the door open in rage and pushed against the open doorjamb. The car slowly started to roll.

"Keep pushing!" he yelled as he jumped in and tried to start the engine in gear.

The car lurched but didn't start.

Now directly in the middle of the intersection, he put the car in neutral and jumped back out to push again. After picking up a little more momentum, the engine fired. We jumped in and rumbled home.

Later that night from the top bunk, I offered encouragement.

"It's not so bad, but it'll need some work."

David replied, "I am not keeping that *piece of shit*. End of conversation. Good night."

Two days later, Grandpa bought the car back for $300. Two days after that, Mom kicked in $1,200 and David became the proud owner of a light blue, 1972 Ford Courier pick-up truck. The old farmer we bought it from made one modification: the stick shift was a chrome knife-handle.

With his newfound freedom, David landed a job as a busboy at Cooper's Coffee Shop. Back then, nitrous oxide, also known as "laughing gas," was an aerosol propellant and a small amount of the gas sat undisturbed inside brand new whipped cream canisters. *The trick was not to shake the canister first.* There were no tamper evident safety labels at the time (the Tylenol Scare hadn't yet happened).[8] Mr. Cooper had no way of knowing that all his whipped cream sat mostly flat–and contaminated with saliva–in the refrigerator.

One afternoon, I sat at the counter drinking a vanilla milkshake–free of charge– and noticed an old man sitting a few stools to my left. We were the only two people in

---

8   In September 1982, seven people died after ingesting cyanide-laced Tylenol. This event led to a revolution in product packaging and tamper-evident safety packaging eventually became the standard. For more on the Tylenol murders, check out *The Tylenol Mafia: Marketing, Murder, and Johnson & Johnson* by Scott Bartz. Fascinating.

the place, other than my brother, the cook, and the tall, pretty waitress. The old man's clothes were tattered and dirty. White stubble covered his face.

We never made eye contact–he just stared into his bowl of vegetable soup.

He looked *frail*.

Slurp . . . slurp . . . sluuuuuurp . . .

Brown soup spilled down his chin and onto the white counter.

Watching him out of the corner of my eye, I suddenly felt uncomfortable and sad.

He ate *slow*. His hand trembled slightly as he brought the spoon to his mouth.

Slurp . . . slurp . . . sluuuuuurp . . .

I finished the ice cream and slipped a dollar under the parfait glass. (Free ice cream didn't mean stiffing the waitress.)

Something about watching a frail old man drip hot soup down his face triggered a reaction in me. I wanted to hug him. I wanted to say, *You are not alone.* Instead, I rushed out the door with tears in my eyes thinking, *I could never work in a restaurant.*

A few days later, Mom took Trish and me there for French-dip sandwiches (her favorite). I gazed at the empty stool, hoping the man would walk in so I could say hello. Maybe invite him to join us. But I never saw him again.

We walked out, Mom grinning and proud as can be, after leaving the busboy an absurdly large tip.

• • •

David worked to support the new vice: the weekend cruise. The three-mile-route was well established: up and down Olive Avenue with jaunts down 2nd, Porter and Main. Prime time was from 8 p.m. to midnight every Friday and Saturday night.

I was in the eighth grade and David, a high school sophomore, was not about to try to impress girls with his little brother in tow.

But I would not be denied.

Sherman Smith was a junior at Monache. He drove a souped up, dark green, 1971 Pontiac Grand Prix and didn't mind that his cruising partner was just fourteen. We'd pass David and his best friend, Richie Morris, on the cruise and nod–nodding was cool, waving was not. David incessantly played Aldo Nova's *Fantasy*–a song unique for its pulsating intro, culminating in machine gun fire and laser beams. Sherman and I countered with Queen's *Dragon Attack*.

At midnight, most kids went home. For Sherman and me, midnight was when things got interesting.

Someone had painted white lines a hundred yards apart on the country road parallel to the Porterville airport. Sherman's two door coupe was primed for *drag racing* and that's what we did. He was my personal Danny Zuko which, I suppose, made me the equivalent of Doody, or, if you must, Putzie. (I'd never claim to be Kenickie-like since we were three years apart and I was yet to claim my cool.) When we blasted off the line, I'd scream encouragement over the roar of the engine, but Sherman was all business: eyes fixed straight ahead, hands firmly on the wheel, foot mashed all the way to the floor. I don't remember ever losing.

When his car was in the shop, we'd take out his mom's VW bus–for cruising, not drag racing. The bus didn't have a radio so he rigged a record player, complete with home stereo speakers, behind us on the floor. With every bump and turn, the needle jumped on the record.

Whether it was the Grand Prix or the bus, we stayed out well past midnight. David was already in bed by the time I tiptoed in the apartment. Imagine your fourteen-year-old kid out until 2 a.m. every Friday and Saturday nowadays. Incredible.

• • •

Sherman raced BMX and turned pro on his twentieth birthday. At a national in Long Beach, California, he crashed and broke his neck. He survived the devastating injury but had to have the vertebrae in his neck permanently fused together. Though he could no longer turn his head, he went on to have a successful 9-year pro career.

Sherman, I love you man.

• • •

John Belushi died on Friday, March 5 of a cocaine and heroin overdose. Gone at 33. Best known for his role as Bluto Blutarsky in *Animal House* ("I'm a zit, get it?") his popularity knew no bounds.

One VHS tape that I've nearly worn out is *The Best of John Belushi* on Saturday Night Live. My favorites include *Samurai Delicatessen*, *The Thing That Wouldn't Leave*, Belushi singing *King Bee* and his absurd over-the-top impersonation of Joe Cocker singing *With a Little Help From My Friends*.

I saw both of Belushi's final movies, *Neighbors*, (a quirky movie about suburbia with sidekick Dan Ackroyd) and *Continental Divide* (a romantic comedy that fell flat) at the Porter 3 theater. It's a shame that Belushi's last two movies were largely forgettable.

• • •

8th grade graduation picture. Can you say Dork?

We held our eighth grade graduation at the Memorial Auditorium on the campus of Porterville High School and the event felt *big*. Big in the sense that life was *really* about to change–whether we were ready for it or not.

Rebecca, a pretty blonde brainiac with glasses, gave the valedictorian speech about how far we'd come.

Blue-collar Mike–best known for his Atari 2600 tournaments–was salutatorian. Mike's achievement surprised a lot of people since he didn't shy away from fist fights and *literally* chased a kid all the way home one day after school. The scene was both comical and tragic: Kid in question running, Mike and a group of ten guys, including myself, twenty five yards behind.

"Kick his ass, Mike!" and "Quit running you sissy!" added fuel to the fire. The kid ran *for a mile without stopping*. We admired Mike's bravado, too, since this kid lived right across the street from him. Things ended in a standoff with groups of posturing kids in their respective yards. When the cops came, we ran into Mike's house for another Air Sea Battle tournament.

So Mike, all red-headed, freckles, and muscles, a guy known for crooning Joan Jett and the Blackheart's *Crimson and Clover* during recess, spoke to his fellow graduates about the future. *The future is upon us. We are no longer kids.*

The junior high choir sang Styx's *Come Sail Away* and I sat on stage in my cheap JC Penney suit with clip-on tie watching the last night of junior high tick away. *We're no longer kids. Hmm . . . no longer kids.*

When I crossed the stage to receive my diploma, Sherman jumped up in the packed auditorium and yelled, "Right on, Tommy!"

People laughed and I smiled with tears in my eyes.

• • •

When I graduated from Monache four years later, I sent Ms. Smith a graduation announcement. She sent me a check for ten dollars. I wasn't going to cash it but Mom said, "You'll only disappoint her if you don't."

I ran into Ms. Smith ten years later at lunch in Porterville. With pulse racing, I interrupted her, not entirely sure it was her.

"Excuse me, but are you Jane Smith?"

She looked up from her Italian food.

"Yes."

I smiled at her in silence. "Do you remember me?"

She smiled and her eyes narrowed. "I know you," she said, the words trailing off.

"Tom," I said.

Then she said, "Tom. Tom Harvey."

I didn't remind her that I was *Tom Harvey, makes farting noises in class.*

We spoke briefly and she introduced me to her father. She said she was now a wife and a mother. Wow!

I thanked her for the "drama days" and her well-wishes upon my high school graduation. It was an awkward conversation, but, at that moment, she was more dear to me than ever.

I looked at her dad. "You've got yourself a great daughter here."

He smiled and gave a quick nod.

She blushed and looked at the floor.

"Can I give you a hug?" I asked meekly.

"Sure."

She stood up and we embraced.

I walked out feeling sad that ten years had passed. Sad that I hadn't appreciated this special lady back in the day. Sad about the farting noises.

1982 Fun Fact #2:

Cal executes "The Play" against Stanford–a kickoff return involving five successful laterals and one heavily-damaged trombone–to beat John Elway's Stanford team, 25-20. Had Elway run a few more seconds off the clock, Stanford would have ran the clock out and won on their last second field goal.

CHAPTER 6

Joe and I became best friends despite his teasing about the tights incident. He said his ability to talk to girls and my looks would take us far. He was confident.

He was also right.

His girlfriend was a mystery since she hadn't gone to Burton and lived across town. I had never met Jenny before the night we went to her house. Jenny had a friend over–Pam–and Pam was eager to work on her kissing skills. That was all I needed to know.

Our problem was a distance of five miles.

As motivated, resourceful fourteen-year-olds, we called on Porterville's public transportation system: Dial-A-Colt.

Dial-A-Colt was the town's only cab service–two cars in all–that, for a dollar per person, would take you anywhere within the city limits.

Within the city limits.

The car picked us up at Joe's house. We gave the guy two dollars and away we went.

"She better not be ugly," I said for the tenth time.

We looked good: Levi's 501 jeans and collared Le Tigre shirts. Neither of us could afford Izod. The cab reeked of Brut aftershave.

It was not yet nightfall when the cab pulled over two miles short of our destination.

"End of the line fellas."

"What?" we asked in unison. "This is a parking lot!"

"*This*," he answered, "is the edge of the city limits. This is as far as I can take you. What do you expect for a dollar?"

We got out with a frown and the car sped off.

"Uh, what now Einstein?" I asked.

"We'll figure it out," Joe responded and put a dime in the pay phone outside the small grocery store. "Jenny? We'll be a half hour late, but we're on our way."

We jogged, then walked, then jogged the two-mile winding country road. By the time Jenny's white house came into view, we were drenched in sweat.

Jenny and Pam sat on the porch, smiling. Oh, and Pam was *cute!*

Joe waved at them as we approached, but Jenny put her finger to her lips. *Shhhhhhh.*

We approached in silence.

"My dad is asleep so we'll have to be very quiet," she whispered. I thought, *Holy crap, her dad is in the house? This is nuts!*

I looked at Pam and smiled. "Hi."

By the looks of it Mission Control was go for launch.

We tiptoed in the house and into Jenny's room, but this was no ordinary bedroom—the only thing separating her room from the living room was a curtain of beads. *There was no door.*

Joe and Jenny claimed half of the queen size bed and began groping each other. Pam and I engaged in small talk at the foot of the bed.

"So," I asked, "you went to Bartlett, huh?"

"Yeah. You went to Burton?"

"Yeah."

"Known Jenny long?"

"A few years."

"Known Joe long?"

"A few years."

The moaning intensified in the dark room. Jenny sat up and said, "Uh, you two should just get on with it. We haven't got all night."

I looked at Pam in silence, unsure what to do next.

Pam said, "If we lay back on the bed, I bet we could imagine there's stars on the ceiling."

"Uh, OK."

We laid on our half of the bed, my back parallel with Joe's. Pam lay under my left arm. Jenny under Joe's right arm. Pam then placed my right hand on her well-endowed left boob and, somewhere in my brain a voice shouted, *LET THE FUN BEGIN!* With four bodies in motion on the bed, Jenny huffed and led Joe out of the bedroom and into the adjoining bathroom.

Pam and I adjusted our positioning.

More room.

Cool.

We continued kissing for fifteen minutes. Pam was right–*I was seeing stars* even though my eyes were closed.

The beads flew apart and a terror-struck Jenny whispered loudly, "MY DAD IS UP AND HE ALWAYS CHECKS MY ROOM!" I franticly looked around. No closet. Nowhere to hide! We dashed into the only locked room in the house: the bathroom. Jenny locked the door while Joe and I looked for an escape route. The window was too small to shimmy through.

Bam, bam, bam!

"Jenny, what are you two doing in there? I have to get ready for work!" her dad yelled. He was a mere four inches away, and . . .

We.

Were.

Trapped.

Though I never actually saw the man, I imagined a Hells Angel biker dude. A big guy who would slam his fist through our chests for the atrocities committed under his roof.

"Pam and I are, uh, washing our faces! We'll be out in a sec!" She cranked on the faucet to full blast.

My heart pounded.

Joe was white as a ghost.

"Hurry up, then! I have to get ready for work!"

Jenny kept her finger raised and pressed against her lips: SHHHHHHH! I thought for sure the sound of my heart slamming inside my chest would give us away.

Jenny listened, trying to determine where her dad was in the small house. After a few long moments of silence, she cracked open the door and peered out, ready to slam it closed. He was in the small kitchen, just out of our line of sight. Joe and I stood trembling in the bathtub with the shower curtain pulled.

"Not yet . . . not yet . . . wait . . . *now!*" she whispered.

We flung back the shower curtain and, as one, the four of us made a beeline for the front door. Joe and I leapt out of the house and Jenny quickly shut the door but not before whispering, "Don't go just yet." The porch was pitch-black with the light off.

Her dad went from the kitchen into the bathroom and turned on the shower. The door closed and locked behind him. He missed us by a matter of seconds.

The front door cracked open and Jenny and Pam's faces peered out, they were both flushed and smiling.

"Well," Jenny said, "*that* was exciting."

"Same time, same place tomorrow?" Joe laughed.

Pam extended her hand through the open door. "It was really nice to meet you," she said. I held out my hand, dumbstruck, and she shook it. I always found it odd that I went from boob stroking to a handshake in less than ten minutes.

It took the entire two mile jog back to the pay phone before our adrenalin subsided. The supermarket at the edge of town was deserted. Joe called Dial-A-Colt but got their answering machine–they were closed for the night.

"What do we do now?" I groaned. We were on the rough east side of town–in a darkened parking lot. Our safety was far from assured.

Joe's brother, Ted, came to the rescue.

• • •

That summer we existed in no man's land–no longer in junior high but not yet in high school.

A few weeks before school started, I received a flyer in the mail that listed the freshman "walk around" day at Monache High School. Held in the school cafeteria, this marked the beginning of the high school journey. The choices made that day determined classes for the entire year. Joe and I agreed we'd go together.

There were a lot of new faces since multiple junior highs made up the freshman class. Nervous and excited, we became separated in the bustle of the packed room. The day was also a fashion show: flipped-up collared shirts, hip-hugging jeans, and new shoes abounded. One face that wasn't new was Pam's. From across the crowded room I waved at her. My right hand, after all, was on a first name basis with her left boob. She looked back in horror and ducked out of sight. I didn't make further contact.

After signing up for my classes (World Studies, Algebra 9, English 9 Honors, PE, Physical Science, and Spanish 9), the hard work was done.

Note: it only took me a few minutes to remember those classes, in that order, nearly thirty years later. Am I pathetic or do I just have a good memory? You tell me.

A group of guys, including David Fine and Ryan Bernasconi, milled around one table, so I walked over to see what they were doing. Joe was nowhere to be found.

"What's going on?" I asked.

David said, "We're signing up for football. Sign up with us."

The three of us played *flag* football at Burton so we thought we knew a little something about the game. This was *tackle* football, though, and something entirely different. Surrounded by the chaos of the room, I looked at the dozen or so names on the signup sheet and only recognized a few.

Suddenly the room was quiet. All I could see was the next empty line on the page. I was mesmerized.

"Well?" Ryan asked, snapping me out of my trance, "you going to do this or what?"

With a blank grin and shaky hand, I added my name.

• • •

We unhinged the top bunk and moved it into my sister's room and I said *adios* to David as a nightly bunkmate. Trish slept in Mom's room anyway. Two posters of bikini-clad supermodel Paulina Porizkova adorned the walls, along with a poster of Finnish motocross racer Heikki Mikkola and a cartoony towel of a basset hound peering through round glasses. I secured the 8-track/radio from the living room and relished my newfound privacy.

• • •

This new commitment, *high school tackle football practice*, preceded the start of school by a few weeks. Junior high, not even ninety days in the past, felt like it was a lifetime away.

With David working at the coffee shop and Mom finishing her nursing studies, I walked the mile and a half to practice, alone.

Walking into the locker room on that hot August summer day in 1982 was eye opening: big lockers, small lockers, offices, and *one community shower*. Showering with the fellas was going to take some getting used to.

Coach Randy Quiram welcomed us by having us run up and down the grassy practice field. We immediately took to the man—he was in his mid-thirties, a PE teacher with a legendarily pretty blonde wife. With a bushy moustache and manicured beard, he ran laps with us and quickly memorized everyone's names. He and assistant coach, Rich Lambie, sized up the collection of nervous, not-yet-freshman players.

"Who's a quarterback?" Coach Quiram shouted.

A few guys, including Ryan Bernasconi, raised their hands. I smirked. *News to me.*

"Who's a running back?"

Different guys raised their hands.

"Who's a receiver?" More hands, different guys.

After each question, he pointed to an area where the respondents congregated. I didn't know what I was, so I just knelt on one knee unsure what would happen next. David Fine, my drama buddy from Burton, knelt beside me. What was left was a mix of little and big guys.

Coach Lambie yelled, "OK, all you linemen, over here!" and away the bigger guys went.

Coach Quiram looked over his remaining players. While I tried to muster a look of calm self-respect, I felt like the last kid getting picked for dodge ball.

"OK, I want all you guys to join the receivers and run routes for our quarterbacks."

I smirked at Bernasconi who stood with two other guys beaming with the instant recognition. He hadn't even thrown a pass and he was moving up in the world. I felt like saying, "Oh, yeah . . . um . . . I'm a quarterback, too," but knew I'd only embarrass myself when I tried to throw the ball.

• • •

The day before high school started, I asked David his advice on this new chapter in my life.

He said, "Have as much fun as you can, but kick ass in school."

I nodded.

"Hmm. Anything else?"

"Yeah, don't walk around alone or you're likely to end up face first in a trashcan."

Ah, yes, the infamous freshman hazing.

"So, the fact that you're my older brother doesn't offer me special protection?"

"Nope," he answered with a grin, "in fact, you might just be a target."

Swell.

That summer I studied David's sophomore yearbook like a kid possessed. I was particularly interested in all the pretty older women I would soon rub shoulders with in the hallways.

Hey, I'm David Harvey's little brother!

That had to account for something.

A freshman named Betsy sure looked cute. Shannon, too.

So many girls. So little time.

<u>*1983 Fun Fact #1:*</u>

McDonald's introduces the McNugget. At 100 milligrams of sodium per piece, who needs salt the rest of the day?

CHAPTER 7

The first day of school was September 7.

At 5' 7" and 134 pounds, I was an average sized fourteen-year-old. I rode to school with David in his mini-truck and nervously sought out my home room class.

It was a cold morning. Mist hung in the air.

Mr. Bierman assigned our seats in alphabetical order and, as fate would have it, my ex-girlfriend, Ellen, sat *right behind me.*

Now, what are the odds of that? Same homeroom? Thirty kids and no one's last name fell between H and M?

Not at all happy with the thought of her staring at the back of my head every day, I turned around and growled, "Anybody but *you!*"

She scoffed. "Anybody but you, too!"

I wandered around the sprawling campus that day with the rest of the wide-eyed freshman, collecting textbooks, greeting my Burton friends and thinking I'd finish the day without incident.

I could not, for the life of me, find my seventh period Spanish class. The bell rang for the last class of the day, and I found myself standing in the auto shop. Not to sound like a total geek, I asked someone, "Where the *hell* is Mr. Briscoe's class?" The guy nodded at the woodshop building. Auto and Woodshop were on the back forty of the campus and I thought, *This just isn't right.*

Sliding back a set of heavy double doors, a makeshift classroom sat at the far end of the large room. Mr. Briscoe, standing behind his desk at the head of the room said, "Ah, buenos tardes! You must be *Senor Harvey?*" Thirty strangers looked at me blankly.

"Yes, I am," I said with a mix of relief and embarrassment finding a seat in the very back of the class. Looking around at large cutout trees and racks of costumes, I asked a pretty blonde girl I didn't know, (Debbie was her name I'd discover), "What is this place?" She cheerfully answered, "*This* is the prop room for the drama department."

"What the hell are we doing in the prop room?"

Gregg, a sophomore with blonde curly hair and thick glasses, answered, "They ran out of classroom space."

"Do we even have drama at this school?"

"Nope, they axed the program at the end of last year," he replied.

With all hombres accounted for, under a Rydell High School sign and a cutout of a 1955 Buick, Mr. Briscoe began his lesson. No one in the back heard a word.

It was a busy first week as David and I went to our first concert ever: Van Halen at the Selland Arena in Fresno. He, in turn, rounded up Sherman, and his friends Bill Bushey and Jason Patterson. Sherman offered to drive the Grand Prix. After school on that Thursday afternoon, Sherman picked us up in the high school parking lot. From there, we stopped at the Joy Jug liquor store.

"Ante up boys!" Sherman announced.

We pooled our money and he marched into the small liquor store. I thought, *He isn't old enough to buy alcohol.*

What I didn't know was that the middle eastern guy at the Joy Jug would sell alcohol to anyone. Sherman walked out carrying a brown paper sack, smiling from ear to ear.

David handed out the booty: The Club brand miniature aluminum cans of pre-mixed hard alcohol. We passed around a Fuzzy Naval, a Long Island Iced Tea, a Screwdriver, and a Harvey Wallbanger (purchased simply for the name and nothing else). By the time we piled out of the car in Fresno, I couldn't feel my face and my stomach burned.

In an odd pairing, After The Fire opened the show. The crowd showed no mercy and pelted them with empty cups, full cups, smuggled in beer cans, and rolls of toilet paper. The rowdy crowd came to see David Lee Roth and the Van Halen brothers, not this unknown New Wave band. I thought, *Is this how all warm up bands are treated?*

Van Halen, in the middle of their "Hide Your Sheep" tour for their Diver Down album, had a sold out crowd including thousands of girls in tank-tops and skin-tight jeans. There were no floor seats–just a human mosh pit–and when the lights went out, a cloud of smoke quickly settled over the crowd.

David yelled in my ear, "That's marijuana!"

No, really?

The next day we wore our Van Halen concert shirts to school and instantly connected with the Stoners.

Sidebar #1:

High School Cliques

Speaking of Stoners, the cliques (pronounced "clicks"), in no particular order, were:

<u>Stoners</u> (also known as Metal Heads)–guys with long hair who wore concert shirts to school. Even if you didn't smoke weed, a guy could find himself in this clique based on clothing alone.

<u>Preppies</u>–open to both sexes, a Prep wore collared shirts (preferably of the Izod variety), Sperry Topsider shoes, and sweaters tied around their necks. Generally speaking, most of the cheerleaders and Student Council members fell into this category.

<u>Jocks</u>–every school had these, whether it was the varsity football players or the varsity volleyball players, jocks covered both sexes (a bruiser upperclassman named Curt and a solid girl named Liz come to mind–I had the hots for Liz in a weird sort of way).

<u>Cowboys, also known as Shit Kickers</u>–open to both sexes, these students wore skin-tight Wrangler jeans, cowboy boots, and cowboy hats. Most were members of the Future Farmers of America (FFA) club (We had a different name for the acronym pertaining to a guy's sexual orientation but it wouldn't be polite to state it here). You didn't want to get in a fight with a Cowboy in fear of getting kicked by those pointy boots.

<u>Vatos, also known as Cholos</u>–this referred to Hispanic students who wore black pants, white T-shirts, and black shoes, *religiously*. Some of the guys carried boom

boxes (also known as ghetto blasters) on their shoulders between classes with Grand-master Flash's *Scorpio* cranked.

Geeks, also known as Computer Nerds–Interestingly enough, this group wasn't looked down on or treated poorly. Usually an undersized guy with glasses, this was the person to go to for help with Algebra, Trig, and Computer Programming. God knows I needed their help.

New Wavers, also known as Punks (short for Punk Rockers)–these were guys and girls with funky, cropped haircuts and colorful, zippered clothing. They were defined by their music. To give you the true flavor, here's an excerpt of what a New Waver named Jay (also known as the Spudboy) wrote in my freshman yearbook:

Nu-Wave shall reign supreme in the kingdom of MHS. There will be masses of new wavers the likes of which the world has never known. And I, as the New Wave Emperor of the World, will see to it that no "Black Sabbath," no "Ozzy Osbourne" and certainly no "Sammy Hagar" will be played within the boundaries of MHS. DEVO, OINGO, Wall of Voodoo, B-52s, Sparks, and all new wave shall win the day! Stay ultra cool and think "new wave."

Many students didn't fall into any of these classifications and some changed their stripes over the years. *Some of us (hint, hint) worked hard to change classifications.*

I fell into the Stoner class based on my long hair, peach fuzz moustache, and concert shirt despite the fact that I was an honors student. When I was offered a joint and declined that first week of school ("Only a dollar" the kid said), the stereotype took a hit.

• • •

We played our freshman football games on Thursday afternoons on the varsity practice field. I saw Coach Quiram during PE the day of that first game. He asked, "Are you ready, Tom?"

"Yes, Coach. And we're going to win!"

He looked at me for a moment without responding–for just a second, he looked sad. The look confused me.

He answered quietly, "We're going to give it our best."

What he knew that I didn't was that our first game was against Visalia-based Redwood High School, and we hadn't beaten them at any level of football in recent memory. After school we lined up for our game jerseys randomly handed out of a large cardboard box. When I reached the front of the line, number 21 was at the top of pile. I held it out proudly. The guy behind me jabbed me in the back. "Move! We haven't got all day!" It's been my favorite number ever since.

Redwood crushed us that day. We didn't even score.

At practice the next day, I noticed that I was the only one still wearing tennis shoes.

Going down the line of stretching players, Coach Quiram asked quietly, "Are you going to get some cleats, Tom?"

"Yes, Coach."

Trouble was, Nike cleats cost more than forty dollars, and I didn't want to ask Mom for the money. I had the weekend to figure it out and ended up raiding the cookie jar–at the expense of that weekend's video gaming–and went to Payless Shoes. I walked out with a pair of twelve dollar Pro Wings. Barely passable as athletic shoes, they were made of cheap white plastic with little nubs for cleats. I was so embarrassed that I razor-bladed off the brand markings and scuffed them up in the dirt. I was the only player wearing them.

We went 1-9 that year and I'd bet that, as our starting right cornerback, I still hold the record for *giving up* the most touchdowns in Monache High School freshman football history. While the memories of most of the games escape me, thankfully, I do have specific recollections.

Golden West ran back the opening kickoff and, later, I was flagged for a fifteen-yard facemask penalty. Coach Lambie pulled me out of the game and, grabbing my facemask, flung me from side to side screaming, "Is this how you're supposed to tackle?"

The game at Mount Whitney was delayed because our bus driver couldn't shift the bus out of second gear. For the entire thirty-five-mile drive, the bus lurched along, the engine wound out and smoking. Cars stacked up behind us on the two lane road, honking incessantly. A few impatient drivers flipped us off as they sped by. The poor lady bus driver was reduced to tears long before we made it to Visalia. We arrived an hour late and everyone patted the sobbing driver's shoulder as we unloaded.

Whitney beat the living hell out of us.

The one game we won, 20-8, was at Selma. Selma, California, is the self-proclaimed "Raisin Capital of the World." The high school's mascot is a raisin. Coach

Quiram turned play calling over to our quarterback, Colin Crow, midway through the second half. Colin handled it like a pro.

On the ride home, I pictured their pep rallies:

"We are . . .

Selma . . .

Raisins!"

I felt sorry for those guys–they had to live with the world's lamest mascot *and* they just got beat by a really crappy team. [2012 update: While driving through town on my way from Fresno to Porterville recently, I noticed a sign that read, "Welcome to Selma–Home of the Bears!" I'm not sure when they changed their mascot but someone was using their noodle!]

When I got home that night and didn't mention the game, Mom asked about it. She was used to the usual report– "Oh, we lost."

As nonchalant as I could muster, I replied, "Oh, we won."

"You did?" she screamed and gave me a crushing embrace.

At one of our home games, I sat on the bench chatting with the other defensive cornerback, David Facio. Coach Quiram yelled, "Tom, you're in!"

I jumped up and looked at the field, confused. "But we're on offense!"

"I know, get out there!"

"Oh my God!"

Coach Lambie said, "Oh my God is right!"

With our starting running back, John Snyder, limping off the field, my heart raced as Coach Quiram gave me the play.

"Dive 34."

I ran into the huddle.

Silence as ten guys waited for me to speak.

"Dive. Thirty. Four." It was the simplest play in the playbook.

Quarterback Rick Short barked out the play, "Dive 34 on two, on two!"

We responded in unison, "Break!"

I was on the field as the tailback! Number 21 in the backfield! Call the newspaper! Take a picture!

I looked straight ahead, conjuring up the meanest, toughest look I could muster. The middle linebacker locked eyes with me. My eyes narrowed menacingly.

The play is deciphered as follows: *Dive* meant a running play up the middle.

In our numbering scheme, the quarterback is number 1, the center is number 2, and the fullback is number 3. A dive play starting with 3 meant the *fullback* runs the ball. The gaps between the linemen were numbered 1 through 5, from right to left, so the 4 in 34 is the gap between the center and the guard, to the left of the center.

Had Coach called Dive 44, or Dive 43, I would have run the ball because the tailback is number 4 in the numbering scheme. Our big fullback, Frank Tate, ran the ball straight ahead for three yards.

The next play John Snyder resumed tailback responsibilities and I returned to the bench. It was my only offensive play of the year.

Later in the game, I stood across from the wide-receiver as the other team lined up in punt formation.

The punter kicked the ball straight up in the air. Coach Lambie screamed from the sideline, but I had no idea what he was saying. Looking straight up in the bright sky, I was determined to make a play. At the sound of loud breathing–like a horse exhaling–I glanced down and locked eyes with that same middle linebacker. His foot pawed at the ground like a bull ready to charge. Thinking that Lambie was screaming *catch the ball*–he was actually screaming *get away from it*–I made the split second decision to stay put. Time to be a hero! Maybe I could run the botched punt back for a score! Time to turn this game around!

The split second the ball touched my outstretched fingers the defender hit me like a Mac truck. I flew off my feet, landed on the back of my head, and crumpled to the ground. In football terms, I muffed the ball–meaning that because I touched it, the other team could regain possession.

The good news was that a teammate pounced on the ball.

The bad news came when I sat up and looked at my right hand: my middle finger was angled ninety degrees, completely dislocated at the middle joint. I wobbled off the field, holding my hand out in front of me, trying not to puke or pass out.

Coach Lambie didn't even acknowledge the injury and screamed, "I told you to get away from it!" Coach Quiram grabbed my hand and popped the joint back into place–oh, *that* hurt. He locked eyes with me and calmly said, "You're OK. That was a good effort. Go sit down and catch your breath."

I sat down on the bench and tried to make sense of what had just happened. I felt lightheaded. Hell, I probably had a concussion. My finger throbbed with waves of hot pain.

Coach Quiram, always the quiet leader, walked over and taped my middle finger to my ring finger and said, "When we're on D, I need you back out there." I smiled weakly as my swollen middle finger grew darker shades of black and blue with every passing second.

Even though Ryan Bernasconi started the season as our third string quarterback, he saw a lot of action due to Rick Short's suspension for possession of chewing tobacco and Colin Crow's broken arm. We used to joke that every pass of Ryan's was a dying quail–it sort of arched in the air then dropped out of the sky. But, God bless Ryan. He tried his hardest, and he led us to the finish.

We finished the year with a shutout loss (0-13) to our cross town rival, Porterville High. The only consolation was that we were Braves and they were Kittens. (Both schools have three-tier mascots as follows: Brave, Chief, Marauder for Monache; Kitten, Cat, Panther for Porterville.) Lord, it would have been tough to be called a kitten but at least the Porterville High players lost that designation after their freshman year. The Raisins in Selma weren't so lucky.

Sidebar #2:

The Traveling Evangelist and the Evils of Rock Music

David brought home a flyer beaming, "We are going to *this!*"

A traveling evangelist was setting up a tent outside of town to preach about the spreading evil of rock music. The flyer promised that the *insidious evil known as backmasking would be revealed.*

Wikipedia.org defines backmasking as:

Backmasking (also known as *backward masking*) is a recording technique in which a sound or message is recorded backward onto a track that is meant to be played forward. Backmasking is a deliberate process, whereas a message found through phonetic reversal may be unintentional.

Wikipedia.org further says:

Backmasking has been a controversial topic in the United States since the 1980s, when allegations from Christian groups of its use for Satanic purposes were made against prominent rock musicians, leading to record burning protests and proposed anti-backmasking legislation by state and federal governments. Whether backmasked messages exist is in debate, as is whether backmasking can be used subliminally to affect listeners.

Straight out of Neil Diamond's song, *Brother Love's Traveling Salvation Show*, this guy did not disappoint when it came to the image in my mind of a traveling evangelist. The guy setup a white tent in a dirt field on the outskirts of town and word spread quickly–the place was packed with a hundred or more teenagers. David and I settled into our folding chairs and waited for the proverbial fireworks.

A heavy set dude in his late thirties with dirty blonde hair and wire rimmed round glasses took the stage breathing fire and brimstone.

Rock music was manipulative!

Rock music was dangerous!

Rock music was evil!

For an hour, the guy paced back and forth working himself into a frenzy. Oh, he had a lot of ammo: The Rolling Stones' album Goat Head Soup was a mockery of the lamb of Christ. Black Sabbath's Heaven and Hell album, depicting angels smoking cigarettes, was blasphemy.

He unleashed on Led Zeppelin's classic, *Stairway To Heaven*, and all the devil-inspired references to change a person's path *away* from heaven.

We learned about Aleister Crowley, founder of The First Church of Satan (if such an institution exists)–Ozzy Osbourne's inspiration in *Mr. Crowley*. He held up Ozzy's Speak of the Devil album and simply shook his head in disgust (Ozzy hurling a big glob of raspberry jam–classic if you ask me).

He ranted against AC/DC, Black Oak Arkansas, and Judas Priest. Even the most innocent of artists weren't safe.

"Your kids are listening to Olivia Newton-John sing about getting physical! She wants us to let our bodies do the talking!" He berated Pink Floyd ("*Pink* Floyd? What are they, a bunch of homosexuals?").

The crowd listened with mild interest and hushed amusement. Bashing the likes of Black Sabbath and AC/DC was expected. We were there for the good stuff–the promise of subversive messages played backwards on a record player. We were there for *backmasking*.

He took one more shot at the teenage sex advocate, Olivia Newton-John, took a deep breath, and fired up the record player.

Everyone leaned forward in their seats.

"If you don't think the obvious messages are bad enough," he breathed, "take a listen to *this!*"

The familiar bass riff of Queen's *Another One Bites The Dust* played through the loud speakers–a hundred teenage heads nodded in time to the music. At the point where Freddie Mercury begins repeating the title, the preacher forced the record backwards against the needle.

The place let out a collective gasp.

"Do you hear it?" the preacher screamed. "DO YOU HEAR IT?"

In quirky distortion, Freddie's high-pitched voice warbled, "Start to smoke mary-wanna." David and I looked at each other and burst out laughing.

The preacher pulled the needle off and his assistant slapped down another record.

"How about the 'great' Beatles White Album?" he screamed, emphasizing the word great sarcastically. "Anyone familiar with the song, *Revolution 9*?"

The record played and the words "number nine" repeated over and over and over. "Listen to this," he whispered.

Spinning the record backwards, every "number nine" morphed into "turn me on dead man"–again and again and again.

The crowd gasped.

I never knew how "turn me on dead man" was satanic, but it *was* interesting.

For the coup de grace, he said, "Remember that sweet ballad, *Stairway To Heaven*? The power of Satan is strong with this one! Let's play this one backwards."

The distorted words of "Here's to my sweet Satan, there's power in Satan, he will give you 666" played through the speakers. Whoa. OK, *that* was wild.

Amid the controversy, Led Zeppelin's record company, Swan Song Records, issued a statement regarding backmasking: "Our turntables only play in one direction–forwards." And Led Zeppelin lead singer Robert Plant denied the accusations, saying: "To me it's very sad, because *Stairway To Heaven* was written with every best intention, and as far as reversing tapes and putting messages on the end, that's not my idea of making music."[9]

The preacher passed the hat and I put a dollar in. David scoffed.

As we shuffled out with the murmuring crowd, the preacher yelled, "Come back Friday night with your tapes and records! Help me put Satan back in his place! Rock music is evil! Come back on Friday for the big bonfire!"

"So," I asked warily, "we gonna burn Highway To Hell?" If any of our records were evil, it was that one.

"Are you crazy? That album cost me ten bucks!" he snorted. "Hell no!"

We passed on the bonfire finale. Satanic or not, it would have been too painful to see all that good music go up in flames.

• • •

---

9   Source: Wikipedia.

The year cruised along and I found one class, Physical Science, to be a real test of my intellect. Mr. Forrest looked the part of a scientist: a small guy in his late fifties with short gray hair, half-moon spectacles, and two fingers on his right hand partially missing. *Blown off in a lab experiment gone wrong.* To this day, that's still the theory.

The class was college prep—open to freshman only and in its first year of existence. He may as well have called it Advanced Physics for Pre-Med Students, as far as I was concerned. For starters, we had to memorize the Table of Elements—not just know how to use it—we had to *memorize* it. With this knowledge, we tried to solve chemical equations so long that the formulas stretched across the top of the page and down the side.

On one hot afternoon, Mr. Forrest described the atmospheric structure of each of the planets—I will say that, of all the topics, astronomy wasn't totally reliant on complicated equations—so I was mildly interested. Pam (of boob-stroking lore), sitting in front of me, raised her hand and asked innocently, "Mr. Forrest, how far across is Uranus?"

Mr. Forrest put his chalk covered half fingers to his lips and pondered the question.

Painful seconds passed in silence.

I burst out laughing.

At that moment, Pam raised both of her arms to stretch and I grabbed them and pinned her backwards on my desk. Looking down at her upside down face, I blurted, "Good one!" This caused a chain-reaction of riotous laughter—just the outlet needed for everyone stifling their laughter at Pam's question—and Mr. Forrest, oblivious to the joke, glared at me with fire in his eyes. He snapped, "Tom! I am permanently moving you away from Pam!" He pointed his stub at an empty desk across the room. I collected my books and barely made it to my new locale, tears streaming down my face.

• • •

Now every guy has a story about either kicking someone's ass—or having said ass kicked—and I had not one, but two, encounters my freshman year.

The first incident started after our football team's winless streak hit four—frustration was high. Our starting wide receiver, a tall, lanky guy named Rob approached me one day and said, "Me and Jaime think you suck! You should quit the team!" Jamie was a starting linebacker—both he and Rob had cops for dads.

71

While his point was valid, I responded, "I don't really care what you and Jaime think."

His eyes grew as big as his evil smile. "I'm going to tell Jaime you said that." He turned and skipped away in glee.

Later that day, Jaime approached with Rob at his heels. Jaime's fists were clenched.

"Rob told me what you said," he growled.

"I didn't say anything," I calmly replied. "Rob did all the talking." I tried to act nonchalant but my heart raced.

Jaime continued, "I think yer nothing but a pussy!" He pronounced it *pus-see*.

I was no match for this stocky kid. He would have beat the living hell out of me.

"You can think what you want, Jaime."

"If I knew I wouldn't get kicked off the team, I'd kick your ass right here and now!"

I said nothing and intentionally kept my arms at my sides–defenseless–hoping he wouldn't sucker punch me.

Rob's smile faded.

Jaime spit on the ground, turned, and walked away seething.

• • •

Jaime and I later became friends and at our twenty year reunion, he disavowed all recollection of the incident. I guess it wasn't that memorable to him.

• • •

The other incident occurred in PE class–and this time it was more than just words and spittle.

Rain forced our volleyball class into the gym. Multiple courts were setup and a stray ball bounced at my feet. I picked up the ball and flung it back–and hit a kid named George in the face. He grabbed his nose and doubled over in pain. Shocked at what had happened, I walked straight at him with my arms outstretched, palms up.

"Oh, man, I am so sor . . ."

It happened fast.

Out of the corner of my left eye, his fist swung around.

SMACK!

But he didn't punch me.

He *slapped* me.

I stood there, stunned.

The games instantaneously stopped. Mr. Kavadas, our PE teacher, was nowhere to be seen.

The next few seconds played out in super slow motion.

My fists instinctively clenched.

A series of rapid fire thoughts went through my mind.

Would I be blamed for starting a fight?

Does it matter who started it?

Can I kick this tall kid's ass?

I took a half-step forward to deliver the retaliation. It was almost like a reflex.

At that instant, George's fat friend took a half step forward.

My next thought.

This guy's going to jump in. I'm going to have to fight both of them.

Long seconds passed as I looked between both of them.

I unclenched my fists and relaxed my shoulders.

"What are you doing?" I pleaded. "I was just apologizing to you!"

"You meant to do that!" George snapped in his heavy Spanish accent. He and his buddy were *cholos*.

"No, I didn't!"

My face stung.

George's buddy–I never knew his name but the guy outweighed me by at least fifty pounds–said, "You just gonna take that, Holmes? Let's see what you got."

Mr. Kavadas broke through the circle of spectators and said, "What's going on here?" All eyes turned to me. I could have ratted George for his sucker slap but knew it would only make things worse.

"Nothing," I said finally.

When everyone reluctantly returned to their game, George's fat friend whispered, "We'll be seeing you in the parking lot, Holmes."

I remained paranoid about getting jumped for a month or so, but the bad blood eventually dissipated and nothing ever became of that errant volleyball throw. In fact, I never spoke to George again.

• • •

The annual "Battle of the Bands" was a coveted lip-synching contest held in the school cafeteria. David joined a band named "First Glance." I tagged along at one of their rehearsals–in an orange grove with David's truck stereo providing the music–after overhearing David and Richie discuss which song my brother would lip-synch. They decided on Sammy Hagar's *Fast Times At Ridgemont High*. I sat in the truck and rewound the cassette tape, over and over again, as the "band" kicked up dirt practicing synchronized dance moves. As practice wound down, I meekly asked, "Uh . . . room for one more?" I was a freshman among upperclassman. It was a bold question.

L to R, Roger Isom (Sr.), Kelly Cooksey (Sr.), Dean Larsen (Sr.), David Harvey (Jr.),
Richie Morris (Jr.), myself (Freshman), Lisa Thomas (Sr.), and Allen Raye (Jr.)

Everyone looked at each other, a domino reaction of shrugs. With smiles and nods, I was in.

Fourteen bands auditioned for three spots. With each band auditioning two songs each, it was a long night of watching the competition. But it was worth the wait–"First Glance" made the finale! After much deliberation, I chose *On The Loose* by Saga with Sammy Hagar's *Remote Love* a close second.

We practiced in orange groves all over town.

When the big night arrived, the cafeteria was packed. By random draw, we went second. We nervously walked through the crowd, then back outside to the side stage entrance. The loud music and applause stopped, the door opened and the guy running the music said, "Five minutes!"

Drenched in sweat, an upperclassman from the first band said, "You're gonna love the first five rows, dude!"

Lisa, in her First Glance T-shirt and candy cane spandex, stood facing the closed curtain holding the dead microphone. We positioned behind her with guitars that weren't plugged into anything–some of them didn't even have strings. I stood at a small keyboard. David sat at the drumset. Colorful stage lights, both in the floor and overhead, operated by a student just off to the side, were black.

From our side of the curtain, we could *feel* the electricity of the crowd. The kids in the packed cafeteria were *in to it.*

Sporting my only pair of Jordache jeans (yes, Jordache made jeans for guys, too), I tied a purple bandana around my leg figuring it was something Mike Reno, lead singer of Loverboy, would have approved of.

The curtain rose and the hot spotlight lit Lisa up in all her splendor. For a second, we stood there in silence staring into the blinding light. *Shadows of the Night* by Pat Benatar blasted out of the speakers and our glorious hour began.

After my eyes adjusted to the lighting, I understood about the first five rows: all girls.

Our set-list included *Stand or Fall* by The Fixx, *Only a Lad* by Oingo Boingo, *Emotions in Motion* by Billy Squier, *Finger On The Trigger (Love Is In Control)* by Donna Summer, *Don't Fight It* by Kenny Loggins and *Night Ranger* by, of all groups, Night Ranger. Between songs the stage went black–but the curtain stayed up–and we stumbled into position for the next song. It never occurred to us to just stick to one instrument the whole hour.

We tripped over microphone stands.

Singing "On The Loose" into a dead microphone. Note Jordache horse head on pocket and bandana around leg. David in the background strumming a dead guitar (as if he knew how to play it in the first place).

We crashed into each other.

When it was my turn at the drums, I whispered in panic, "Where are the drumsticks?" I had heard of an air guitar; but, air drumsticks? Richie, in his camo pants and knee high moccasins ran them back to me at the last second. He had taken them with him to the keyboards.

Midway through the hour, I performed my song, *On The Loose*. God bless that mob of front row girls–not a one of them a freshman–for making the youngest kid on stage feel like a rock star.

No.

A rock god.

They squealed. They screamed. They pawed at my legs. It was priceless.

The curtain came down on our hour and *we were spent*–and thrilled. We hugged and congratulated each other. *Wow*.

As we passed the nervous members of the third band in the side door, I said to one of the guys, "The first five rows are bitchen, man."

We walked out into the cool night air to catch our breath. What a difference the hour made. I no longer felt like the freshman among upperclassman–suddenly I belonged.

First Glance didn't win. We weren't preppy enough, but we were too excited to be disappointed.

On Monday, I felt a new awareness around school. Students whispered, "*Hey, that's him!*" as I walked by. Girls giggled. Guys nodded. Rock star for an hour. I highly recommend it.

• • •

Nowadays, songs that are considered oldies keep me occupied during my 34-mile daily one-way commute. Some days I'm Michael Hutchence belting out the INXS classics. Some days I'm Bono fronting the best rock band in the world. Some days I'm Zack de la Rocha raging against the machine. And *some days*–to be perfectly honest–I'm Rick Astley singing about the six things I'd *never do* if you were my girl.

When I'm lost in the music saturating my Mini Cooper, I don't visualize strutting around a sold-out Madison Square Garden or L.A. Coliseum. The pretty teenager girls that are Betsy, Mary, Mari, and Jennifer are *forever* in the front row, laughing and singing along. In my mind, my rock star lives on the small stage in the Monache High School cafeteria. He'll always be 18 and I'll always love that guy to death.

• • •

As the school year came to a close, Joe and I mulled over the best way to improve our girl meeting opportunities. Despite my temporary rock star status, my grandiose plan of dating a varsity cheerleader hadn't panned out. I needed a different strategy.

We interviewed for two open positions on the yearbook staff with the following conditions: 1) they had to accept both of us or neither of us, and 2) we would be photographers. We knew nothing about photography. The interview committee agreed to our demands.

1983 Fun Fact #2:

KISS appears on MTV without makeup for the first time. The traveling evangelist said the acronym stood for "Kings In Satan's Service" but, really, who cares? I wanna rock and roll all night . . . and party every day!

CHAPTER 8

The crappy, 1972 Ford Courier farm truck, just before its candy apple red paint job and camper shell. With all mods complete, the truck would later be featured in "Truckin'" magazine.

David decided on another trip to Walla Walla.

That same thousand mile drive in the sweltering June heat we had taken with Mom two years earlier–only this time we had an eleven-year-old farm truck, and I only had my learner's permit. David was seventeen and not legally old enough to supervise my driving. He didn't ask permission–he simply informed Mom of the plan: drive straight through and I'd chat it up all the way to keep him awake.

For eighteen hours.

We hit the road on a hot morning with the plan to stop only for gas, the bathroom, and food. We figured it would take less than a day.

We figured wrong.

One of many problems was that David's 1972 Ford Courier was in the process of being modified into a show truck. At that point, it was illegally lowered to the ground, the windows were illegally tinted, and we cranked the music so loud that we had no chance of carrying on a conversation or hearing an emergency vehicle approaching (also illegal). David poured every penny he made at the coffee shop into a candy apple red paintjob with colorful stripes across the louvered hood. (It wasn't enough to just have a drop-dead paint job, holes punched into the hood and tailgate–louvers–were also a necessity.) All of these modifications made the truck standout to the California Highway Patrol (CHP) more than a band of Hells Angels. We didn't get *ten miles down the road* before a CHP cruiser, heading in the opposite direction, flipped around and tailgated us to the county line. He waited for us to do something–anything–to give him reason to pull us over. (Whenever we saw a cop, we hastily rolled down the windows because of the illegal tint job.)

His other customizations posed other challenges:

- The front air dam nearly dragged the ground and meant swerving around even the smallest bump in the road (and slamming on the brakes over every railroad track).
- The Bondo'd-on visor above the windshield meant swerving away from oncoming semi-trucks in fear of the sudden airflow cracking the permanent fixture.
- The speaker box behind the seat meant we sat uncomfortably upright and forward in the small cab.
- The overhead console loaded with two heavy equalizers fell down every time we hit a bump (about every five minutes).
- No windshield wipers–windshield wipers weren't cool.
- No tools to change a flat tire. Who needs them when you don't have a spare to begin with?

These were the things we knew about. Of course, it's the surprises that get you. Little things like mountain ranges. Mechanical failure. Weather. Fatigue.

Just two hours in the trip, the engine temperature indicator (the little arrow that usually resided in the middle of hot and cold) rose and stayed menacingly near the top of the gauge. Turns out that going seventy five miles per hour wasn't going to work so he slowed down to sixty. Going sixty when everyone else is going eighty is hard on the ego, so he pushed the little truck to the verge of overheating, and we'd stop at gas stations to hose down the radiator. After doing this every hour, on the hour for eight hours, David pulled into a rest stop along I-5 and said, "Screw sixty miles an hour!

We're going to wait until night then make up our lost time." The math didn't quite work in my mind, but I was just along for the ride. Literally.

We waited for the cool night air and started out again.

Around midnight, we hit the Mount Shasta area of the Cascade Range near the Oregon/California border and learned another something about that truck: it could only do forty miles an hour up a steep grade. Big rigs blew by us, up and down the harrowing terrain.

The other modification–a chrome front grill with four square headlights (because the stock round headlights had no place on a show truck)–put us at the greatest risk of all: he never adjusted the headlights correctly so they were pointed two feet ahead of the truck. Thanks to the funky wiring (necessary to power the heavy amplifiers that kept crashing down on our heads), we blew a fuse every couple hours. When this happened, we lost our headlights *and* taillights. When we ran out of fuses, David jammed a nail where the fuse went–it didn't occur to us that we were ripe for an electrical fire. So while we could barely see ahead of us in the best of circumstances, we must have looked like a defective golf cart to those fast moving big rigs on the dark and winding highway.

But, hey, we looked good.

By the time we hit Ashland, Oregon, we were eight hours behind schedule and a combination of the heat, our long pit stop to wait for nightfall, and the white-knuckle adrenalin rush of driving through the Cascades equaled one thing: fatigue.

We pressed on.

We overshot our exit (I-84 East) in Portland–which is pretty hard to do, getting lost on I-5, that is–and had to stop and ask for directions. Admittedly, I am the world's worst navigator and proved it to my weary, frustrated, sweaty brother. Once pointed east, with the state of Washington across the Columbia River on our left, we perked up.

Only two hundred and fifty miles to go.

The crawl continued.

It was midmorning by this time, sweltering hot, and the wind off the Columbia River blew hard against us. People in backpacks hitchhiked along the highway. We had never seen anything like it and before I said a word, David said, "We are *not* picking anyone up." The truck had a custom built camper shell–no side windows–so we could have taken on a couple guys in the back. It was a sauna back there but it was plausible.

"Not even for gas money?"

"No."

Just outside of the The Dalles, Oregon, with less than three hours to go . . .
WOOOOOOOOOSH!

Boiling hot green liquid flew out of the louvered hood and splashed against the windshield. We bolted upright out of our stupor.

The temperature arrow sat all the way north on the gauge.

David swerved the truck to the side of the highway and we jumped out in panic. Lifting the hood we discovered in horror that the radiator hose had burst. Big rigs flew by, blowing hot air and dirt in our faces. David looked at the hose, then at the migrating hitchhikers slowly making their way toward us.

"What are we going to do?" I asked.

"Whatever we do, we have to stay ahead of *them!*" he yelled, pointing to the people trekking along the highway–now just a half-mile away.

It was as if the hitchhikers were the undead–*zombies*–shuffling along the highway. In our exhausted state, we were actually *afraid*. It didn't help that, moments earlier, we cruised by their outstretched thumbs, stereo cranked to Rick Springfield's Living In Oz cassette.

David climbed in the back of the camper shell and emerged with a wide roll of silver duct tape. Lucky for us, the radiator hose hadn't completely exploded; fluid spewed from a two-inch long crack along one side. As I held the shiny candy apple red hood in the bright sunlight (no latch for the hood, *that wouldn't have been cool!*), I imagined that the slog of people approaching us *were going to eat our brains*. The hood was a beacon.

The ground was boiling hot. The air was boiling hot.

I watched David in silence. Sweat poured down his face.

Finally, I said, "Hurry, man, hurry!"

He looked over his shoulder at the scraggly hitchhikers and taped faster.

"There! That should hold us for awhile!"

We scrambled in the truck and pulled onto I-84 with a hundred yards to spare before the first group of hitchhikers reached us. We honestly thought they would beat the living hell out of us.

A mile down the road, we pulled into a Chevron and explained our problem to the geezer who multi-tasked as the cashier, the mechanic, and the guy who pumped the gas (you can't pump your own gas in the state of Oregon, by the way). He shuffled into the locked garage in no particular hurry. A few minutes later, he emerged holding a shiny black rubber radiator hose.

It was the most beautiful radiator hose I'd ever seen.

He handed it to David and said he'd have to trim it to fit. David borrowed his knife and got to work. After handing us a gallon of Prestone antifreeze, Grandpa Chevron announced the bill: $38.

$38? I stood in stunned disbelief.

The grizzled old fart stood there smiling proudly, his hands tucked in his dirty blue overalls. He had us and he knew it. No sympathy for the kids in the neon-painted farm truck with California license plates.

I handed him two twenty dollar bills–a significant part of our total travel budget–and waited for the change. He shuffled back in the office and came back with two grimy dollar bills.

As we pulled away, he said, "You fellas have a nice day now."

Hanging out the window, I replied, "Yeah. Merry Christmas, *cheesedick!*"

We pulled into Walla Walla at five p.m.–989 miles from Porterville, seventeen hours behind schedule and forty dollars lighter.

Lorne lived with our uncle Bart and Bart threw down the rules. "Lorne, don't you get these guys drunk tonight." Lorne assured him that *everything was cool*–the plan was to have some of Grandma Bun's blackberry cobbler then *maybe go to a movie.*

That was partially correct–we did have cobbler. Then we went to a party where everyone was drinking Jack Daniels and Coke. Van Halen blasted through the crammed apartment.

Knowing nothing about proper whiskey to soda ratio, (I thought it was 50/50) I proceeded to show everyone how a fifteen-year-old from California could hang with these twenty-something's. The revelers couldn't believe my heavy mixing hand–then couldn't believe I drank the awful mixture. I swallowed it like a chump–I mean, *a champ*. It burned like fire but I didn't know any better.

On the totem pole of brotherhood, it's unwritten that the youngest brother gets the floor when all beds and couches are taken. I was only horizontal on the floor for a minute before staggering to the bathroom, fighting back the churning, burning mess rising in my throat.

Extrication was imminent.

After the fifth projectile vomit in the general direction of the toilet, I looked up through blurry eyes and there stood Uncle Bart in nothing but his white Fruit of the Looms. His arms were crossed. His frown was legendary.

"I think I got a touch of food poisoning tonight," I croaked between wretches. Bart didn't say a word.

The next day I awoke face down on the floor. My face, hair, shirt, and the pristine white carpet were covered with drying, partially masticated blackberry cobbler. White carpet fibers clogged my crusted nostrils.

The brothers in the summer of 1983.

My stomach boiled. My head ached.

David looked down from the couch and said, "Whoa. Look at all the blackberry seeds!"

Lorne was grounded. For a month.

A week later we left Walla Walla in the evening and drove down the more direct I-97 South through Bend, Oregon. Surviving the second harrowing trip up and over Mt. Shasta, ten hours into the drive, David pulled over on the side of the freeway.

Without saying a word, he proceeded to *climb in the back of the camper shell*. It was 8 a.m. and the sun was just beginning its blazing assault. He never bought a boot to connect the cab with the camper (*so not cool!*) which meant there was no way to communicate with him back there.

He laid out a sleeping bag (at least we had thought of that much) and was asleep as soon as he laid his head down.

I was on my own behind the wheel.

I pulled onto I-5 and prayed to God that the truck wouldn't break down, or I wouldn't get pulled over for any number of infractions the truck was guilty of. I wasn't sure that I could keep myself awake in the blistering heat of the morning but it helped that the overhead console swung down and hit me in the head every five minutes. With sole control of the music selection, I blasted Tears For Fears' Songs From The Big Chair and sang as loud as I could.

• • •

One craze that began around this time was the brainchild of inventor Xavier Roberts: the Cabbage Patch Kid. Demand far exceeded supply and we watched the news in awe and amusement: New York City moms throwing blows over the one homely doll on the shelf.

What was special about these simple dolls with oversized plastic heads and soft, fabric bodies wasn't so much the doll itself–it was the *story* behind the doll.

According to Mr. Roberts, the dolls were *orphans*. Not only that, but if they weren't adopted they'd spend their "lives" toiling in a pit doing hard labor. Each doll had a name and, the *coup de grace*, a birth certificate.

Every kid in America, including my eight-year-old sister, *had* to have one. Thus began the quest for the seemingly unattainable. Each night we'd watch the news for Cabbage Patch sightings: *Channel 5 reports that the Fresno Gottschalks in the Fashion Fair Mall has 25 dolls . . .*

Before Mom could run to the phone, hoping to beg Gottschalks to hold one, the reporter continued: ". . . *the dolls lasted all of ninety seconds as shoppers grabbed them as they were placed on the shelf. No blood flew but there was some pushing and shoving. Let's now cut to another Cabbage Patch brawl in New York . . .*"

Mom would not be denied and called her brother in Atlanta. Soon a package arrived from our good Uncle Harold with huge block letters: TO BE OPENED BY YOUR MOTHER ONLY. I MEAN IT!

Mom locked herself in her bedroom, let out a shriek, and emerged with, perhaps, the only Cabbage Patch Kid in Tulare County. It wasn't my sister's birthday, it wasn't Christmas, it wasn't even Kwanzaa, but it was a day that would forever be a part of Trish's childhood: the day she adopted her very own Cabbage Patch Kid.

It was a girl with thick strands of red yarn for hair. Her name, Jenny McFlowerypants, or some damn thing.

Trish carefully filled out the adoption papers and pinned the birth certificate on the wall. This gave her two loving brothers an idea.

On more than one occasion, my sister returned from school to find little Jenny dangling from a noose, complete with an official-looking death certificate.

Kids.

A couple years later, the Topps Company parodied the lovable dolls in the form of trading cards and stickers via the Garbage Pail Kids. With names like Adam Bomb, Stinky Stan, and Douche Bag Dennis (OK, I made up that last one), the vile Garbage Pail Kids were an instant hit with kids and teens alike.

In the 1986 Rodney Dangerfield comedy, *Back To School*, we see another parody reference via the Melon Patch Kids–dolls that weren't orphaned, they were abandoned.

In a movie no one saw in 1987, *The Garbage Pail Kids Movie*, Paramount Pictures tried to keep the flicker of interest alive but Topps was eventually sued for trademark infringement and the back country third cousins to the Cabbage Patch Kids soon dropped out of the mainstream.

In the 1997 black comedy, *Grosse Pointe Blank*, John Cusack plays a guy who returns to his hometown of Grosse Pointe, Michigan for his 10-year high school reunion.

In a coincidence I find ultra-cool, John's character graduated in 1986.

The soundtrack is New Wave all the way featuring songs by The Clash, English Beat, Violent Femmes, Echo & the Bunnymen, The Specials (who *I absolutely love*), The Cure, Siouxsie and the Banshees, Pixies, and so on. It also has two of my favorite funk songs, *Let It Whip* by The Dazz Band and *White Lines (Don't Do It)* by Grandmaster Flash & Melle Mel. I listen to this CD religiously these days–such a departure from what I used to listen to.

There's a point to this ramble, trust me.

So I was cruising along in the Mini-Cooper the other day, trying to keep up with Faith No More's *We Care a Lot* (another song off the soundtrack) and nearly ran off the road when I heard the reference. If you listen closely, (it takes a bit of concentration because these guys have *heavy* British accents) you will hear a reference to the Garbage Pail Kids in this song!

To think it only took 15 years of listening to finally hear it.

Even today, you can find Garbage Pail Kids trading cards at your local store. Not too far, in fact, from the descendents of Jenny McFlowerypants, gathering dust on the shelf.

1984 Fun Fact #1:

George Orwell got it wrong in his classic novel published in 1949: Nineteen Eighty-Four. Thankfully, Big Brother's totalitarian society remains a few lifetimes away . . . I think . . . the book did spur a great song by Oingo Boingo, though—Wake Up (It's 1984).

CHAPTER 9

I learned the proper protocol for riding in my brother's truck to and from school. Not that he had much of a choice. For half of my sophomore year, I was his passenger–under the following conditions:

1) You do not wave to anyone.
2) You may nod–and nod only–but only if it's in response to a wave or nod.
3) The entire JV cheerleader squad is eligible for a ride home. If we stop to pick up a girl, she'll ride between us. If we pick up two or more, I ride in the back.
4) If we pick up Dayna, Teresa, or Renee, I ride in the back.

We started our day together on the road and in the classroom, sharing Mr. Briscoe's first period Spanish 2. The class was a riot since no one learned anything from his first year class (and if you took Spanish 1 from Mr. Briscoe, you *had* to take Spanish 2 from him, for that very reason). Mr. Briscoe was too lovable and not nearly strict enough. With Chevy Chase's film, *National Lampoon Vacation* in the theaters, he *was* Clark W. Griswold in the flesh–bumbling, lovable, and oblivious.

After Spanish 2, came Typing, Geometry, PE, English, then Yearbook.

It wasn't a common sight for a guy to take typing in 1983. Of the thirty students in my second period class, 90% were girls which was the reason I enrolled in the first place.

That first quarter was rough for two reasons: 1) I was stuck on one of the few manual typewriters (Mr. Fishburn must have figured my fingers were stronger than his average student–you really had to mash down to put print to paper) and 2) memorizing the keys didn't come easy to me. During daily typing drills, we looked straight ahead at a large poster of a keyboard–forbidden to look at our hands. A couple months into class, Mr. Fishburn took the poster down without warning. He knew his deviants and often stood next to me during class. When he saw me peering down in frustration, he'd clear his throat and say, "You're only cheating yourself, Tom."

I finally learned the layout of the keys and was rewarded with an electric typewriter from the second quarter on. To my surprise, I *excelled* at typing and cracked the top ten of fastest typists (displayed on an obnoxious poster for all to see). By the end of the year–at our last timed exercise to determine the fastest typist in the class–it came down to me and a girl named Lori. Tension was high. We locked eyes like two gunslingers at the OK Corral.

Ready? Set? Type!

After the smoke settled on our final exercise, Mr. Fishburn announced, "Lori, congratulations on typing forty seven words a minute!"

Lori looked at me and beamed.

"Tom, congratulations on typing forty eight words a minute! Tom is the class' fastest typist!" I sat back in my chair, not sure whether to be proud or embarrassed.

Despite my brother Lorne's advice to *make math my friend*, math had other ideas. All that side-angle-siding of sophomore geometry made no sense to me. The first time I raised my hand to ask a question, Mr. Reeder snapped, "Class time is my time to teach! If you have questions, see me *before school!*" He hurried through the day's lesson, then sat in the back of the class working on football strategy–he was the JV football coach.

After a D the first quarter (and I did meet with Mr. Reeder–once–before school but found it pointless–the guy had *zero* patience), temptation got the best of me and I cheated off a classmate. Candace was a senior so I figured she understood geometry better than I.

A day after the test, Mr. Reeder kept the two of us after class. Holding up our tests, both emblazoned with big F's circled in red ink, he asked, "These are so wrong and so identical that I want to know who copied off of who."

We stood in silence–in cheating there is solidarity– maybe that was the lesson learned.

"It doesn't matter," he continued. "You're both getting an F for the semester for cheating." With that, he waved us out the door in a mix of disgust and twisted pleasure.

I dropped Geometry that very day and finished the year in General Business.

I enjoyed English 10 Honors with the venerable Margaret Land. She taught writing fundamentals and demanded excellence. While other sophomores read *Catch 22* and *A Farewell to Arms*, we spent months picking apart the complex storyline of Frank Herbert's science-fiction classic, *Dune*. Coincidentally, the movie was released in December 1984, and I went to see it the first weekend–anxious to show my devotion to Mrs. Land's beloved book.

"So I saw *Dune* this weekend. Wow, it was great!" I said before class the following Monday.

"You think so?" she asked warily. "I saw it too and thought it was one of the worst adaptations of a book I've ever seen. Utterly horrible."

I shuffled back to my desk with my head down.

There was no sucking up to Mrs. Land as I found out struggling to learn the comma rules. [10] Hoping she'd go easy on me during her random, sadistic pop quizzes, I employed what I thought was a time-proven technique. The latin term, I believe, is *Ass-kissis Maximus*.

"Mrs. Land, do you drive a blue Celica?"

"Yes."

"I really, *really* like it. When I get my driver's license this year, I hope to get one just like it."

"Really? Well, that's nice . . ."

The class bell rang and everyone sat down.

She continued in the same breath, *"Tom, what are the comma rules?"*

---

10   Here they are for your education. Use a comma to 1) separate elements in a series, 2) after a conjunction to connect to independent clauses, 3) to set off introductory elements, 4) to set off parenthetical elements, 5) to separate adjectives, 6) to set off quotations, and 7) to separate city and states & dates and years.

The last class of the day was Yearbook–a class not at all confined to a class-room. One thing Joe and I learned almost immediately was that being a yearbook photographer was a *hell of a lot of work*. Unlike today's digital age, we shot rolls of film through the most manual 35 millimeter camera ever made: the Pentax K-1000. We learned aperture settings, film speed, and f-stops via accelerated trial and error. While the perks were great–time out of class, free entry into dances, ogling students at rallies and around campus–the workload more than offset the social advantages.

Here's why.

Every roll of black and white film had to be developed, *correctly*, in the dark-room. From there, a proof (a thumbnail exposure of all the pictures on a standard sheet of photo paper) was produced for yearbook staffers. With ink pencil in eager hand, they circled the thumbnails they wanted enlarged for further consideration in their page layouts. We were, then, back in the putrid darkroom with dozens of photos to produce.

The darkroom was nothing more than a small closet that reeked of sulfur within the interior hallway of the science building. The only way there was through one of six science building classrooms and, during seventh period, we interrupted the same teacher: Mr. Funderburk. We called him "Funder Chicken" and he didn't mind it in the least. I never had Funder Chicken as a teacher and what I pulled on him a few years later amazes me to this day–but we'll get to that.

The workload was so great that we had a set of keys to the science building which allowed us in the building evenings and on the weekends. Imagine that today: Giving free reign to a couple of sophomores in a building full of chemicals, lamb eyeballs, and baby pigs suspended in formaldehyde. Oh, the mischief we could have caused.

We weren't exactly angels and embraced a tradition found the first time we closed the sliding darkroom door. There, in all its splendor, were a dozen pictures of cheerlead-ers caught in compromised positions. A note taped to the door was all the instruction needed: "$20 for the best beaver shot of the year. Keep the tradition alive boys."

Once again, I shake my head–now–at the brazenness, the ignorance, *the sheer stupidity*, of what we–a couple of honor students–were doing. Had a teacher–any teacher–walked in the darkroom, slid the door shut and turned around, we would have been in serious trouble.

After a year of photographing our cheerleaders in action, Joe and I contem-plated the finalists. My picture captured a tall blonde Porterville High cheerleader in full leg kick–her right toe practically touched her forehead. (The picture was taken at our annual rival basketball game.) Joe's picture was our mascot (in her very Pocahontas-like outfit) doing the splits in mid-jump. After multiple enlargements of specific regions of our unknowing subjects–to the point of frustrating distortion–we ended in a stalemate. I thought my picture was clearly better and demanded the money. Joe countered that my picture was ineligible because it wasn't a Monache cheerleader. For weeks we argued over it until we nearly asked Funder Chicken to step in and declare a winner. Thankfully, *for all involved*, we decided that wasn't a good idea.

[Note: We left the "Beaver Shot Collection" taped to the inside of the darkroom door and, upon returning for our junior year, discovered the pictures were *gone*. In full-stage panic our first day back as juniors, Joe and I awaited the page from the principal's office, certain we'd start the first week of school on suspension.

The week passed. Nothing.

After the second week, we figured we were in the clear and a new collection began. I can only imagine what became of those pictures–but I like to think they're aging gracefully in some retired, appreciative, janitor's garage.]

Our yearbook advisor, the lovable, aged, Mr. Schoenfeld, had his hands full overseeing the yearbook production staff and had no idea what his photographers were doing most of the time. He only taught yearbook that year because his daughter was a senior–a varsity cheerleader at that.

One rule of the Beaver Shot competition was that crotch shots of Mr. Schoenfeld's daughter were strictly out of bounds since he could have dropped in on us in the darkroom at any time and it would have been well within his right. Lucky for us, he never did.

When the seventh period bell rang we were rarely in the yearbook classroom and got busted, on more than one occasion, playing hacky sack. (Hacky sacks were the size of Ping Pong balls, filled with sand, and made of leather. Kicking the bag around a small circle of guys was all the rage at the time, though I was never good at it. Sperry Topsiders were the best shoe for the game, but they were too expensive for me at $54 a pair.)

With the advent of the digital camera, anyone can be a photographer without the laborious task of processing and developing film–the darkroom, as we both loved and hated it, is a thing of the past for all but true aficionados.

But, oh, the inside of that darkroom door.

Being a yearbook photographer definitely raised us up a notch on the ladder of popularity–people loved to have their picture taken. Thanks to the yearbook, I found my first high school girlfriend. I'll call her Lynn.

Lynn was part of the hardworking yearbook page designers. She was blonde, pretty, and a junior–yet again another older woman in my life.

One fair night in the last months of 1983, I joined the ranks of the *educated*. In my insecurity and uncertainty, I applied one condom–and then another. It wasn't out of a fear of AIDS (that only affected gay males, right?)–it was simple fear from a naive, fifteen-year-old kid. [Note: That's much, *much* too young. Teenagers, take note! Keep it in your pants. You'll be glad you did.] There, on my small twin size childhood bunk bed, under two posters of the swimsuit-clad super model, Paulina Poriskova, my virginity became a thing of the past.

I thought I had a good idea of what went where after watching my first ever porno a few days earlier: *Insatiable* starring Marilyn Chambers. One of David's friends brought over the video after-school–along with his VCR since we didn't have one–and fifteen teenage guys huddled intensely around our 19" Philco. We thought we were pretty smart by dead bolting the front door which allowed a three second warning that Mom was home when she tried to open the door–*we never dead bolted the front door.* I have to credit the kid manning the VCR–he had that tape swapped out after my panicked, "Mom's home!" announcement. By the time she unbolted the upper deadbolt, we were casually watching John Travolta ride the mechanical bull in *Urban Cowboy.* Mom looked at the overflowing room of red-faced, cross-legged guys and smiled. She never said a word.

After *Insatiable*, I never looked at a pool table quite the same way again.

• • •

A few weeks before my sixteenth birthday, Mom drove up in a severely oxidized reddish-pink 1977 Honda Civic. She didn't say where she got it or why she had it but I secretly thought, *God I hope that's not for me.* That sounds horribly inconsiderate, I know.

My sixteenth birthday!

After my trip and back to the DMV on February 8 (95% on my driving test; docked 5% for not turning my head while changing lanes on Main, damn!), Mom handed me a small box wrapped in birthday paper. Inside, the keys to the Honda. I hugged her.

The best thing about that car, as Lynn and I discovered, was that the front seats folded completely horizontal. We, uh, *practiced* under the cover of darkness in one of the thousands of acres of orange groves around Tulare County.

One night we decided on a change of venue and ended up at the rural Porterville airport. There was a large perimeter chain link fence around the property but the double wide gate was open. I drove down the crushed white gravel road and pulled off to the side–a hundred yards from the road.

As we enjoyed each other's company in the pitch black of night, a four-wheel-drive truck barreled down the gravel road toward us. He must have had quite a laugh when he spied a crappy Honda Civic rocking on the side of the road and skidded to a halt two inches from the rear bumper. White gravel showered the back of my car. I jumped into the driver's seat and sprayed gravel all the way to the main road–what a sight, two half-naked teenagers speeding away from the scene of the crime.

Our adventures weren't limited to the inside of my small car, though. Some entrepreneur opened a rent-by-the-hour hot tub business at the base of the Mustang Waterslides in Tulare. He should have called it the "Mustang *Ranch* Hot Tubs" since use of the hot tubs was discreet and cheap ($8 per hour, per person). Picture that now: by-the-hour hot tub rentals. *Gross.* Back then, it was a $16 thrill (and we went dutch. How can you lose?). And, who was kidding whom? The guy who took our money and handed us clean towels (at least I *think* they were clean) knew exactly what was going down behind those locked doors. Sixty minutes later, we'd emerge with bloated, pink skin and semi-permanent smiles on our faces.

The hot tub portion of the Mustang operation had a short life–in business less than a year. The waterslides, as far as I know, are still there. You can't have sex on a waterslide, though, can you? Hmm, now there's a thought.

• • •

Tragedy struck in May when an eighteen-year-old senior, Mark Zaninovich, died in a single car accident. He fell in the cowboy clique in his Wranglers, boots, and handlebar moustache. As the entire school discovered, his sudden death transcended the cliques. Our beloved principal, Mr. Boehme, addressed the school on the intercom system in tears, declaring that written notes would not be necessary for students who missed class due to the funeral. St. Anne's church was filled to capacity with hundreds of students left to stand outside.

Mark had been ejected from his four-wheel drive truck in a high speed rollover accident and died of massive head injuries. Alcohol, people whispered, must have been a factor. In an effort not to get caught up in the emotion of it all, I said to David, "Well, that's what happens when you drink and drive." He grabbed me by the front of my shirt–his eyes on fire–and cocked his right fist. I held my breath. Finally, he said, "You don't know what you're talking about so shut your fucking mouth!" He released me and I stepped back in wide-eyed surprise.

Fifteen hundred kids wanted to do something to honor Mark and, within a few weeks, money was raised to purchase a memorial bench. The following school year, the bench sat at a busy intersection between classrooms. His name, birthday, and death date, were engraved in the granite.

For weeks, no one dared sit on the bench.

Mark's sister, Paula, provided the picture I am most proud of in two years as a yearbook photographer. The vibe was strong the day I approached the area–Paula sat on the bench engrossed in a textbook, oblivious to the two hundred students and teachers surrounding her in hushed reverence.

The picture is special for a few reasons: 1) I had color film in my camera and we only had two weeks out of the year to take color pictures for the yearbook, 2) Paula is wearing her varsity volleyball jersey with her last name on the back, and 3) the picture isn't posed. I burst into the yearbook classroom that day with the news that I had captured the moment–poignant and perfect.

Word quickly spread that Paula used the bench and other students followed suit. Thanks to Paula, people no longer avoided the bench. Even in death, Mark brought people together.

He was buried in a Catholic cemetery on a hill south of town, and I used to go there alone and stand in silence over his grave. I never told anyone because he and I had never spoken a word to each other. I felt sad thinking that he was out there all alone.

Death is tragic and confusing, isn't it?

1984 Fun Fact #2:

After watching him as Gumby and Buckwheat on Saturday Night Live, Eddie Murphy hits box office gold with Beverly Hills Cop. I watched it in the theater, twice.

CHAPTER 10

Rekindling my love of football, I discovered that the varsity coach, Mr. Rice, ran a summer passing league. Since the Central California summers are blisteringly hot, this entailed running around in shorts and a T-shirt–learning pass routes and catching passes.

I discovered something that surprised everyone: I ran the forty-yard dash in 4.5 seconds, second fastest on the team. Every day I showed up to practice, Coach Rice (and his son, the "other" Coach Rice) smiled widely, and nodded their approval–*Hell, I'm a varsity football player! I'm the second fastest guy on the team!*

What I didn't realize was that the coach gladly accepted all-comers–*anybody*– because he needed bodies. Despite my speed, I was only 5'9" and 155 pounds. I hadn't played since my freshman year, and, let's be honest, I sucked.

The program for the first home game listed me at six feet and two hundred pounds. Coach Rice was quite the optimist.

• • •

David and Richie decided to inner tube down the Tule River which ran from the small mountain town of Springville, north of Porterville, through the River Island golf course and into Success Lake. I invited myself along but had to come up with my own tube.

The Tule River raged from an unusually high snowmelt that summer, and my automobile tube paled in comparison to their tractor tubes. We drove past the country club and parked on the side of the winding road. After a small hike, we stared at the raging river. This was to be no leisurely float.

We laughed at my little tube.

"It's now or never." I jumped onto the tube and the ice cold current whisked me away.

Just around the bend, I slammed into a tree lying across the expanse and the tube exploded on a jagged branch. Frantically trying to pull myself onto the tree, the force of the current pulled me lower and lower. Shoulder deep in the frigid water, I looked down at a pool of blood circling under my chin. My bare chest bled from rough abrasions.

I was stuck.

The deafening noise of the water rushed around my ears. My feet were caught in a web of branches and debris just beyond the large trunk and *I knew* that letting go meant I would drown.

"Help! Help me!"

Time slowed.

My fingers began to turn blue.

The raging force pulled me lower into the river.

I started to sob in panic, choking on bloody water tumbling over my head. Ice cold water poured into my eyes.

My arms began to ache. Starbursts flashed in my distorted vision.

The water was taking me. I was going to drown in the swirling web of debris under this fallen tree. The voice in my mind calmly said, *People drown in the Tule River all the time. Today it's going to be you. Look on the bright side. Your name will be in the Porterville Recorder tomorrow.*

My grip loosened.

I closed my eyes. The world became dark and quiet.

The moment was *peaceful*. I was alone and today was my day to die. My last thought in this life: *Mom, I'm sorry. I'm so sorry.*

"I've got you!" David screamed, his voice muffled and distorted, a thousand miles away.

I opened my eyes. David's wavy, angelic face appeared, surrounded by bright sunlight.

He was under red streaky water.

No.

I was under red streaky water.

As he knelt on top of the tree, both of his hands locked onto my left forearm.

"I've got you! Don't let go!"

He tugged upward and I drew in a large gasp of air.

I slipped back. With just the top of my head and arms above the rushing water, I was caught in a life-or-death tug of war: My brother versus the strong grip of the current.

He knelt forward and yanked upward with all his adrenalin-fueled strength. My bare chest ripped across the rough bark as he lifted my shoulders clear of the water. How he didn't break my forearm, at that odd angle, is a miracle.

Noise rushed back.

Pain.

Cold.

I sobbed uncontrollably.

He yanked again and draped me over the tree.

He yanked again and pulled me to my knees.

Safe.

Saved.

He steadied himself and sat back, exhausted.

I gasped and coughed for air, spitting blood and pieces of wet bark. My body convulsed uncontrollably.

"You saved my life," I croaked. Tears poured down my face.

He looked at me, expressionless.

"I don't know," he smiled, out of breath. "You should see yourself."

The entire front of my body was bright red and bleeding. I had bitten my lip and blood trickled from my mouth. My fingers were blue and bleeding. I was a mess.

"I guess that little tube of yours wasn't such a good idea after all," he said matter of factly.

"You saved my life today," I sobbed.

"I thought I lost you for a second."

"In another second you would have."

This is what had happened.

As soon as I hit the water, David and Richie knew I was in trouble. They jumped in after me and watched as I was swept away on the tiny inner tube. I hit the tree on the left side of the river, the tube exploded on a branch, and they jumped off of their tubes onto the right bank. As I held on for dear life, David tried to figure out how to cross the rushing water. He ran up the bank, crossed at our entry point, then ran back toward me. By the time he crawled onto the fallen tree, I was just losing my grip. The whole thing took three minutes.

I crawled off the tree and limped back to the truck. Every part of me hurt. When we got home, Mom just about had a heart attack.

• • •

Wednesday, July 18, was like any other hot day in the valley until every channel began broadcasting the live coverage of a siege in San Diego.

At a McDonald's of all places.

I watched the rampage in shocked disbelief. Bodies and blood, lots of blood, could be seen through the shattered windows of the restaurant. News cameras shook as cameramen jostled for protection behind buildings and police cars.

Gunfire.

Chaos.

Death.

A SWAT team sniper ended the ordeal on live TV after an hour and seventeen minutes of sheer madness and murder. In all, twenty two people died, including the deranged gunman.

What became known as the San Ysidro McDonald's Massacre changed how police departments across the country prepared for such incidents. Trained tactical units with higher power firearms became more the norm than the exception.

The site was razed and a memorial built.

1985 Fun Fact #1:

Coca-Cola changed its formula and launched "New Coke." Cuban dictator, Fidel Castro, called New Coke a sign of American capitalist decadence. (There's that word again.) Not that we gave a rat's ass about what Castro thought, but in less than 3 months we were back to "Coca-Cola Classic."

CHAPTER 11

I mourned the loss of my brother and his friends–they all disappeared via that life changer known as high school graduation. David and Richie and Allen and Eric–and a slew of others–just weren't there anymore.

As for my dream of playing varsity football, reality crashed down when the regular players strolled on the field and reassumed their places on the team. Coach Rice moved me from wide receiver to tight end. Not only was I too small for the position at 155 pounds, I was a *distant* third stringer. I couldn't block and didn't know the plays. I was an offensive lineman only on paper.

Despite getting kicked to the curb at a position I'd never play, I did have a spot on the kick off team. Not special teams, *just the kick off team*. This ensured the absolute minimum field time as logistically possible.

It was truly a matter of pride to me–to be on the varsity squad–after spending all summer practicing. Plus, the varsity cheerleaders were more womanly than the JV cheerleaders and, c'mon, that's important.

Our first game was at home against powerhouse Redwood High School. We played our home games at the Porterville College football stadium and made the four mile drive in the team bus in uniform. No one said a word. The moment was intense.

Pregame warm-ups included running routes in front of bleachers filling with students and parents. Working into the rotation of wide receivers, I sprinted thirty yards and stretched out to catch Jack Sussoev's pass. In full extension, I missed the ball, landed on my head, and rolled in the freshly cut grass. The near capacity home crowd roared its approval. I ran back with the ball, smiling inside my unblemished gold helmet. Looking at the stands out of the corner of my eye–the cheer wasn't for me, the band had just marched out on the track. Damn.

The first game glory lasted until kick off. Two positions from our kicker in the middle of the field, my job was to go straight to the ball and make the tackle. In full sprint, I made it fifteen yards before a defender threw his forearm into my throat and I crashed to the ground gasping for air. I scraped myself off the grass and coughed my way back to the bench. It was the only time I stepped on the field.

Redwood laid the wood to us, 35-0.

The following Monday at practice while I was on the ground stretching, Coach Rice stepped into my line of vision, blocking out the bright sun. The man spoke a total of a dozen words to me and this is ten of them:

"I want you to drop down to the JV team."

I sat up in disbelief as he walked away.

Anger.

Betrayal.

There was no way my pride was going to accept this demotion. Hell, I had already paid twenty dollars for my customized varsity jersey! The JVs didn't have their names on their jerseys! The JVs were the opening half of the Friday Night double headers with the Varsity teams in primetime. And, and . . . the varsity cheerleaders were just more *womanly!*

No way in hell I was dropping down.

For the next two weeks, I pretended the request was a figment of my imagination. Coach Rice didn't bring it up again and the JV coach never came looking for me (The fact that I flunked out of his geometry class probably had something to do with it).

Mike Wells, a proud member of the JV team, approached me.

"Hey, they've been calling your name when they take the JV roll call."

"There must be some mistake."

He looked at me, unconvinced.

"You know," he continued, "if you *did* drop down, you'd be the starting tight end."

"That's nice, but I'm on the *varsity* roster. I already paid for the jersey."

Mike shrugged.

The next Friday we played at powerhouse Mount Whitney High. At halftime, when it was obvious our winless record was comfortably intact (the scoreboard showed twenty four points and none of them were ours), I approached Coach Rice as we retook the field.

"Coach, I'm fresh."

He walked on, clutching his clipboard, trying to ignore me.

"Coach, I'm fresh."

Not even a sideways glance.

"COACH, I'M FRESH *GODDAMNIT!*"

In its simplest terms, the words meant, *Coach I'm not tired, let me play*. It also meant, *Coach I gave you my whole goddamn summer and I've been on the field once after a game-and-a-half.*

Amid the clicks of forty players' cleats on the parking lot asphalt, Coach Rice stopped and looked at me. Players click clacked around us. It was a look of compassion, a look that said he understood.

"OK," he said quietly.

Late in the fourth quarter, with the scoreboard reading 31-0 and the other team playing their third stringers (and, likely, any kid from any local junior high who wanted to play), we marched inside the ten yard line our one and only time.

"Harvey, in! Leppert, out!" Coach Rice yelled. Hey, he knew my name after all.

Leppert had the height at 6' 3", but it didn't matter who was lined up at receiver. There was no way we would pass the ball so close to the goal line.

Leppert threw a fit. "What the hell? What the hell, Coach? What the hell? What the hell?"

Coach Rice held up one stern finger and Leppert sulked away, spewing obscenities.

I ran into the huddle, my spotless white jersey and gold pants the cleanest on the field. My helmet had one little scuff from me intentionally dropping it in the parking lot. My heart pounded.

"Dive 44," Jack said.

I ran out to the far left flank and locked eyes with the defensive cornerback. I nodded as if saying *hello* but the guy just pawed his foot on the ground. He was going to hit me all right. We waited for the snap of the ball.

And waited.

And waited.

I looked down the line to our quarterback. Jack pointed at me frantically. I pointed to myself, *You talking to me?* It suddenly occurred to me that I was off the line of scrimmage which would have penalized us five yards for illegal procedure. With two seconds left on the twenty five second clock, I stepped forward–making the formation legal–and he ran the dive play.

At the snap of the ball, my defender knocked me to the ground.

Our running back, Kenny Mariboho, met a wall of third string defensive players and fell back. No gain.

I ran back in the huddle.

"What the hell, dude? Get on the line of scrimmage you idiot!" Jack hissed. He didn't even know my name.

Still wide eyed, I nodded. Holy crap, I sucked.

We ran the play again with the same result.

We huddled again and I looked over at our sidelines. Leppert paced around, complaining to anyone who would listen. I smiled.

On third and goal from the two yard line, Kenny finally broke through. Touchdown! Our sideline erupted. Our band played. I was on the field when we scored–the moment was *good*. When I tried to run off the field, Coach Rice waved me back in for the try. I lined up at tight end and ran into a kid who made no effort whatsoever to block the kick.

We kicked the extra point and, with five seconds left in the game, tried an onside kick. Since I was on the kick off team, I was on the field a record number of successive plays: five. The onside kick failed. Game over.

Mount Whitney: 31, Monache: 7.

Week Three had us back home against a team from Bakersfield, Highland High. I made it on the field twice in the loss.

Highland: 35, Monache 7.

After three straight losses with a combined score of 101-14, Coach Rice was *pissed*.

"Starting Monday, we will have *two* practices a day! *Before and after* school! I want to see if anyone on this team has any heart!"

We loaded the bus and made the somber drive back to school in silence. Sitting next to Ruben Zamora, I said, "I'm done. I don't need this abuse."

I never stepped on the field again.

In retrospect, I regret that decision. The JV and Varsity teams that year went a combined 1-19, but, so what? I should have swallowed my pride, taken my place on the JV team (where I rightfully belonged), and played for the sake of playing–for the fun of it. My only moment of glory–and I mean that in the most fleeting of ways–occurred while listening to an away game on the local radio station one Friday night in my bedroom. The broadcast went something like this:

"And Monache continues to struggle this year. Looks like their winless streak will continue . . . Coach Rice is starting to substitute freely now . . . we have a new wide receiver on the field . . . don't know who it is . . . let me look at my roster . . . hmm . . . could be Harvey but I'm not sure . . ."

I bolted upright in my bed and laughed so loud Mom came in my room.

"What's so funny?" she asked.

"The radio announcers think I'm on the field."

She hugged me. "You're first string in my book, baby."

• • •

I guess you could say I was fickle since my interest in Lynn eroded after six months. It wasn't as if I had my eye on anyone else, either. In my sixteen-year-old mind, it was simply time to move on. No more orange grove adventures. No more trips to the steamy hot tubs.

What attracted me initially to Lynn was her long blonde hair. When she chopped it all off one day, I realized our future wasn't so bright that I needed shades. The timing of the breakup, in retrospect, was cruel. I look at the picture now–the March 1985 "Hearts and Flowers" dance–and can't help but be reminded that I broke up with her *that very night*. I can see the pre-breakup tension in our faces. She wasn't surprised when it happened–just angry. The picture makes me sad. She deserved better.

My bachelorhood lasted just over a month. *True love* happens when you least expect it, right?

Tiffany was exotic with long brown hair, brown eyes, and an olive skin complexion–half-Portuguese on her dad's side. I passed her in the school hallways and knew that she was a senior based on her circle of friends. She was on the tennis team. She played the flute in the band. And she drove the coolest car in town: a brand-new, 1985, red Pontiac Fiero. License plate: FOOTLSE.

I had to get to know this girl.

Her tennis partner was a mutual friend, Paula Zaninovich. My inquiry began with her.

"Paula, tell me about Tiffany."

"What do you want to know?"

"Does she have a boyfriend?"

"Well, she's sort of seeing a guy from Porterville High but I don't think it's serious."

"Why do you say that?"

"He has the only other Fiero in town. It was sort of an attraction of cars. Kinda weird if you ask me."

Great. She liked cars and I drove a faded pink Honda Civic piece of crap.

Paula and I smiled at each other in silence.

"I'm going to come out and watch your match after school, if you don't mind."

Paula grinned. "That would be fine. I'll tell Tiffany she has an admirer."

After school, I stood in a small cluster of observers as the team filed two-by-two onto the courts. Tiffany strolled by with a grin on her face, her hair in a single ponytail, her tan legs long and slender, her eyes hidden behind a blocky pair of brown Vuarnet sunglasses. I hid behind my red cat-eye Vuarnets, trying to act nonchalant. In her collared white shirt, white tennis skirt, white ankle socks, and white tennis shoes, she was stunning.

Her serve was weak and her return, inconsistent. I watched in twisted humor as this gorgeous girl (and her partner, Paula) ran around the court handily getting pummeled by the opposition. Seeing that they were on track to lose 0-6, 0-6, I left before the end of their match. What a gentleman, concerned about her feeling embarrassed for losing so resoundedly.

The next day, Paula and I resumed our conversation.

"That was a pretty tough team you played yesterday," I said, trying to sound empathetic.

"Not really. We're not very good and we know it. We're just out there to have fun. She wants you to know that she doesn't have a boyfriend."

"Bitchen."

"And, she told me to give you her phone number so here it is."

She handed me a piece of paper.

"Is this her handwriting?"

Paula nodded.

I slipped the small piece of torn paper–this treasure–in my pocket. *Her phone number in her own handwriting*. The seven had a horizontal line through it–even her handwriting was exotic. The phone number of that beautiful girl with long brown hair. The *FOOTLSE* girl. Unbelievable.

I paced around my bedroom that night, heart racing, palms sweaty, trying to work up the nerve to call. Finally, I punched in the numbers. The phone rang twice as my heart rate jumped to triple time. Sweat dripped off my face.

"Hello?" It was a pleasant woman's voice, the kind you can hear smiling as she spoke.

Boom, boom, boom, my heart thundered.

"Hi . . . is . . . um . . . Tiffany home?"

Pause.

"Is this Thomas?"

Holy crap . . . I don't know . . . is it?

"Um, well my name *is* Thomas but most people call me Tom."

"I'm Tiffany's mom and *we've heard all about you.*"

Boom, boom, boom.

BOOM, BOOM, BOOM.

My facial muscles twitched.

Her mom continued. "You were at the tennis match yesterday, right? Red sunglasses? Moustache? Kinda look like Tom Selleck?"

"Um, yes, that was me."

BOOM, BOOM, BOOM.

"Yeah, I was standing right next to you. Tiffany's at work right now. She works at Longs Drugs but she told me to tell you that you could meet her after work in the parking lot. The store closes at nine."

"Really? Wow! OK, thank you!"

I hung up the phone and ran into David's room.

"I'm meeting Tiffany after work in the Longs parking lot!"

He looked up from his Dirt Bike magazine. *Urgent* from the Foreigner 4 album played on the record player. "Cool."

A few minutes after 9 p.m., she walked out of Longs wearing a white dress with blue trim. After two showers, and a liberal application of Polo cologne, I casually leaned against my car–parked next to her gleaming Fiero–wearing 501s and my favorite red Le Tigre polo shirt–collar flipped up.

"Hi," she said shyly as she approached. Her voice was deeper than I expected. Deep and exotic.

No formal introductions were necessary.

"You play a mean game of tennis."

She laughed, then I laughed.

"Yeah, right," she said with a wry smile. It was bullshit and we both knew it. "You're a yearbook photographer. I've seen you around taking pictures. You took the tennis team picture."

"I did?"

"Yes, you did."

We smiled at each other.

And that's where my first love bloomed. Right there on Henderson Avenue, in the parking lot of Longs Drugs. April 12, 1985, 9:05 p.m.

We talked for an hour in the dark parking lot. She told me about her aeronautical engineering scholarship to the University of Southern California and her upcoming valedictorian speech. The girl was beautiful *and* brilliant.

I called her the next day, a Saturday, and after a few minutes of working up the nerve, invited myself over.

"So . . . how about I come over and help you wash your car?"

She agreed and gave me her address.

"I'll be over in half an hour."

After a quick shower, I pulled up to her house and she was already hosing off her car in the driveway. (I soon learned that her car was kept spotless–at all times–and the last thing she needed was help washing a perfectly clean car. I could have asked to come over and mow the lawn, or paint the house, or bake cookies, and the answer would have been the same: yes.) Her parents, Anthony and Kate, greeted me with loving smiles.

Two weeks later, she accepted my class ring. Soon, a metallic clip replaced the yarn she used as a spacer. I loved the initiative.

One day after school, the *coup de grace*: She held out her car keys and said seriously, "*No one* has sat in the driver's seat except me."

It was one of those *take notice* moments.

I slid behind the wheel, started the car, shifted into first gear and . . .

The car jerked forward . . .

And stalled.

She looked at me like I had just kicked her cat, Pickles.

I tried again with the same results.

The design of that sports car, damn near lying down in the angled seats, was harder than it looked. After the third time, I managed to shift-up to second gear and we were off. That night I received my first traffic ticket for running a red-light–*hey, the light was yellow when I entered the intersection!* That bright red boutique car attracted a lot of attention.

• • •

I look at our 1985 prom picture and she is radiant in her ruffled white dress. Her curled dark hair sprawls over her bare bronze shoulders. A moment forever captured in time, two kids in love.

• • •

As the school year wound down, I was ready to complete my transformation to fully immersed Prep and the way to do that was to be on the coming year's Student Council. But you had to be elected–it wasn't as simple as checking a box next to "Seventh Period Student Government."

I decided that "Entertainment Commissioner" sounded like the most fun. One other junior, Jenny, filed papers to run. She was tough competition–very pretty, very smart, and she dated our star running back.

Joe and I canvassed the school with flyers and campaigned to anyone who would listen. At the last rally of the year, everyone running for next year's Student Council gave their election speech to the standing-room-only gym. After that, voting began back in class.

Over the intercom, the winners were announced.

And . . .

I lost.

I blamed it on the freshman boys. Of the group of people Jenny and I knew the least, it was the freshman boys. And if they didn't know us–as a guy–I knew who I would have voted for. When in doubt, vote for the pretty girl.

Jenny was humble about her victory, and I congratulated her sincerely, but the defeat stung. Bad. *Maybe I wasn't cut out to be a Prep after all. Maybe time to break out my Sammy Hagar Three Lock Box concert shirt . . .*

The next day, our president elect, the one and only Paula Zaninovich, stopped me in the corridor. I figured she wanted to offer her condolences.

"Hi, Paula. Congratulations on becoming next year's student body president. How cool is that?"

"It's going to be great. A lot of fun and a lot of work."

I nodded.

She continued. "I'm going to need help and I need hard workers."

Again I nodded, thinking *those damn freshman boys screwed me!*

"You know," she said, "not every Student Council position was filled. Take, for example, School Board Representative. No one even ran for that."

"I didn't know that," I said but the new information–coming from her–got my heart pounding. Where was *this* going?

A few seconds passed. We smiled at each other. It was almost like the awkwardness of asking someone on a date.

Finally, she said, "Would you be interested in . . ."

"YES."

She started again.

"Would you be interested in being next year's . . ."

"YES."

She giggled.

". . . School Board Rep on the Student Council?"

"YES."

"Good. It's done then. You're on the Student Council." She turned and walked away. "Oh, by the way," she said over her shoulder, "I've never seen Tiffany happier."

• • •

The culmination of many California high schools, just short of the actual graduation ceremony, is Grad Night at Disneyland. Throughout the month of May, the Happiest Place on Earth opens to hundreds of high schools whose students enjoy the park from dusk to dawn.

As soon as we walked through the gates, we knew exactly where to go: The Tahitian Room. Dinner and a stage show on a first come, first served basis. I was one of a handful of guys selected from the crowd to do the hula on stage. I look at the pictures now and it's weird—the guy next to me ended up marrying Tiffany. Small freaking world.

While we ran for the restaurant, others (namely three of our varsity cheerleaders) ran for the nearest restroom. What happened next became part legend, part myth, and all gossip since they ended up as guests in the Disneyland Jail for the rest of the night. And I'm not talking about that cell in The Pirates of the Caribbean with the toothless pirate and furry little dog.

Didn't know Disneyland had a jail? Neither did I.

These girls—popular, pretty *leaders* of our little San Joaquin Valley school—will remain nameless and forever innocent until proven guilty. Not the smartest decision to cram into a bathroom stall to snort *aspirin*. That was their story anyway. To further humiliate our school's finest, Disneyland officials wouldn't release them to anyone but their parents. So instead of simply sitting around for twelve hours waiting to board the bus back home, these girls had to call their parents to come get them.

Now.

Pronto.

Immediately if not sooner.

Porterville to Anaheim: 187 miles. One way. Up and over a mountain range.

We later learned that had there been a way to round us up, Disneyland officials would have kicked the entire school out of the park that very night. Imagine the overhead page: *Will all the students from Monache High School meet at Gate A? You're all expelled from the park and your buses are leaving in 20 minutes! Yeah, we know you just got here!*

I guess they figured if the cream of the crop of our student body snorted white powder in their crapper, everyone at the school must be an asshole. Disneyland also took it a step further and served notice that Monache was banned from future Grad Nights.

Banned from Disneyland. That's so much worse than being banned from Pizza Hut.

After an aggressive campaign effort from our school administration, months later, Disneyland officials added Monache back on the list of invitees. You can't just ban an entire school for eternity due to the actions of a few morons, right?

"Calvin & Hobbes" makes its debut in thirty five newspapers. For years I wanted a tattoo of the duo but could never decide on the stuffed or live version of Hobbes.

CHAPTER 12

For the second summer in a row, David decided that we'd take his modified farm truck to Walla Walla. We were both, now, licensed drivers.

But I suffered from a serious case of Love Sickness and suggested he make the trip alone. Having none of it, he agreed to wait a week–after my trip with Tiffany and her parents to Morro Bay to visit Tiffany's grandparents.

In early June, with Tiffany and I, giggly, in the back seat, and her parents gleefully in the front seat, we hit the road.

We stopped for lunch at the midway point of the three hour drive, a large, roadside coffee shop. (I drove by it many years later and it was boarded up and abandoned. What a shame.)

The place was packed.

The mood was light and playful. Tiffany just graduated valedictorian and was on her way to USC, her mom was excited to see her parents, and her dad was just happy to be there–he was always happy.

Tiffany's mom, Kate, thought she'd apply a little torture to her daughter's new boyfriend.

"So, Tiffany, I guess we should tell Tom about Bruce. After all, you and Bruce have *quite* a fondness for each other."

I stared back, not knowing how to react.

Tiffany giggled but said nothing.

Kate turned to Tiffany's dad, Anthony, and pressed on. "Yes, Bruce really, *really* likes Tiffany, wouldn't you agree?"

He smiled and nodded.

I felt my teeth gritting.

Kate continued in a playfully mocking tone. "We really *should have* told Tom about Bruce, huh?"

I thought, *There must be a point here.*

Tiffany put her hand on mine and said quietly, "Bruce is a black Lab–my grand-pa's legally blind and Bruce is his seeing eye dog."

I exhaled in relief and everyone laughed.

These people were still strangers to me–and me to them–and it was a timeless moment. It was a magical feeling, the love and kindness–the acceptance–of these kind and funny people.

"Yeah, we sure love Bruce," her mom trailed off. "We were at lunch one day and I looked down at him. He had a new collar on with a heart shaped nametag. I looked down to get a better look at the tag and turned to Nana . . ." (Tiffany's grand-mother's nickname) "and asked, 'does Bruce have a heart on?'"

Anthony started choking on his fries.

I looked at him, puzzled.

"Nana looked down, grabbed Bruce's hind leg to get a better look and said, 'No, I don't think.'"

I burst out laughing.

I mean, *I burst out laughing*, raised my hand over my head, and slammed my open palm down–hard–on the table. Silverware, glasses of water, and empty plates rattled and bounced off the table with so much racket that the entire restaurant stopped and stared.

I looked around at the now completely silent, filled-to-capacity restaurant, and laughed even harder. Spit flew from my mouth. Tears rolled down my red face. It was, without a doubt, the funniest thing I'd ever heard. I have never laughed that hard in my life–not before or since.

Kate beamed.

We spent the weekend with her grandparents–in separate rooms under Kate's watchful eye–and I met Bruce the black Lab. He was as endearing as Kate's description–smart, lovable, and handsome. He still had the heart shaped dog tag, too.

Tiffany and I drove into San Francisco and spent the day walking around Pier 39. She bought me a stuffed animal–a small, yellow Lab (they were out of black)–and for an extra two dollars a guy with a Sharpie wrote "Tiffany" on the collar.

Upon my return to Porterville, my acute medical condition, *Lovesick-itus Gigantis*, raged. David would not be denied and was chomping at the bit to hit the open road. Being the obedient little brother, I climbed in the little truck without a fight. Resistance was futile.

Tiffany–the stuffed animal, not the girl–went with us.

I'll admit that, even at the time, a lovesick seventeen-year-old guy clutching a stuffed animal was pathetic. The drive to Walla Walla the second time around (third if you count the 1982 trip with Mom) was long and uncomfortable but we didn't break down. No blown fuses. No blown radiator hoses. Just one long, hot drive.

We stayed at our grandma's house our first night in town, and I'll never forget the confused look on her face when I curled up on the couch clutching the stuffed animal. I didn't even bother defending myself–I was miserable. I was also mortified after leaving the remains of a wet dream on her crushed velvet, gold-colored couch.

All sense of cool goes out the window when you're in love for the first time. I moped around the week we were there, counting down the days until we made the long drive back.

We cruised the town with Lorne once again–not too lovesick for that–and learned the *proper* ratio of Jack Daniels to Coca-Cola (closer to 10/90) and kept the

The bro's at Cypress 33.

blackberry cobbler digested. But I was only there in physical form–my mind yearned to be back in the presence of my beautiful, radiant brunette.

On the drive home, a thought occurred to me. A thought of *epic* proportions– something that would go down in the history of my life as one of the coolest things I've done. I asked David what he thought. He mulled it around then said, simply, "Cool. Go for it."

My brother is a man of few words.

The moment we swung back in our apartment complex at 3 p.m., I jumped in the shower–tired or not I was going to see Tiffany *immediately if not sooner*.

I drove to her house but she was at work.

"Do you have an extra set of keys to her car?" I asked her mom.

"Uh . . . yes . . ." Kate said, skeptically.

"I need them."

When Tiffany walked out to her car at 9:15 p.m. that night, she found a single red rose on the driver's seat. When she got home, she found another rose on the walk leading from the garage to the front door.

Then another.

Then another.

Then another.

A red rose every three feet.

She picked them up as she walked along. I heard her heels click, then stop, then click, then stop. She opened the front door and continued gathering flowers. The trail continued down the short hallway. Anthony and Kate giggled from the living room.

She opened her bedroom door and the trail ended with me sitting at the foot of her bed holding the last rose. She took the flower and gave me the slowest, most memorable kiss I've ever had. We were smiling and crying at the same time.

Apart a whole week.

For the rest of the summer we were inseparable.

One hot day–they were all summertime hot–we sat cross-legged and facing each other on the living room floor–with both of her parents at work (God love the summer and working parents)–Tiffany sheepishly asked, "Do you want to see something?"

House to ourselves–check.

Girl asking a promising question–check.

Boy ready for more–check.

"Yes," I smiled, trying to control my heart rate.

She stood up on her long, smooth legs, straightened her white shorts and red spaghetti strapped tank top and disappeared into her bedroom.

My heart pounded.

Do I follow her?

"Are you sure you want to see this?" she called.

Cyndi Lauper's voice sang in my head: "*Catholic* girls just wanna have fun!"

I stood up and yelled at the ceiling, "*YES! YES! I WANT TO SEE IT! I WANT TO SEE IT! CATHOLIC GIRLS JUST WANT TO HAVE FUN!*"

I stripped off my shirt and bounded into her bedroom.

No, actually I didn't.

I blinked.

The vivid daydream passed.

"Are you *sure* you want to see this?" she asked again, her voice still in her bedroom.

"Sure!" I replied in a shaky voice. A bead of sweat rolled down the side of my face. Was she slipping into a terrycloth robe or pink lingerie? *A guy can dream.*

She re-emerged, grinning. Her clothing hadn't changed and she carried a small black suitcase with square corners.

She sat down in front of me and started giggling.

"Promise not to laugh?" she asked.

I leaned forward and kissed her on the lips. "I promise." I thought, *Please Lord, let it be nude photos of her taken by a girlfriend. C'mon nude photos!*

She opened the case and watched my reaction.

I smiled but said nothing.

"You think I'm a geek, huh?"

I blinked, not knowing what to say. In a million years, I would have never guessed the contents of the case.

She pulled out Darth Vader and held it up. "Look at the detail. I have *two* of him."

It was a collector's case full of Star Wars action figures in pristine condition, eighty in total: Obi Wan Kenobi, R2-D2, C-3PO, Boba Fett, Chewbacca. You name it, she had it.

"Wow," I said with amazement, "you must have them all."

"Actually, I'm on the look out for Admirals Piett and Ackbar," she replied dreamily.

I almost burst out laughing. I picked up Princess Leia and moved it to the Darth in her hands.

In my best female voice: "Oh, Darth, what a large light saber you have."

She pulled Darth back and frowned.

Oh God, I've offended her. The tension held for a few seconds until she relaxed her shoulders.

"Leia, release the cinnamon buns on your head and give big bad Darth a little sugar," she replied in her deepest Darth Vader impersonation. God, I loved her deep voice.

I tackled her and Darth and Leia dropped to the floor.

• • •

With car, girlfriend, and the free time of summer, I needed a job–something that didn't involve killing gophers or matching wits with four hundred pound hogs. The job market for a high school student primarily consisted of the handful of fast food restaurants in town: McDonald's, Del Taco, and Burger King. Lynn's employment at McDonald's ruled that out. I *really* didn't want to wear the grease-splattered, burnt orange, skintight, polyester uniform and come home reeking of French fries and Big Macs.

Outside of fast food, the only other employment opportunities were Longs Drugs, K-Mart, Montgomery Ward, and JC Penney–in that order of coolness. At the time, we hadn't even *heard* of Wal-Mart and the nearest Target was forty miles away. There was one large grocery store (Save-Mart) and one local grocery store (Smith's). Pickings were slim.

Here's an interesting side note.

According to local legend, while scoping out Porterville for his West Coast distribution center in the late eighties, Sam Walton walked into a stationary store intent on supporting a local business. Mr. Walton, a down to earth type of guy, believed strongly in superior customer service. When no one waited on him–or failed to even acknowledge him–he turned around and walked out. Little did the owners of the store realize that the *richest man in the country* had just been snubbed. Despite this, he did build a distribution center and, later, a store in Porterville. But the stationary didn't come from the locals.

Back to the story.

I decided I'd try K-Mart since it had a variety of attractions: an electronics department, a cafeteria (*spin the wheel for a chance at the one cent banana split!*), sporting goods, auto, and clothes. I filled out an application and received a call a week later. It was a walking interview–which put me at ease–with one of the floor managers. I met the gal at the front door and we walked through the large, bustling store as she asked questions. The interview concluded like this:

Manager: "I can see you as a cashier up here in the front. What do you think?"

Me: "No, I want to push the blue-light-special cart around. That's the job for me."

(For those unfamiliar with a longstanding K-Mart tradition, all K-Marts have "blue light specials"–as in, *Come on over to the Health and Beauty section K-Mart shoppers! For the next five minutes, Charmin toilet paper is on sale for twenty nine cents a four pack! Look for the flashing blue light! Get 'em while they last! Ya know you need 'em!*)

People took to the blue light like moths to a bug zapper. Yeah, *that* was the job for me–pushing the cart around the store ahead of eager geriatric patrons. I could've been the Pied Piper of the store. *No!* I could've nonchalantly pushed the cart around the store gathering old folks in my wake. I could've reached for the blue light switch–gauging the eagerness in people's eyes–then bolted down another aisle. I could've *messed* with people. *That* would've been fun. Hell, I'd have done that for free!

K-Mart never called.

David said, "I can't believe you're a K-Mart reject."

"Easy there, dishwasher."

Without a doubt, the coolest job in town–reserved for the upper echelon of high school kids–was Longs Drugs. While it was a full blown pharmacy, it also sold food (*and alcohol!*), toys (Teddy Ruxpin's went fast, even at $89.99), electronics, and greeting cards. It had a photo department, a cosmetics department, and a small jewelry counter. The place was happening.

I bounded through the small aluminum swinging doors (that are still there, by the way), up the narrow stairs, turned right to the manager's office, and read the sign:

WE ARE NOT ACCEPTING APPLICATIONS TODAY.

The sign was *permanently* mounted on the manager's door.

I looked around and thought, *Hell, I'm already here, I may as well give it a try.* Mr. Salvador Petrucelli, the revered store manager, sat at his desk staring at a piece of paper. I lightly rapped on the unwelcoming sign. He looked up. "Yes?"

"Hi . . . um . . . I see that you're not accepting applications today . . . but . . . um . . . I was wondering when you *were* accepting applications . . ."

He waved his hand in the air. "Try back next week."

This scenario happened every Wednesday afternoon for four consecutive weeks. On the fifth Wednesday . . .

"Hi . . . um . . . I see that you're not accepting applications today . . . but . . . um . . . I was wondering when you *were* accepting applications . . . "

Mr. Petrucelli looked at me for a long moment then said, "Come in here and sit down."

I walked in and sat down in the chair facing his desk. From this perspective, a guy could look out over the whole store from a wall of glass that made up one side of the office.

"You've been coming in here for the past month. You get the persistency award. *Who are you?*"

"My name is Tom Harvey. I'm going to be a senior at Monache and I'd really love to work here, Sir."

He put his pen down. "My daughter's going to be a senior at Monache." This, I knew. Hey, it was a small town.

"*Really?*" I asked with my best look of surprise.

"Her name's Linda. Do you know her?"

"Linda Petrucelli? Of course! Who doesn't?"

He leaned back, beaming. After a long moment, he picked up the phone and paged the Assistant Manager, Johnny Gonzalez.

Johnny was a short, stocky, no nonsense guy. When he appeared in the doorway, Sal said, "Johnny, I want you to give this guy the psych and math test."

"Well . . . we don't have any openings at the m . . ."

"Just do it, Johnny! This kid won't leave me alone!" Sal smiled broadly and waved me out the door.

I followed the grumbling Assistant Manager into the adjacent office. Johnny frowned and said, "I don't know how you did what you just did but I got to hand it to you."

I smiled weakly.

I struggled with the hundred question multiple choice test with questions like: If you saw a coworker take five dollars out of the cash register, would you:

A) Report it to your supervisor immediately
B) Pretend it didn't happen
C) Tell him/her to put it back
D) Demand $2.50 of it

A variation of this question was asked ten different ways. I breezed through the simple math test.

Johnny told me to come back a week later for the results. I was on my way!

The next week I bounded up the narrow stairwell with nervous anticipation. When I appeared in Mr. Petrucelli's doorway, he and Johnny sat on opposite sides of the desk.

Johnny beamed. Sal frowned.

"Come in, Tom." Sal said glumly. I looked at the stocky Assistant Manager. He grinned like he had just come from the Mustang Hot Tubs.

"You didn't do so good on your psych test," Sal continued.

"You are kidding."

"No, I am not kidding. In fact, you basically flunked it."

My face began to burn as the two managers looked me over.

Johnny continued to grin and crossed his arms. *So much for pulling back the veil, so much for working at the coolest store in town.* I wanted to drop through the floor.

"Still . . ." Sal said. He looked at Johnny with a straight face.

". . . despite bombing the psych test, I like you." Sal's locked eyes never left Johnny's. "I like you so much, in fact, that I'm going to offer you a job."

I looked between the two men and watched their expressions change–Sal's frown morphed into a smile and Johnny's smile morphed into a frown.

"I can't understand flunking the psych test, Mr. Petrucelli. Perhaps I can take it again?"

"No, you flunked it because you answered the questions the way you think we wanted them answered, not the way you should have instinctively answered them. That's the trick of the test. No matter. Would you like a job?"

"Yes, Sir!"

Johnny snorted. Sal ignored him.

"Since I like your persistence, and since I think you'll do just fine, I'd like to offer you a rate above minimum wage. How does that sound?" Sal beamed. He enjoyed this part of the job.

"It sounds great!"

"Ten cents above minimum wage it is. Johnny, set it up and let's get Tom a green jacket and out on the floor."

I followed Johnny out of Sal's office, feeling elated and embarrassed at the same time.

Johnny said, "I don't know how in *the hell* you did that since I have a hundred qualified applicants who didn't flunk the psych test and we don't even have an opening."

I shrugged.

"But . . . Mr. Petrucelli gets what he wants so I need to make room for you."

I smiled.

He finally smiled back and said, "Welcome aboard."

And that's how I earned $3.45 an hour–a dollar more an hour on Sundays. I was a clerk–stocking shelves, rounding up shopping carts in the parking lot, and manning one of the eight cash registers when needed.

My first job. How could I have known it would also be the funnest job I'd ever have?

My first paycheck was $84 and I promptly bought my first pair of Sperry Topsiders for $39.99.[11] My transformation to full blown Prep was on course.

• • •

Tiffany's parents taught us Pinochle and we discovered that playing barefoot allowed us to pass cards under the table. Little did I know that Tiffany's mom knew all about our cheating ways but she didn't care–she loved that her daughter chose to hang out with her appreciative parents. I discovered that, the one time the guys took on the girls, Anthony had his own method of subtle hand gestures and eye movements. The guy was a cheat, too! When normal play resumed, I felt no remorse for our game of barefoot cards.

On Sundays we went to church. I was baptized Presbyterian, so the rituals of the Catholic Church were foreign, to say the least. During Mass, I didn't know when to stand, when to kneel or what to say when the congregation murmured in unison. It was downright creepy the first service I went to. ("The Lord be with you"–*And also with you.* "Give thanks to the Lord."–*It is right to give Him thanks.*) After a few Sundays, I was ready to fake it and receive communion, but Kate forbade it. A guy kind of feels like a leper when everyone in the church lines up to receive the wafer–and I mean *everyone*–except for the schmo sitting next to his pretty girlfriend. Now that's love.

---

11   The burgundy-colored Sperry's were on sale–I couldn't afford the *really* cool blue pair.

The priest's name was Father Sweat but I referred to him as "Sweat Dog." Kate didn't appreciate it. She asked when I would begin my conversion to Catholicism ("classes are starting up soon!"), and I honestly didn't know what to say.

Classes to go to church? What the?

Tiffany burst out, "*Mother!*"

End of discussion.

Tiffany's dad was the captain of his slow pitch softball team and the guy was *competitive*. The three of us cheered from the stands and Kate would yell, "C'mon lover!"

He'd get up to bat and I'd yell, "C'mon lover!" A dozen people laughed and Kate jabbed me in the ribs.

One night on the pitcher's mound, Anthony took a shot–and I mean a *line drive*–to the nuts. The ball hit him, he grabbed his testicular region and fell over like an oak tree. I mean, he got *tagged*. We ran out to the mound where he lay red faced and gasping for air (think Richard Gere in *An Officer and a Gentleman* after Lou Gossett, Jr. kicks him in the balls). Anthony was in agony–his night, in more ways than one, was clearly over.

• • •

As the summer wound down, we took a trip to Los Angeles to finalize Tiffany's living arrangements at USC. She ended up on the eighth floor of Pardee Tower, better known to the students as "Party" Tower, much to my chagrin. We walked around the picturesque campus, took pictures at Tommy Trojan, and bought T-shirts.

I bitched and moaned the entire day. "Is there anything good about this place?" I picked up a school newspaper. "Look at this! The crime section of the school paper is as big as the Porterville Recorder!"

Tiffany huffed off.

We drove the three hours back to Porterville in silence. I was such an asshole.

• • •

We moped around a few days before she left for college. USC was just 3 hours away but the short distance was no consolation.

Kate insisted we say our goodbyes the night before Tiffany was to leave–she didn't want her daughter driving to Los Angeles in tears.

We had a teary, exhaustive, goodbye the night before.

The next morning Tiffany was to leave at 7:30 a.m. Against Mother's Orders, I drove over and parked a block away, next to an empty lot across the street from her house. The front door opened and Tiffany quickly slipped into the side door of the garage with her parents in tow. Her dad saw me instantly and waved. Kate jabbed him in the ribs and put her hands on her hips in disapproval.

I didn't move.

As the shiny red Fiero backed out of the driveway, Anthony waved me over. Tiffany climbed out of the car and we held on to each other like we'd never see each other again. I breathed in the smell of her skin. Tears mixed with our saliva at yet another tearful goodbye. It was one of the purest moments in my life.

As we held each other tight, our perfect summer was over.

Things would quickly change.

On live television, talk show host Geraldo Rivera wastes two hours of our lives opening Al Capone's vault. What did he find? Absolutely nothing. Andrew Dice Clay would later use the Geraldo flop in his stand-up routine. Gotta love the Dice Man for that.

CHAPTER 13

Leaving the Stoner behind, this is classic Prep–note the knit tie and sweater. If this were a color picture, you'd also see that the shirt is pink.

I knew that I had some final year makeup to improve my GPA so signed up for three Honors classes (where A's were worth five points instead of four): Humanities Honors, Civics Honors, and World History Honors. Rounding out the schedule was Geometry, Computer Programming, and Student Council. My resulting grade point average (4.3) meant I shared the highest GPA of anyone in the school that year. (Doing the math, I was only able to earn a B in Humanities. The rest were straight A's.)

Seriously, I wasn't a total screw off.

Mrs. Land's Humanities class was the closest thing to college there was–research papers, oral presentations, and essay tests. We feared, loved, and respected this woman. I spent more than one all nighter cramming for her exams. We couldn't fake our way through questions like: *Compare and contrast the Athenian way of life vs. the Spartan way of life* and *Discuss a typical day in the life of the great Greek historian, Thucydides*. The day became infinitely easier after first period.

I repeated Geometry and understood it just fine from a teacher who cared to impart her knowledge. As an added bonus, thirty-something Mrs. Samperson (blonde hair, blue eyes, always smiling) was the prettiest teacher I'd ever seen. I didn't even mind that she was pregnant. With only three seniors in the class, I took the liberty of referring to her by her first name, Laura. She never corrected me but no one else followed suit. I was usually late for her fourth period class since Student Council activities kept me occupied during the fifteen-minute "brunch" between third and fourth period. One day, she announced to the class that I was to be punished with detention. Had I known that simply meant spending the lunch hour flirting with her at her desk, I would have begged for the punishment a lot sooner.

Hans Budnarowski taught Computer Programming, and two of my best friends, Kellie and Brock, joined me in the class. Hans, like Spanish-teacher Briscoe, was also a Clark W. Griswold-like character (lovable, interested, and clueless), except that Hans had a huge brown beard. Computers in 1985 were nothing like they are today–with small monochrome monitors and five and a quarter inch floppy drives, we learned how to write computer code. Known as *strings*, computer programming was a combination of math, logic, and typing accuracy–the challenge being to write commands that executed simple programs. (My best example is my year-end project where I wrote a slot machine program that was a simple random number generator. It took about twenty five taps of the return key on the bulky keyboard for all three numbers to arrive at seven at which time the screen flashed in monochrome splendor: *Congratulations! You've just won a 1986 Porsche 944!*

On weekends, I led a small contingent of friends who decorated houses with toilet paper in the dark of night. A dozen of us would meet at Joe's house and determine the night's targets. From there, we'd caravan to Smith's Market where an instant line formed of kids purchasing multiple packs of whatever toilet paper was on sale. We'd say something like, "Grandma's feeling *real* sick" and the clerk would just laugh. Subtlety wasn't our strong point.

Mr. Bud's house on West Grand Avenue had a *massive* tree in his small front yard which made the long, dangling strands of TP semi-permanent. One night it rained TP in that yard. The following Monday, I said with a smile, "Mr. Bud, I drove by your house this weekend and it looks like you're doing some redecorating. Can't say that I fully understand your vision, though." He looked at me with a smirk but there was a glint in his eyes.

The next day, *my desk* was covered with toilet paper. "Tom, I see that you're decorating your desk, but I don't really get the big picture," he quipped in his thick German accent.

Touché, Mr. Bud.

Brock and I walked by a table where a stodgy young Marine stood giving his best recruitment speech to a few nervous looking guys. I turned to Brock and said, "Looks like we better join before we get drafted!" (One of my favorite lines from the Bill Murray comedy, *Stripes*.)

Brock looked at me with wide eyes and whispered, "What the hell are you doing?"

The Marine snapped, "*What* did you say?"

We broke into a run, the safety of Mr. Bud's door loomed fifty feet ahead. *The Marine gave chase.*

We ran in and slammed the door just as the bell rang. The door flung open behind us and the steely-eyed Marine walked in without hesitation. A bewildered Mr. Bud said, "What's going on here?"

I shrugged innocently. Brock fled to his desk.

Our lovable teacher turned to the Marine. "Can I help you?"

"Yes, Sir. Seems I have some business with this gentleman right here." He nodded at me.

"No, I don't think so," I said.

The class sat in silence looking between me, the Marine, and Mr. Bud. I looked at Mr. Bud with pleading eyes and shook my head subtlety. *No, please, no.*

The German broke into a wide smile. "Yes, perhaps you *do* have business with this *gentleman*." He shoved me out the door. "Take *all* the time you need soldier."

We bestowed "1986 Male Teacher of the Year" on Mr. Bud as nominated by yours truly.

• • •

Free from yearbook duties, I went from behind the camera to in front of it. With football season in full bloom, one of the main responsibilities of the student council was Friday pep rallies.

I have to say that speaking–and *motivating*–1,500 people was a rush and my ego knew no bounds.

The best rally of the year was our Christmas production. I conjured up a scene out of the movie lighting up the box office, *Rocky IV*, in *true* David and Goliath fashion.

Steve was the hero at 5' 5" and 125 pounds. In the opposite corner, our favorite German exchange student, Philipp Gutzwiller, at 6' 6" and 240 pounds.

The mural at the center of the gym became the boxing ring.

I stepped to the microphone.

"Can you believe that Porterville High is talking trash *again?*" (The word "smack" wasn't yet invented.) A couple hundred students booed.

"I said, 'can you believe that Porterville High is talking trash about our glorious Monache High School?'"

The boo's intensified.

"We've put together a little boxing match to decide who the better high school is, once and for all!"

The crowd cheered.

"I'd like to introduce Porterville High's athlete. His name is Philipp Dra-gooooooooooooooo!" As Philipp bounded in front of the crowd, wearing the orange and green of our cross town rival, the boo's rained down on him. Holy crap, the guy was huge.

"And now give it up to everyone's hero! Our champ, Steve!"

Steve ran out, waving his gloved hands in the air–the crowd *roared*.

As they squared off in the middle of the gym, Philipp towering over Steve, it couldn't have been more ridiculous. I stood back and laughed. Good God, it was brilliant.

In spectacular fashion, the little hero and the gargantuan villain boxed three quick rounds as I improvised commentary.

They weren't *really* throwing blows but little Steve was getting knocked around pretty good.

"And Steve's taking some serious abuse now! Oh no, he's down! Steve's down! Can it be possible? Is Porterville High the better school? Philipp Drago thinks he's got the win! Say it isn't so!"

BOOOOOOOOOOOOOOOOO!

"Can Steve get up? He needs the crowd's energy to get off the mat! Can he do it? Let me hear you Monache!"

ROOOOOOOOAAAAARRRRRRRR!

"Steve needs a knockout for the win! Can he do it? CAN HE DO IT MOOOOO-NAAAAAAA-CHEEEEEE?"

Steve bobbed. He weaved. He leapt up and connected with Philipp's big, square chin. On cue, the big German flopped in spectacular fashion.

Fifteen hundred students leapt to their feet. The cheers, deafening.

Steve's corner men carried him around the gym on their shoulders. He waved, he blew kisses, the crowd freaking loved him. Philipp and his crew slunk away in mock defeat.

I hugged the big German later that day.

"Philipp, that was a thing of beauty. You deserve an Academy Award!"

"Yah! Dat was fun!" he beamed. The guy had the biggest smile I'd ever seen.

We talked about it for months.

• • •

Tiffany found the aeronautical engineering classes at USC to be anything but easy. She was no longer the smartest in the class–every kid in every class was the valedictorian from their high school. I have to take the blame for her distraction–in the days before email, we wrote and called each other on a daily basis. She also mailed cassette tapes of one-sided conversations–things like, "I hope you had a nice day" and "I have so much homework that I don't know what to do" and "Some geek asked me out today but I told him I had a boyfriend." I still have the cassette tape of her singing *Crazy For You* in a $10 recording studio–the pre-cursor to today's karaoke. At the end of each *Crazy For You* wail, she added the word *Thomas*.

On Saturday morning, October 5, I tiptoed out of the apartment and left Mom a note: *Took the car. Be home later tonight*. I didn't bother elaborating that I was going to Los Angeles. Navigating the L.A. freeways–in the days before GPS–was not for the faint of heart. Somehow I managed to find the university in the rough East Los Angeles neighborhood (but not before stopping at a Chevron where no one spoke English).

We went to the homecoming football game and blended in with thousands of cheerful students making their way to the Coliseum. I knew the venue from the 1978 Warren Beatty movie, *Heaven Can Wait*, and was thrilled to see it firsthand. The electricity of 70,000 screaming fans was amazing. All of Porterville *times two* could fit in this stadium.

We sat in the hot sun enjoying each other's company and watched the Rodney Peete-led Trojans destroy Oregon State, 63-0. After the game, I drove the three hours home and simply told Mom that I had been "out and about."

On November 2, I took my second trip to USC–this time divulging my intention to spend the night since Tiffany's roommate was gone for the weekend. Mom frowned but said nothing. If she had an opinion, she kept it to herself. USC crushed Washington State, 31-13, that day.

Tiffany's shared dorm room on the eighth floor of Pardee Tower wasn't much larger than a single car garage at twelve feet by fifteen feet. The eighth floor was all female, meaning I had to sneak down to the all male seventh floor to use the community restroom. While brushing my teeth, a guy walked in and eyed me suspiciously–three months into the school year these students knew everyone on their floor.

"Hell of a game, huh?" I mumbled.

His eyes narrowed. "Uh, yeah. You new or just visiting?"

"Just visiting. My girlfriend's upstairs and her roommate is out of town. We'll try not to keep you awake, if you know what I mean, hyuck, hyuck, hyuck."

He laughed and walked out.

Though it was the first time I spent an entire night in the same bed with a member of the opposite sex, it was clear that sex was *not* on the agenda. From the start, she was clear that being Catholic meant a lot of things, one of which was no premarital sex. I didn't have a problem with it. Unfortunately, neither of us knew how to share a twin bed (spooning was completely unknown to us) so we had a miserable night of tossing and turning.

We spent the next day at a Golf 'N Stuff miniature golf course (the one in the movie *The Karate Kid*) before I drove home bleary eyed and exhausted.

Sidebar #3:
The Hit of All NFL Hits

The hit inspired the blockbuster movie, *The Blind Side*, and made multimillionaires out of professional left tackles in the NFL.

On November 18, 1985, Anthony and I were watching the Giants take on the Redskins during an otherwise routine Monday Night Football game. Tiffany was at college and Kate was in the kitchen making lemon squares.

Just after Lawrence Taylor, the most feared linebacker of the day, smacked Redskin quarterback Joe Theisman from the blindside, Anthony and I bolted upright in our chairs.

"Did I just see what I thought I saw?"

Anthony said nothing but his otherwise dark Portuguese face was white.

The broadcasting trio of Frank Gifford, O.J. Simpson, and Joe Namath struggled for the right words. What *are* the right words to describe a compound fracture of the tib/fib on live TV?

I wasn't a big Redskins fan but did like Joe–the only quarterback in the league with a single bar facemask–even in 1985, he was old school. There he lay, writhing on the ground while millions of people across the country tried not to projectile-vomit their Hungry Man dinners. The injury was *gruesome*. We watched his leg explode in slow motion from the reverse angle. Nice.

The Redskins won the game, 23-21, but Joe never played again. Poor Joe. Holy crap.

● ● ●

Tiffany came back for my Christmas Ball but the strain of being apart was taking its toll. We argued at the dance, made up, then argued some more. The joy of her prom, just seven months earlier, was a *distant* memory.

On the weekends she didn't make the drive home, I continued going to church with her parents. Sulking in the back seat to and from St. Anne's, her mom would say cheerfully, "I bet Tiffany's at the beach right now!" or "Did you hear that she's applied to be a Hellene Girl?[12] I sure hope she gets it!" I tried my best not to resent Kate for her enthusiasm; after all, USC is not an inexpensive venture and Tiffany deserved to enjoy her college experience. At the time, I didn't want her having *any* fun at all. I was 17, naïve, and a dick.

---

12   The USC Hellenes are the all female "official hostesses" of the University. I saw it as one
     nonstop party where tan, rich college dudes could hit on my girl.

Sidebar #4:

The Army Recruiter

The strongly worded postcard arrived in January stating that I was *required* to register with the Selective Service. As I stood in the long line at the Porterville Post Office, postcard in hand, I mulled over the bad taste in my mouth. Everyone else was mailing packages. To me, I was standing in line for the draft.

Yeah, it was overly dramatic.

I wasn't being drafted.

I wasn't being singled out.

I'm not sure what mode of notification would have been all right for me; probably nothing.

Not long after performing my act of civil obedience, I returned home. The phone rang. David answered and, chortling back laughter, called me to the phone.

"Hello?"

"Yes, is this *Tommy* Harvey?"

"Uh . . . yeah . . . who's this?"

"This is Sergeant Reeves, your local Army recruiter. I've called a couple times for you now, *Tommy*, and each time your brother tells me you're *very* interested in enlisting. I'd like to setup a time for you to come in my office and sign up."

I glared at David, choking back his glee.

I repeated what the sergeant said.

"Let me get this straight. My *brother* told you I'm anxious to enlist?"

David burst out laughing.

"Yes."

Thinking it would put the kibosh on the conversation, I lied, "You know, sergeant, I'm now thinking of joining the Navy, but I appreciate your interest in me."

"Well you *have* to come in and see me then. The Navy's for losers! How about you come in tomorrow after school?"

"How about I don't?" I wasn't used to being disrespectful to an adult but this actually felt pretty good considering the day I was having.

"Then I will keep calling you until you do, *Tommy*."

David kept laughing and pointing at me. I waved him away.

"Fine. How about 3:30 tomorrow?" The final school bell rang at 3:15.

"Fine. See you then, *Tommy*."

I turned to David. "Thanks a lot, asswipe."

The military recruiting offices shared a small, common parking lot at the corner of Putnam and Hockett. The four offices–Army, Navy, Air Force, and Marines–looked identical, and I opened the first glass door I came to.

A guy in a black uniform looked up.

"This the Army recruiting office?" I asked.

"Come on in!"

It only took a minute to realize that I was in the *Marine* recruiting office but the guy wasn't in the least concerned about me missing my appointment next door. For the next hour, I learned all about the Marines, too intimidated to walk out.

That evening, the Army sergeant called again. I told him what had happened.

If he was at all miffed about me missing the appointment, he didn't show it. We set up another meeting. Walking past the Marine recruiting office the next day, I glared at the guy inside. He looked back blankly.

When I walked into the Army recruiting office, there sat my persistent sergeant in his olive green, wrinkle-free uniform with polished black shoes. I thought, *This is what a soldier looks like?*

He offered me his hand, exuding an air of self confidence. "So," he asked, "you ready to join the exciting life of a soldier and serve your country?"

"I'm here to learn more. How about we start with that?"

He asked about my home life. I told him I had two older brothers and he jotted it down.

"Let me show you the latest and greatest in technology," he gushed and pulled out a TV on a mobile cart. Underneath the TV was a laserdisc player. If you don't know what a laserdisc is, picture a CD the size of a phonograph record. He loaded the large, shiny gold disc and we sat back. Set against a thumping soundtrack, soldiers jumped out of airplanes, ran across open plains shooting M-16s, and finished the day chowing down on huge platters of steaming food. A soldier's life looked pretty good.

After the fifteen-minute promo ended, the sergeant pulled out forms in triplicate and said, "OK, let's take the next step in your bright future."

I frowned.

"I came here to learn more and because you won't stop calling me. I'm not ready to make any commitments today."

He looked back expressionless.

"You have two older brothers?"

"Yes."

"Would you say that, as the youngest brother, *they* made all the decisions around you growing up?

"Uh . . . I guess so."

"Did you, as the youngest brother, *ever* make a decision that *they* had to live with?"

"Well . . . no."

"I think it's time you show them, right here and now, that you are *a man*. Show them that you can make your own decisions."

Tense seconds passed.

"I tell you what, if you can get me into West Point, I'll sign right this second." I didn't know anything about West Point but thought the military school life in the movie *Taps* looked cool. I was dead serious.

He looked at me, puzzled, the gleam in his eyes fading.

"Do you have any idea the process for getting into West Point?"

"No idea."

"Among many factors, you have to be nominated by your local Congressman."

"Really? Isn't it just a special form in your desk?" I honestly didn't know.

"Not even close."

"Well, I'm happy to say that my grandpa was in the Army, and I'll consult with him about our conversation today." With that, I stood up and walked out without looking back.

He stopped calling, thank God.

• • •

On January 28, 1986, I walked into Mr. Crichlow's second period Civics Honors class. Every seat was still occupied by his first period class. Everyone was glued to one of the few TVs on campus, mounted in the corner of the room.

I looked around and broke the silence. "What are you guys watching? A porno?"

Mr. Crichlow snarled, "Sit down and shut up! The space shuttle just blew up!"

For weeks leading up to the Challenger launch, intense media coverage followed the first schoolteacher in space, Christa McAuliffe. Out of 11,000 applicants, the history teacher from Concord, New Hampshire, was President Reagan's first educator in his "Teacher In Space Project." It was to be a shining moment for the entire country. Instead, seventy three seconds into that fateful launch, Mrs. McAuliffe and six other crew members lost their lives on live television.

I looked up at the TV–tendrils of white smoke spread across the sky, falling back to earth in every direction. Moments after the explosion, NASA's flight control operator stated, emotionless, "Flight controllers here looking very seriously at the situation. Obviously a major malfunction." *That* was putting it mildly.

For the next forty five minutes, we watched the coverage in disbelief. No one moved. We hardly breathed. Images of the launch and subsequent explosion played over and over again. Students openly wept. Some glared at me for my ill-timed joke. I looked at the floor in shame.

• • •

In February, the council adopted a member of the faculty for a week–a "Secret Santa" kind of thing–where we left small gifts for our randomly assigned teacher. To accomplish this, we had access to the faculty lounge.

For years, I watched teachers walk into the administration building and disappear down the hall leading to the principal's office–headed to their only place of refuge–strictly off limits to students–the hallowed ground of the faculty lounge.

We drew names and, through divine brilliance, the name I drew was Mr. Funderburk–"Funder Chicken" himself.

Small gifts began appearing in each teacher's inbox the next week. The girls on the council baked cookies and banana bread. The guys left candy bars and packets of gum. During the Friday lunch hour, we revealed our identity. It occurred to me that I had nothing to give Funder Chicken about the time I drove into the parking lot that morning so I diverted to 7-11 in a panic. This was the pinnacle of the week–a grand event–another Snickers wasn't going to cut it. What made me grab what I did still strikes me with a mix of humor and horror. What the hell was I thinking?

The small faculty lounge was packed with jovial students and teachers.

My heart raced.

My palms were sweaty.

How would my fifth and final gift be received by the lovable Funder Chicken? *I never had him for a class so we really didn't know each other–maybe he wouldn't appreciate my sense of humor. Oh my God, I am so screwed!*

I peered into the brown paper bag and my heart sank. *What have I done?* I had no backup plan.

My rational voice screamed, *Get out now! Make it up to the Chicken later. Flee while you can!*

My irrational voice said, *Be cool. He's gonna love it. You're untouchable!*

Seizing a moment of maximum chaos in the noisy room, I stepped up to Mr. Funderburk and said, "I hope you've been enjoying your Snickers and Bubblicious but you're *really* going to appreciate the finale." He chuckled with smiling eyes, pleased that I was his secret student council admirer. Maybe it was going to work out after all.

Don't do it! Turn and run!

Be cool. It's too late now anyway!

People swirled around us. I held up the brown bag and raised the contents half way.

His eyes bugged out.

Sweat rolled down the inside of my shirt.

He grabbed the bag before I could remove it completely.

"I . . . I'll have to appreciate this later," he stammered.

It was the last time I saw the February 1986 *Playboy* again.

• • •

Sidebar #5:

AIDS/AYDS in 1986

It's generally regarded by most scholars that Acquired Immunodeficiency Syndrome (AIDS) made its first appearance in the United States in 1981, but as late as 1986, AIDS wasn't a topic in any of the conversations I was having. The disease, frankly, wasn't well understood because it didn't initially have a name. The first name it did have, Gay-related Immune Deficiency, or GRID, didn't help in gaining the attention of the mainstream.

When the disease was given the name we all now know and fear, misinformation and conflicting information was the norm:

Only gay males can contract AIDS.

You can contract AIDS *giving* blood.

You can contract AIDS from a mosquito bite.

I specifically remember AIDS in 1986 based on a conversation I had with Mom after hearing on the radio that people were dying of *AYDS* in New York City.

"Can you believe that people are dying of AYDS?" I asked incredulously.

Mom nodded, a grim look on her face.

"I can't believe we stock it at Longs."

139

She looked at me, confused. "What are you talking about?"

"AYDS. We stock it at Longs. It's an appetite-suppressant candy. I tried one and they taste absolutely nasty." And then, "Whoa, I could have died!"

"Uh, AIDS is a disease not a dietary supplement."

"Really? Wow, AIDS is a disease *and* a dietary supplement. That's got to be the worst product name ever!"

In no time, our supply of *AYDS* disappeared into the trash, never to return to the retail shelf.

• • •

The Battle of the Bands turned into a much anticipated annual event each April. We called ourselves "Strike Zone" after the Loverboy CD of the same name. The guys (Bruce, Brock, Ryan, and me) dressed in white pants, white shirts, and *pink* bowties. The girls (Kellie, Wendy, and Linda) wore colorful spandex of their choosing (with matching Sheena Easton-esque headbands).

The front page of Monache's school newspaper, the Tribal Tribune.

We felt, to borrow a Pat Benatar song, *Invincible*. We were the odds-on-favorite preppy band all the way.

I kicked off the hour singing Robert Tepper's upbeat Rocky IV anthem, *No Easy Way Out*. We added risqué humor when Ryan and Brock dueted Atlantic

Starr's *Secret Lovers*. With the growing paranoia of AIDS, it was far from politically correct. Either we'd be kicked off stage mid-song or the school's administration would play along with our jest. Lucky for us, everyone had a sense of humor.

The duet with my pretty blonde band mate, head cheerleader Wendy, (Whitney Houston's duet with Jermaine Jackson, *Nobody Loves Me Like You Do*) went over like a lead balloon with one person in the audience: Tiffany.

Caught up in the fun of that hour on stage, we finished the show in togas to Otis Day and the Knights' *Shout*, pulling people on stage from the front row to dance in the finale. (Jennifer, I apologize, again, for letting you flop on your face when I jerked you up by your outstretched arm.)

Strike Zone won.

After the trophy presentation, I found Tiffany standing in the corner in tears, her lower lip spasming in utter misery. It is one of those moments that I reflect on with mixed emotion. Surrounded by the chaos of celebration, I felt disappointed and bitter with her reaction. *It was only one dumb song! It was all just an act! Hell, we won! After four years of trying, we won!*

But it wasn't just that one song.

The tension of our different lives culminated at that moment. Selfishly, I refused to spend the night patching it up. The celebration awaited and Tiffany—my first love, my exotic, beautiful, smart girlfriend—felt nothing but pain, confusion and betrayal. I left her standing with her friends as a group of revelers swept me out the door. I drank away the pain and resentment later that night.

The next evening, we sat on her bed—the spot of the end of my glorious trail of roses ten months earlier—and I asked for my class ring back. She handed it over in tears and I fled past her bewildered parents in the living room.

She deserved better.

• • •

It was a slow night at Longs. Co-worker and classmate, Brian Massey, and I didn't have much to do. Brian was voted "Best Looking" by the class of '86. While I took the "Prep" route, he took the "New Wave" route—he was the Michael Hutchence of Monache—and I freaking worshipped the guy.

He sprung his idea on me to which I replied, "Oh, hell yeah." I went in search of plastic spoons.

When I climbed on top of the industrial freezer in the corner of the warehouse, he was already there with the gallon of blueberry ice cream. The freezer was at least fifteen feet high and with our backs against the wall, we were virtually invisible to anyone below. Even with my heart pounding from stealing our treat and utensils–not to mention that we were doing *nothing* to earn our $3.45 an hour–we sat in silence. Sitting shoulder to shoulder, picking at the ridiculously sweet ice cream, I finally said, "Can you believe it's almost over? In a few weeks we'll graduate and everything we've known these past four years will change."

"I can't wait to get out of this town."

"Really? You think leaving all this behind will be easy?"

He looked at me, grinning, and repeated what I had said ten minutes earlier, "Oh, *hell yeah*." And then, "We'll be in Hawaii in a few weeks then I'm moving to L.A. and not looking back. It's time to get on with the real world. Oh, and I'm giving my girlfriend a pearl necklace after work so life is good!"

The pearl necklace comment registered about a week later.

"I don't know," I said. "This has been a pretty sweet four years, Mr. Best Looking.

He started to answer but the overhead page echoed through the warehouse: "MR. MASSEY. MR. HARVEY. CART SERVICE OFF THE LOT, PLEASE."

"Time to get back to work, Mr. Best Personality," he laughed.

We climbed off the freezer, tossed the contraband in the trash, and raced out into the warm night air.

• • •

They awarded scholastic medals to the top 10% of the class. For all the hard work patching up my GPA (I finished with a cumulative 3.5), I graduated 30th.

Two hundred ninety graduates.

Top 10% receive a medal.

Do the math. I did.

Damn it.

On June 6, 1986, 290 teenagers accepted their diploma under the school's glorious, arching palm trees and the chapter on the Monache graduating class of 1986 came to a close.

The Phantom of the Opera opens at Her Majesty's Theatre in London. Over the years, I've seen it a dozen times in Los Angeles, San Francisco, Sacramento, and Seattle.

CHAPTER 14

THE SUMMER OF 1986

All year long, a couple dozen seniors scrimped, saved, and dreamt about a week of fun in Hawaii. It was a monumental time to go for two reasons: 1) it was our last chance to get together before scattering in the directions life had in store for us, and 2) the drinking age in Hawaii was eighteen, to be changed to twenty one in November. We were going to take full advantage of current Hawaiian law–it's what we law-abiding citizens do, right?

A group of us planned where we'd stay, what we'd do, and who we'd do it with. All year long, I implored–I begged–Mike Wells to come with us. The five hundred dollar price tag was too steep for him–as for me, I kicked in fifty dollars a paycheck.

As fate would have it, Mike's grandparents gave him exactly five hundred dollars for graduation.

The flight from LAX to Honolulu left four days after graduation, Tuesday, June 10, 1986. After learning of his financial windfall, my assault on Mike intensified.

"Mike, this is your one and only chance to come to Hawaii and party like it's 1999!"

"I'm saving up for a new car stereo."

"A new car stereo? This is Hawaii, man! You have to come. The drinking age is eighteen for only another few months!"

"I'm not eighteen, Tom. I turn eighteen in *August*."

"Details, details. They probably don't even card anyone anyway. We are going to drink profusely and stay in a perpetual state of numbness . . . with girls we know. Hell, Mike, your virginity's on the line here!"

Mike looked back with a thoughtful expression but said nothing.

I was packing my graduation present (beach towels) when the phone rang Monday morning. It was Mike.

"I'm in."

An hour later, we walked out of Argonaut Travel. He was pale and slightly off balance holding plane tickets in one hand and one dirty quarter in the other.

No travel package.

No accommodations.

Just a seat on a plane–a middle seat, at that.

"That was the most money I've ever had in my life," he mumbled. "All I have left is twenty five cents."

I slung my arm over his shoulder and said, "Now, let's talk about the demise of your virginity . . ."

Twelve hours later we were in a van on our way to LAX in the dark. Most of our group was on the same United flight and we left Mike to find his way to the now-defunct World Airlines gate.

"See you on the other side!" I yelled. "We'll have a cold one waiting for you!"

"This better work out!" he yelled back.

We had a drink just after checking in at the Moana Surfrider Hotel–four *strawberry daiquiris*–across the street. Not the most macho of drinks but it's a fact whether I like it or not. We took pictures of ourselves buying eight-packs of Lowenbrau. Why that beer? Maybe it was the fact that Lowenbrau came in eight-packs instead of six. Maybe it was the silver-foil-wrapped caps. Maybe it was the first beer we saw. We walked back to the hotel, filled our trashcans with ice, opened the doors to our rooms and declared to no one in particular, "The bar is now open!"

I found a green, canvas cot in a janitor's closet and set it up between our queen size beds. "Mike is now officially taken care of," I declared to my roommate, Steve.

An hour later, we stumbled back outside in search of the International Market Place–everyone needs an oyster guaranteed to have a pearl in it, right? As we stood on the hot, busy sidewalk, feeling no pain from the mix of daiquiri and bitter Lowenbrau, a familiar voice pierced the drone of traffic.

"Bruce! Bruuuuce!"

From out of the touristy masses, Mike appeared carrying a suitcase in both hands. He looked like he had just trekked across the Sahara: sweaty, red-faced, and grinning from ear to ear. He wore white shorts, a pink tank top, and a white T-shirt *tied around his head*. He looked ready to collapse.

We rushed to him, laughing.

"Where have you been? Didn't your flight land a few hours ago?" I asked.

He spoke in short, out-of-breath, erratic bursts: "Got on the wrong bus. Headed inland. Damn it's hot. Got on another bus. Headed back to the airport. Found the right bus. Dropped me off a mile back. Got rained on. Damn it's hot. Walking ever since."

145

"Buddy," I said, "you need a drink."

We had another round of daiquiris (banana this time, good God) but Mike's *virgin* drink put everyone in a dour mood. The locals *did* ID the hordes of high school vacationers so Mike's youth presented a problem. We returned to our room, presented Mike with his cot, and mulled over this serious setback.

Mike was ten weeks short of the Promised Land. This was my problem to solve.

"Let me see your driver's license."

He downed a cold Lowenbrau, grimaced, and handed it over.

California Drivers Licenses' at the time didn't have the security features they do today–no laser-inscribed watermarks, no red ink that read, "This person is a minor until his birthday in xxxx." The thing wasn't even laminated. I studied the license in silence.

And smiled.

Mike perked up. "What?"

I began laughing.

"What? WHAT?"

"Buddy, it's a good thing you were born in August and not any later or this wouldn't work."

"What? What are you going to do?"

"We've only got one shot at this so let me concentrate."

With the skill of a half-inebriated surgeon armed with a steak knife from a room service cart, I performed the operation.

"What are you doing?" Mike demanded.

"Shh!"

Nick.

I handed the license back to him. "There, go rub some dirt on it and we are good to go."

"You defaced my driver's license?"

"Your birthday is now *March* 22nd, the 8 is now a 3."

"What am I supposed to do with this when we get home?"

"We will worry about *that* a week from now. Now, when's your birthday?"

"Uh, *March* 22?"

Oh, yeah it was.

"*When's* your birthday?"

"March 22!"

At my insistence, our group ended up at a strip club called Lollipops. Huddled around a small table next to a small stage, we ordered a round of beers and sat there looking like dumb high school kids. What came next is an image permanently burned in my memory.

The lights went out, the music started, and out pranced *a woman* lit up by a spotlight. She had to be at least twenty five. It didn't take long for her to strip down to a g-string–*and nothing else.*

The way we situated ourselves around the small table, I was closest to the stage with the guys behind me. When the gal knelt down and shook her big boobs at us, I turned to my partners-in-crime–I was going to yell, *See! This was a good idea after all!*

I didn't have to say a word.

When I turned, they all had the same frozen expression: drink halfway to mouth, mouth wide open, eyes glazed over in a thousand-yard stare. It was the first time any of us had seen a pair of *womanly* boobs up close and personal. Ah, the innocence of youth.

We went to the USS Arizona Memorial the next day. I met a girl from Porterville High, Rachel, and we hit it off immediately. Realizing that this was a moment in our young lives that wouldn't come around again, it was time for a little *carpe diem.*

You can't go to Hawaii and meet a pretty girl without taking a long walk on a moonlit beach. We walked. We talked. We stopped at every beachside bar where we both downed a Flying Squirrel.[13]

I couldn't feel her lips when we kissed because I couldn't feel my face.

We stumbled back to her hotel room.

And then . . . the sounds came.

The gurgling stomach.

Involuntary belches.

Houston, we have a problem.

Rachel's pretty face turned white and clammy.

She began groaning, "Uhhhhhhhhhhhh."

I grabbed the trashcan as she swayed on the bed.

At exactly this moment, the door flung open and her cousin Frankie and his two friends walked in.

"What's going on here?" he demanded.

---

13   Consisting of tequila, Triple Sec, sweet and sour mix, orange juice, and lime juice–an easy-to-drink, dangerous combo.

"UHHHHHHHHHHHHHHHHHHHHHH . . ."

Rachel fell over on her side as I stood up in the same motion. I figured it would help my chances in avoiding a royal ass kicking if I wasn't in physical contact with Frankie's inebriated cousin. He immediately took my place as his two friends blocked the door, arms crossed.

And then, the first projectile vomit.

The pink mess flew the distance between the beds and splattered on the green shag carpet–*Ah, she had the seafood buffet too*. Frankie pulled her partially puked on hair away from her mouth and said, "Just let it go."

And she did, wretch after wretch into the trashcan.

I sidestepped the two guys and made a hasty retreat out of there. Oh, I felt bad for poor Rachel.

That was as close to romance as I got that week. I apologized to Rachel the next day. Luckily, I never saw Frankie again.

• • •

I saw Rachel once after our return to California. We met at Murry Park and sat in her Buick Regal listening to Janet Jackson sing about "control." We laughed about Hawaii and hugged goodbye.

• • •

Seven years later, I was back in Porterville working at the local hospital. The article in the Porterville Recorder read: "Benefit Dinner To Raise Money For Cancer Victim."

I called the number in the article. *Rachel* answered the phone.

"Hi Rachel, this is Tom Harvey. Do you remember me?"

Her voice was weak but she laughed. "Do I remember Tom Harvey? Yes, I remember Tom Harvey."

She was battling ovarian cancer.

I searched for encouraging words and she was upbeat.

We ran out of things to say and said goodbye.

I mailed her a note to stay away from flying squirrels–our own private joke.

She died two weeks later at the tender age of twenty four. Heartbroken, I went to her funeral, alone. Of the hundreds of grieving mourners, I was the first to pass by the open casket. *I was the lucky guy who walked on Waikiki and kissed this pretty girl under the Hawaiian moon.*

I didn't recognize the girl in the pretty white dress with lace. Cancer had ravaged away her youth. I drove back to work in tears.

• • •

The timing of my high school graduation coincided with David's graduation from Porterville Junior College. With both boys headed to Cal State Sacramento,[14] Mom packed up our lives and hit the road. I was to catch up with them upon my return from Hawaii.

Back from Hawaii (and temporarily staying at Mike's house), I drove back to the only place I knew as home: Unit 133 in the Wildwood Apartments. The front door wasn't all the way shut so I walked in. The blinds were closed and the living room was dark.

Spooky.

I am convinced that apartment is haunted but that's a series of stories I'll spare you.

The empty apartment looked *very small.* Images flashed through my mind: the gray metallic shelves we used in the living room, the green faux leather recliner that matched absolutely nothing, dusty trophies lining the small windowsill, the brown wicker laundry hamper in the narrow hallway.

I went from room to room in silence. My heart hurt.

I sat down on the floor in my empty bedroom and began crying. Dusty outlines were the only thing left of the posters that used to peer down on my youth.

The door flung open.

"What are you doing in here?" the apartment manager growled.

"Oh, I'm sorry. I just returned from my senior trip and was just saying goodbye."

"Your family is gone. You're not supposed to be in here!"

I looked up at her, anger boiling up through the tears.

"This was my home *for the last six years.* I grew up in this bedroom. Do you mind giving me fifteen more minutes?"

She frowned.

"You don't still have a key, do you?"

"Yes, as a matter of fact, I do."

---

14   After striking out at my top three choices: UC Santa Barbara, UCLA, and Cal.

I took the key off my key ring and looked at it for a long second before handing it to her.

She saw the tears streaking down my face and her stance softened.

"Take all the time you need but, please, lock the front door when you leave."

She walked out and left me to my grief.

• • •

I left Porterville the next day. Home was now nothing more than an address scribbled on a piece of paper.

We rented two apartments in the same complex on Fair Oaks Boulevard in Carmichael–Mom, Trish, and me in one and my two brothers in the other. Lorne, having graduated from Eastern Washington University, joined us. We all went in search of jobs. I found a job at a nearby Longs Drug store, Mom got on at American River Hospital, David found a job at a nearby miniature golf course, and Lorne found a job in a loan office.

David said, "We should join a sorority when school starts."

I laughed and said, "Uh, that would be nice, but I think you mean *fraternity*."

<u>1987 Fun Fact #1:</u>

U2 releases "The Joshua Tree" which won the Grammy for Album of the Year. Guns N' Roses releases "Appetite for Destruction" which became the best selling debut album of all time. Michael Jackson releases "Bad" which produced five number one singles in the US. Overall, not a bad year for music!

CHAPTER 15

On the campus of Sacramento State. I could relate to the wood carving: hands up in panic, looking totally overwhelmed and fearful!

I was late for my first day at Sacramento State, underestimating the seven miles of gridlock traffic between our apartment and the university. When I flung the door open to Dr. Syer's "Government 1" class at twenty minutes past 8 a.m., a hundred strangers glared at me. The professor, thankfully, said nothing.

The sprawling campus and the vibe of a four-year-university was both exciting and intimidating. I wandered from class to class in awe of the sheer number of students–it was as if the entire population of Porterville was in a one mile radius.

I declared English as my major and earned a coveted spot in an English 1A class as a freshman. Classes were few, demand was high, and all students were required to pass 1A to graduate. When the instructor walked in that first day, I felt, once again, like a small town guy. With her platinum-white cropped hair, pale-white lipstick, black leather mini-skirt, and black knee-high boots, she exuded confidence. This rebel was an English professor?

Not exactly.

"Laura"—we'll just keep it to first names—was a graduate student whose sole purpose in life, I soon discovered, was to take out her frustrations on her students. I wasn't smart enough to join the thirty-two students who dropped the class after the first two weeks. I commiserated with the only friend I made at Sac State, a pretty blonde named Stacey.

Looking back, I have to think that a twenty percent retention rate for a class in so high demand would have—*should have*—raised eyebrows in the administrative office. In any event, with each paper I grew more and more dismayed. On one paper she wrote, "Well, isn't this just a happy, fairy tale little ending? Don't just go for the easy out. Your conclusion is much too convenient."

Much too convenient? What does that even mean?

After my third D in a row, I confronted her.

"Laura. I've written three papers and they've all come back D's. I don't understand it. I am an English major! This is what I do best! I was a straight A English student in high school!"

She looked back at me blankly.

"Tom, an A in high school automatically equates to a C in college. Didn't you know that?"

I frowned.

"No, I did not know that. If that's the case, shouldn't I have three C's?"

"I don't think you're applying yourself. I think you can do better."

At that I *should* have become the thirty third drop from her class but I assumed that Laura's grading was the new universal rule. I changed my major to Undeclared. Thank you, Laura, you sadistic torturer of ignorant undergraduate souls.

David and I met at "the Quad" between classes—the center of the school—where I'd whine to him about Laura. Just having someone to talk to among the thousands of strangers was comforting. We turned our attention to the dozen fraternity's soliciting for new members and David decided on the one that had the prettiest "little sisters."

153

We'll refer to those knuckleheads (the guys, not the little sisters) as Kappa Dumbass–for their sake.

We participated in all the rituals–we raced around town with twenty other pledges looking for the fraternity's precious lamp-of-knowledge ("*it's been stolen!*"), we created elaborate paddles (think of Kevin Bacon's "Thank you sir, may I have another?" scene from *Animal House*), and we partied furiously at the fraternity house (David, to my knowledge, still holds the record for upside-down Kamikazes at twenty-three[15]). We went on to survive the overnight initiation ritual, (sleeping on the cold floor of an empty church in nothing but a hospital gown was just the beginning) and learned the secret handshake. We made fifty instant friends.

Or did we?

The family depended on our financial-aid to help pay the bills–bills that now included monthly fraternity dues. A snafu in the financial aid office froze our support for a semester, and the Harvey brothers had no choice but to tell our fraternal friends that we couldn't afford the dues.

We became outcasts overnight.

We later discovered that the fraternity had run up such a large tab at the local liquor store that, despite all the pomp and circumstance around *selectively* growing the membership, they really only had three requirements for new members: 1) a penis, 2) a pulse, and 3) the ability to pay monthly dues. Once our financial aid was restored, we didn't bother to re-affiliate with those clowns.

Sidebar #6:

The Reds and the Blues

The Longs in Carmichael fielded a softball team to take on another store and I asked the Photo Manager, a black guy named Duane, if he was going to play. He shook his head *no*.

"It's going to be fun. Why aren't you playing?"

He looked at me seriously.

"Do you know where the games are played?"

"No."

"The games are in south Sac and south Sac is right in the middle of the Reds and the Blues. You can get yourself killed down there for wearing the wrong color."

---

15   It is TRULY a miracle he didn't die from alcohol poisoning.

I had no idea what he was talking about.

He went on.

"Whatever you do, don't wear any red or blue. You could end up getting shot."

I laughed at the absurdity.

My guess is that in 1986, people in Sacramento didn't know the Bloods and Crips by name–they were simply referred to by their colors. Two years later, I learned everything I wanted to know about these gangs in the 1988 movie, *Colors*.

We played one softball game, losing big time–in our *black shirts with white numbers*–before disbanding.

• • •

Despite the sheer masses of students at Sac State, I struggled with loneliness. One afternoon, as I sat on the steps of the music building studying the Circle of Fifths (someone should have told me music was math disguised with notes and clefs), a familiar face approached. I perked up instantly.

"Jennifer. Hi!"

The little blonde girl looked at me, surprised.

"Tom Harvey? Wow."

With that, she passed by without even slowing down.

She was from Monache, now a senior, touring the school's music department. A girl I hadn't said two words to in three years of high school. Now I was practically falling over myself to say hello.

Her chilly reception caused me to pause.

Was I really that big of a snob just a few short months ago? The answer, simply, was *yes*.

• • •

As David and I drove through Carmichael one afternoon, a black Ferrari came up on us in a flash.

"Check out this cool car," I said.

It pulled up on our right hand side. We turned in unison.

With blonde hair flying, the driver belted out lyrics we couldn't hear. He laughed at us, downshifted, and blasted away. What is the ticket for doing a hundred in a forty mile-per-hour zone?

Thrilled at the sighting of our hero, the Ferrari with the plates "REDRCKR" disappeared ahead of us. It's true. *Sammy Hagar can't drive fifty five.*

• • •

The family, just before I left home for good.

As I floundered in Sacramento, the reports from Joe at Cal State Northridge were nothing but positive. Every time we talked, he gushed about hot tub parties in the dorm, pretty girls, and the lively Los Angeles club scene.

I sat down with Mom.

"I've been thinking about this and . . ."

She looked at me with raised eyebrows.

"I'm going to transfer to Cal State Northridge. Joe and I are going to get a place together."

There was sadness in her eyes. At the tender age of nineteen, her youngest son was leaving the nest.

Leaving home is one of those things that doesn't feel like a life changing event. At the time, I simply felt like I'd enjoy my college experience elsewhere. I can only imagine how she felt the day I drove out of sight, oblivious to the major life-changing events in my near future.

"Sledgehammer" by Peter Gabriel wins 9 awards at the MTV Video Music Awards. I always liked "Red Rain" better.

CHAPTER 16

THE SUMMER OF 1987

I made the four hour drive to Porterville and moved into Joe's garage for the summer. He worked for the California Department of Forestry and stayed at the fire station up the winding, mountain road twenty miles away.

Moving back to Porterville and working at my old job made moving away from home easy–the pangs of "leaving the nest"–wouldn't come for another few months.

There were new faces at Longs Drugs–all of my high school contemporaries were gone, replaced by current high school students. One face was the radiant blonde, Nina, a girl two years younger than me. The attraction was immediate.

I took her to dinner, we saw some movies (*Ghostbusters* and *Born On The Fourth of July* come to mind), and it wasn't long before she introduced me to her parents. This seemingly insignificant act changed the course of my life.

She lived in a sprawling villa surrounded by open fields. I met her parents for the first time as they relaxed on their massive backyard deck–paradise, by my definition: palm trees, a dry river bed, pebble trails that wound their way through the perfectly manicured landscaping. And there, in the middle of it all, sat her content father happily drinking St. Pauli Girl beer.

"So *you're* Tom?" her mother asked in her thick German accent.

"Yes, I am."

Nina's dad, a short, rotund balding man with round glasses, stood up. "Please call me Ray. Have a beer."

He either didn't know or didn't care that I was only nineteen. The guy had a taste for all things German. When we ran out of St. Pauli Girl we switched to Becks. After five beers in a two-hour period, I staggered to my car and drove back to Joe's garage with my head spinning.

Over the course of the summer, Ray listened intently as I talked about aspirations of law school. What I didn't fully appreciate about the man–the thing he enjoyed immensely–was that I had no idea how powerful he was in the community. Behind the

Porterville Development Center (a state run housing and medical facility for developmentally disabled people) and the school district, Ray's role as Administrator of the local, ninety three-bed district hospital made him the figurehead for the third largest employer in town. Nearly five hundred highly trained professionals worked for him. While everyone referred to this retired Army Colonel as "Mr. Grant," (that was his last name, after all) to me he was simply "Ray." I saw the soft side of this kind and gentle man that few people knew. We sat on that back porch for hours, with or without his daughter. Oh, that drove her *nuts*.

• • •

On Sunday, August 16, Nina and I had just finished dinner with her parents and turned on the TV. Every station was broadcasting a downed commercial airliner.

Northwest Flight 255 had crashed just after takeoff in Detroit. We watched in horror at the fire and chaos. Mangled, unrecognizable pieces of the MD-82 lay strewn around the runway and adjacent interstate. In all, a hundred and fifty six people died in the tragedy, including Phoenix Sun center Nick Vanos. I remember thinking, *It would be a miracle if anyone survived*. The next day, we learned that a four-year-old girl was the sole survivor. I cried when I heard the news report.

• • •

While I paid no rent for staying in Joe's garage, my part-time work schedule at Longs at $3.45 an hour barely covered the essentials. The summer was almost over and I was a week from my first class at Northridge–and my share of the first month's rent in the new apartment.

A visit to my ultra frugal grandparents was in order. They had moved to a tiny trailer park on the outskirts of the city limits. The drive took all of five minutes. I took my friend Tim Miller with me.

We had a nice visit in the cramped trailer and I immediately regretted not seeing them more over the summer–they were both so happy to see me. But, here we were, and nothing changed the fact that the summer was over and I was desperate. Hell, man, I was *broke*.

"Well, Son, anything we can do for you?" Grandpa asked as if sensing my ulterior motive. Grandma sat back in her dinette chair, a brown, ill-smelling Virginia Slim burning in her fingertips.

"Actually, there is."

The silence hung in the air. My grandparents smiled but said nothing.

I continued.

"I could really use . . . a loan . . ." The words hung in the air.

Having said the words, I realized that I had no idea how much I needed. I had never asked anyone for money before. I felt sick to my stomach.

"How much do you need, Son?" he asked without hesitation.

"How about . . ."

Tim raised his glass of water to his lips . . .

". . . five hundred dollars?"

With that, Tim spewed water across the small trailer. We watched it splat against the faux wood grain paneling. I immediately thought, *Oh, that's too much. Damn it! Damn it! Damn it!* Tim coughed and choked at the brazen request.

Without hesitation, my grandpa said, "Is a check OK? We don't have that much cash lying around."

I pounded Tim on the back, his face red, the veins in his forehead pulsing like a fire hose, and said quietly, "A check would be just fine."

<u>*1988 Fun Fact #1:*</u>

Canadian Ben Johnson wins Olympic gold in the 100 meter dash. Wait, check that. That medal belongs to American Carl Lewis. No medal for anyone who tests positive for steroids, dumbass!

CHAPTER 17

Our three-bedroom apartment in Canoga Park was eight miles from the campus of Cal State Northridge. Joe and his older brother of one year, Ted, furnished it with the essentials: a couch and a TV. Joe and I shared the master bedroom and a king-sized bed.

This took some getting used to.

There's a scene from the 1987 movie *Planes, Trains, and Automobiles* that summed up the first few weeks of this sleeping arrangement. Starting on our respective sides of the bed, invariably we'd awake in a comfortably-spooned position. One night Joe elbowed me roughly after I whispered *oh baby* in his ear.

We were close, but not *that* close.

We eventually put two king-size pillows down the middle of the bed which helped reduce the occurrence of unintended groping. Despite these nocturnal displays of affection–misguided as they were–we went through a month of strained transition.

I had never lived on my own and the three previous months in Joe's garage came with an attached house fully stocked with toilet paper, toothpaste, and clean towels. Joe's mom, happy to have the company, cooked lavish meals every night. I wasn't really on my own that summer–I had swapped one mom for another.

I admit it, to Joe and the world, I was a slob.

I used his towel and threw it on the floor.

I used his toothpaste.

It's a wonder I didn't use his toothbrush.

For the first few weeks, he didn't say a word.

Tension grew to the point where we couldn't look at each other.

"Stop using my toothpaste!" he screamed one day.

"OK," I said mindlessly, "but toothpaste is expensive! Like three dollars a tube!"

"And get your own damn towel! I can't stand the thought of you drying your hairy ass with my towel!"

I nodded. He had a point.

"And we need to establish a toilet paper budget, too!"

I looked at him blankly. His eyes lit with rage.

After a few moments we burst into laughter and, from there on, we established the basic set of rules: use your own toothpaste, use your own towel, and keep the TP stocked. Oh, and always flush the toilet, but I guess that goes without saying.

Fair enough.

$$\bullet \ \bullet \ \bullet$$

Having already spent a year in the area, Joe and Ted had jobs working the graveyard shift at local gas-stations. That wasn't for me. I was going to be a movie star.

After perusing the newspaper, I called one of the dozen or so casting agencies and made an appointment. The guy on the other end of the phone, "George," was eager to meet me. This was exciting.

Navigating my way into Hollywood, I found the dumpy building and sprinted up two flights of musty stairs. George greeted me with enthusiasm. "You must be Tom? Right on time!"

I nodded.

"Let's start by having you fill out this information sheet but, I have to tell you, you've got *the look!*" He made a goal post with his fingertips (thumbs together, forefingers extended) and walked around me as if he were a big shot director setting up a scene.

I wasn't sure what *the look* was, but I was glad that I had it. Five minutes later, he snapped a headshot with a grimy Polaroid and hurried me out the door. Another two would-be future movie stars sat patiently on the lumpy couch. George's schedule was backing up.

I drove back to the San Fernando Valley pleased as can be. Night shift at a gas station for me? I think not.

When I walked in the apartment, Joe reported that George called and needed me to call him right back. My heart raced as I dialed the number.

"George, this is Tom. I just left your office."

"Oh, yes, Tom! Have I got exciting news for you! I've got you lined up for several commercials already!"

"You do? I can't believe it!"

"Yeah, you'll be in a holiday commercial where you serve a computer eggnog and the computer burps. Oh, it's going to be so funny. And then I have you lined up for a clothing commercial, and, lastly, a men's cologne commercial. Oh, but one thing," he casually added. "You'll need to get some professional pictures taken."

"Sure, anything."

"Great, here's my photographer's name and number. Setup a time to meet with him ASAP. This is very urgent."

"I'll call him right now."

"Oh, and one last thing. His fee is three hundred dollars, but don't worry. You'll make that back on your first job."

Click. The phone went dead.

Three hundred dollars? *Who's got three hundred dollars?*

Two days later, I found myself in a North Hollywood living room. Cameras and strobe lights were strewn around the room. On a coffee table sat a stack of headshot photograph's a foot thick.

"So, you got the three hundred?" the guy asked eagerly.

"Actually, I don't. I can pay you half today. Would you mind the other half once I earn my first paycheck?"

"Uh, that's not how it works." He frowned. "Give me what you have today, and we'll have to work out the details."

After an hour of posing, I walked out the front door as the dumpiest, dirtiest Oldsmobile pulled up to the curb. Lo and behold, it was George.

He stepped out of the car and must have seen the look of doubt on my face. "Oh . . . uh . . . rental car . . . my Porsche is in the shop." He actually said that.

"Huh. Well, I'm all done here. The photoshoot was fun, and I should have the proofs in a few days."

"Good."

We passed on the sidewalk and George entered the house without knocking.

As I started my car, George flew out the front door. "Wait! Wait!" The guy was old, but he could move.

I rolled down my window.

"You only paid him half!"

"Yeah, that's all I can afford right now. I was hoping to pay him the other half once I worked a job or two for you."

"No, no, no, no. That won't work. You need to pay him in full! *Now!*"

"If I do that, George, I won't have money for food."

"This is more important! You've got *the look*, kid! We need those photos done as soon as possible. You need to pay him right away." He practically yanked me out of the car.

I walked back in the house and wrote a check for a hundred and fifty dollars, leaving exactly eight dollars to my name.

When I got home, I told Joe what had happened. Joe was *pissed.*

"You just got scammed. You needed to pay in full because that was the only way George was going to get his cut. They just played you for a fool and now you can't kick in for food. They screwed you over and now you've screwed us over. Thanks. Thanks a lot."

I went to bed that night with a knot in my stomach, both from the microwaved potato and the fact that I was so gullible.

I did end up with professional headshots to send to casting agencies but the jobs that George had lined up, oddly enough, were no longer available. I never heard from George again. Maybe I didn't have *the look*, after all.

I took a graveyard position at a North Hollywood Texaco. If you've never worked the nightshift, brother, let me tell you–it ain't easy. If there's a less glamorous job, I'd like to hear about it. (Actually, I wouldn't. That was only a figure of speech.)

And this was no convenience store job.

The job entailed locking oneself in a 4' by 10' booth behind bulletproof glass. My shift started at 9 p.m. and ended at 6 a.m. The first few hours were occupied watching *LA Law* and *The Wild, Wild West* reruns on the twelve inch black and white TV. But after the charismatic James West foiled the train robbery, hit to twenty one on a soft seventeen, *and* got the girl, there wasn't much to do but stare out at the empty streets of North Hollywood.

I had my regulars: the bored Secret Service agents whose only job was to sit outside Ronald Reagan's daughter's house all night, every night. They'd fill up their nondescript Ford sedan and have me throw in a couple of candy bars on their government gas card, all the while grumbling about how much they hated their job. There was the fifty-something Asian businessman in the silver Mercedes, dressed in his power suit– complete with prescription sunglasses which he wore at night–who hit on me regularly.

"What time you get off?"

"Uh, it varies. Can't really say."

"I come back for you. We go to breakfast."

"Uh, thanks, but no thanks."

My favorites were the three teenage black dudes who shuffled across the lot, trying way too hard to look cool for their audience of one. I give them credit for the routine: they'd step into the light, flash what I think were supposed to be gang signs, urinate in large, sweeping circles, then disappear into the night in no particular hurry. The first few times, they flipped me off as they walked away, but we eventually came to a peaceful co-existence. Rather than flash me the bird, they'd nod as if to say, *We still gonna pee, but you all right in our book.* I always knew it was 2 a.m. when the Three Homies made their appearance. When the coast was clear, I'd leave the security of the small booth for my nightly chores: checking the long dipstick that extended into underground storage tanks for a reading of fuel capacity, emptying the trashcans, and hosing off the acrid smell of Gang Banger urine. Holy crap, did these guys eat asparagus *every* night?

When I turned the keys over to the 6 a.m. guy, I drove bleary-eyed back up the Ventura Freeway, exited to Canoga Avenue, and stumbled back to the apartment where I had a choice: Do I fall face forward into bed or force myself to stay awake for 8 a.m. Biology? I tried a power nap once and discovered that there was no such thing as a forty-five minute nap after a sleepless night–once in bed, it was sleep 'til noon.

My grades suffered that first semester–I just wasn't cut out for the nightshift.[16] It wasn't easy on Joe either as we both crashed around the noon hour in Dr. Fischer's Oceanography class. (Perfect name for a Professor of Oceanography, don't you think?) Dr. Fischer was none too pleased to have students taking a siesta on his time. We'd take turns sleeping and keeping an eye out for the roaming professor. The combination of sleep deprivation, a stifling hot classroom, and a less-than-exciting discourse on how the Coriolis Effect impacted sediment along the coastline was too much. We were doomed.

". . . and who can answer the question?" Professor Fischer asked. There he stood, hovering over Joe like a hawk.

Joe, oblivious and sound asleep with his face down on his folded arms, didn't stir. I was half awake (or was it half asleep?) with my face propped up in the open palm of my hand.

---

16   I got a C in golf. Seriously? All we did was pitch range balls in the open field adjacent to the school. How the hell does a guy get a C doing that?

Dr. Fischer scanned the room, glared down at me and then spied Sleeping Beauty.

"How about . . . hmm . . ." He looked around the room in a grandiose sweeping motion–like a pirate surveying a distant shore–but there was no doubt his intention.

". . . you?"

He pointed to Joe with a three-inch-long piece of chalk.

No response.

My half-closed eyes shot open but it was too late to come to the rescue. Joe was screwed on my watch.

Dr. Fischer reared back and bounced the chalk off Joe's head with as much force as he could muster. Pieces of broken chalk scattered across the room. Joe's head snapped up, he wiped drool off his chin, and said, "Huh, what?"

"GET OUT!" Dr. Fischer bellowed. "BOTH OF YOU! THERE IS NO SLEEPING IN MY CLASS!"

We grabbed our books and made for the door.

"Thanks a lot," Joe hissed.

I couldn't help but laugh–I had never seen a teacher break a piece of chalk on a student's head.

"We have to find different jobs," I replied as we furthered the conversation over a game of pinball in the student union.

We tried selling coupon books for a local Chevron station. After one night going door-to-door, we quit.

We tried selling overpriced steak knives to friends and family. After one night, they fired us.

I wasn't cut out to be a salesman.

• • •

One day while perusing The Daily Sundial, Cal State Northridge's student newspaper, a Help Wanted ad caught my eye: *Clerk needed for video store. Evening hours after class. Apply in person.* I ran to my car and drove to the address in nearby Chatsworth.

National Home Video was tucked into a small strip mall. The husband and wife owners, John and Dee Duca, employed their high school-aged daughter and her friend. With four employees, they needed help.

I immediately felt at ease with John Duca, a small, balding man with glasses who sounded just like Yoda. We talked for awhile about our love of movies until he asked me the question that sealed the deal.

"My daughter, Dana, is in high school and you'd be working with her on Sundays. She'd technically be your boss. Do you have any problems with that?"

Without hesitation, I responded, "If she asked me to sweep the sidewalk, I'd say, 'Where's the broom?'" I paused and thought, *Where the hell did that come from? It was genius!*

The phone call beat my ten-minute drive back to Canoga Park. While the pay wasn't great (something less than $5 an hour, as I recall) the fringe benefit was unlimited movie rentals. In fact, part of the job was to watch as many movies as possible so I could recommend movies when asked, "What do you have that's in that's good?"–a question posed by every person who walked through the door.

Behind two white swinging doors was the porn section and, buddy, let me tell you, I took my movie-watching responsibilities seriously. Even Joe and his brother were eager to critique this genre and we watched such timeless classics as *Top Buns*, *Romancing the Bone*, and the never-ending *Where The Boys Aren't* series. Surprisingly, the vast majority of porn renters were *women* and they consistently asked for something *classy yet erotic*. I was happy to oblige.

I found it ironic that the business depended primarily on children's movies (mostly Disney classics at the time) and porn–genres rented over and over again. It's not like someone was going to watch *Beverly Hills Cop 2* more than once–but they'd rent *The Jungle Book* or *Where The Boys Aren't Part 20* multiple times.

VHS tapes were expensive. Most movies *cost* John Duca $64 from his wholesaler. At $2.50 a rental, every new title had to be rented *26 times* before it broke even. Many movies didn't last that long due to sun exposure or machines that ate the tape.

I worked Tuesday, Wednesday, and Thursday evenings and all day Sunday. Sunday's were fun for a couple reasons: 1) no one rented a movie on Sunday, it was all returns from the previous day, and 2) Dana worked on Sundays. The seventeen-year-old was vivacious and pretty and she knew it. We got along swell. Every Sunday we put on our favorite movie, *Grease*, and danced around the store singing every song as we returned movie boxes to shelves. Regular customers returning their Saturday rental joined in on the chorus. Sunday's were hydromatic, ultramatic–they were like greased lightning!

Renting pornos can get awkward. One of my regular customers slipped into the double swinging doors and emerged with *Switch Hitters 2*. It was one of the two bi-sexual films we carried; obvious to me, not so obvious to him apparently. I didn't know whether I should point out that the film *wasn't your average porn film.* I decided to give the guy the benefit of the doubt. That is, when in doubt, don't say a damn thing.

Half an hour later, the guy stormed back in the store and threw the movie on the counter. "This movie is the most disgusting thing I've ever seen! Why didn't you warn me?"

"Uh . . . I haven't actually watched it. I stick to the *more traditional* films. Sorry about that.[17] Go ahead and pick out something else. No charge."

The guy glared at me before slipping back into the porn section.

In April, I received a call from a casting agency. Turns out that the overpriced headshots I had blanketed the industry with actually paid off. The gal told me to report to a high school in Whittier–I was going to be an extra in a movie.

Fighting two hours of southbound I-5 traffic, I arrived at the location at 6 a.m. as instructed and joined a couple dozen other bleary-eyed teenagers in an empty classroom.

We waited.

And waited.

And waited.

We talked about the three "principals" (the "stars" of this particular movie) who would be on set that day: Jill, Donovan, and Brad. The general consensus was that Donovan was the next superstar.

At 8 a.m., a crew member rushed in and said that the hallway shot was setup and she needed background people. Twenty four arms shot up in the air. I immediately thought if the lady needed someone to eat a turd on screen, twenty four arms would have shot up (mine included, sadly). The lady randomly picked four of us, including me, and we followed her like baby ducks following its mama toward the bright lights of the set.

She placed us on marked Xs on the floor and instructed us to have *the liveliest mime conversation we could muster*.

And . . . *action!*

With the camera pointed directly at our foursome, we began a comical silent movie routine. The "principals" entered the scene (the next big star Donovan, the unknown Brad, and the unknown Jill) and began their conversation in front of us. The scene was filmed at least a dozen times and, with each take, the absurdity of the background performers grew.

---

17   As if it was my damn fault!

By the twelfth take, we were doubled over in silent laughter, silently pounding each other on the back like we were reciting Dice Clay nursery rhymes.

With the director finally satisfied, we were told to return to the "holding tank" to wait for another opportunity. Enamored with the lights, cameras, and boom (the microphone suspended just out of camera view), I lingered behind and watched the crew setup the next scene. In strolled a face I *did* know–hey, that's Roddy McDowell from *Planet of the Apes!*

And . . . *action!*

Roddy, and the female lead, a pretty brunette with a gravelly voice, (Jill Schoelen) spoke their lines (a play on the word *principle*. Roddy was *principal* of the high school) over and over and over again. As the takes added up ("Cut! We've got an airplane passing overhead. Cut! We've got an ambulance siren in the background. Cut! Let's do it again faster.), I leaned in closer to the Panavision camera.

Roddy was so focused on his lines that his face was still turned toward the scene as he walked out of camera view.

WHAM.

His faced slammed into mine, knocking me backwards. My eyes flooded with tears from the sudden impact.

"Oh, I'm so sorry, Mr. McDowell," I whispered as he cupped his nose in pain. He looked at me for a moment as if deciding whether to have me thrown off the set. Finally, he smiled, said nothing, and they set up the scene again. No one noticed his bright red nose.

At lunchtime, a large tent was set up by an army of caterers. As the group of bored extras filed into line, we were turned away–this was the lunch for the Screen Actors Guild card-carrying members.[18] They handed out sack lunches to us silent-types and told us to get lost for an hour. As I walked off feeling underappreciated and a bit stupid, a girl in a cheerleader uniform argued with the guy guarding the catered lunch area. "I am *not* an extra!" she snorted and shoved him aside in disgust.

A traveling circus was setting up a tent on the adjacent football field, and I strolled around the swirl of activity.

Seeing her stopped me in my tracks.

The black panther paced back and forth in its small confines. Its large, muscular tail smacked the bars of the cage. It hissed and spit in rage. I looked at my half eaten

---

18   Utter one word on camera and you have to join the union . . . and pay union dues!

ham sandwich and thought, *If that cat escaped, I would be its half eaten sandwich*. It was the most intense animal I've ever seen.

"Isn't she beautiful?"

Without looking to see who asked the question, I breathed, "Awesome. Totally bitchen."

I turned and there stood the star of the movie, Donovan Leitch, son of the British singer Donovan of *Mellow Yellow* fame. He wore a black suit and–get this–*bowling shoes*.

I said, "So all the extras say you're going to be the next big thing."

He smiled modestly, never taking his eyes off the big cat. "I don't know about that. We'll see what happens."

"So what's with the bowling shoes?"

"Oh, don't you know? I'm a psychopath. At one point I kill someone with a bowling ball and mumble, 'Strike!'"

"Are you serious?"

"Oh, yeah."

We both laughed.

"So who's the other guy in this morning's scenes? The blonde haired guy?"

"His name's Brad. Brad Pitt."

"Huh, never heard of him."

He smiled then finally said, "Well, I guess we should get back to work." We walked back to the high school together.

I worked a total of two days on the set and was disappointed to discover, years later, that the scenes I was in ended up on the cutting room floor. Cut out of *Cutting Class*, what a drag.[19]

---

19 But if you pause the basketball game scene, I'm the guy across the court in a bright blue Hawaiian shirt working the serious one-armed fist pump.

Actor Haley Joel Osment is born which is important–he'd later see dead people in M. Night Shyamalan's thriller, "The Sixth Sense." Did I get the twist at the end? Hell no! And neither did you! Be honest now. One of my favorite cinematic lines of all-time: "I didn't know you were funny."

CHAPTER 18

THE SUMMER OF 1988

I returned to Sacramento for the summer hoping to land a job at the California Department of Fire (CDF) station in nearby Placerville. Any hope went out the window as I waited my turn. There, in the front office sat my competition: three volunteer firemen and a pretty girl in her early-twenties. *Hell*, I thought, *I'm in last place already.*

I had no fire fighting experience. The committee of three guys, dressed in olive green CDF uniforms and dirty black boots, leaned forward and asked, "How well can you cook?"

Before I could answer, one guy mumbled, "Everyone takes a turn cooking around here and most guys can't cook for crap."

I said something about BBQ chicken, thanked them for their time, and made a hasty retreat for the door. A few days later, I received the postcard thanking me for my time. I wouldn't have hired me either.

Longs Drugs wasn't hiring so I signed up at a temp agency. When asked what skills I possessed, I wrote, *acting ability–having recently performed in an as-of-yet-to-be-released major motion picture.* When I handed the form back to the chubby lady in the cheap flowery dress, she scanned down my application and burst out laughing.

I made another quick retreat as she passed it to a co-worker, pointing at it in glee.

A few days later Chubs called and said she had a job at the local Pepsi Cola bottling plant.

"They filming a commercial there?" I asked brightly.

"Uh, no."

"They need a typist? Did I tell you I can type forty eight words a minute?"

"Uh, typing jobs are filled by the ladies, Sport. If you want this job, you'll need work boots, long pants, and a long sleeve shirt. The job starts at 6 a.m. tomorrow. Now, do you want the job or not?"

Faced with the prospect of another day watching *The Price Is Right* and *General Hospital*, I reluctantly said yes.

Early the next morning, I reported to the Pepsi plant along with two sleepy black dudes. It was still dark and cold as we stood outside the warehouse door in silence, our hands stuffed in our pockets. The door swung open and out popped an overweight, unshaven, agitated white guy in a hardhat.

"You're on the clock. Let's go!"

He looked at the three of us like we were slime.

"Only three of you today, huh? Well, LET'S GO LADIES."

We followed him in as rows of overhead florescent lights flickered on. Forklifts fired up. Machines whirred to life. What little respect I had for the foreman quickly disappeared.

"You mooks[20] are working on a conveyor belt today, see?"

The three of us yawned in unison.

"You'll unload empty glass bottles onto the belt, see? The belt runs them through the washer. From the washer, they go through a dryer, then they get refilled. You'll need to work fast."

I think the mooks could handle it.

"One last thing," he barked. "This is a Pepsi plant, see? Doesn't mean that the occasional Coke bottle doesn't come back to us. You let a Coke bottle past you and we have to stop the line. *Don't make me stop this line!*"

With that he climbed into an elevated chair next to the belt and, with the push of a button, the conveyor belt sprang to life. Forklift drivers began delivering pallets of empty sixteen ounce bottles.

Perhaps the most well-known episode of *I Love Lucy* is the 1952 "Job Switching" where Lucy and Ethel take a job packaging candy on a conveyor belt. In no time, they fall behind and resort to all kinds of shenanigans to keep up. That is what the long morning felt like. Our supervisor must have thought his hardhat made him the Grand Poobah–either that or Chief Asshole–because he controlled how fast the belt moved. And we couldn't move fast enough.

The quicker we unloaded heavy cases of sticky, empty bottles, the quicker he'd run the belt. Occasionally, a rogue bottle slipped through–a Coke, or a Sprite, or a Mr. Pibb–and he'd slam the red button halting the line, leap down off of his perch, and shove the offending bottle in our faces.

"How'd *this* get through, huh?"

The three of us shrugged.

---

20   Dictionary.com definition: "a contemptible, incompetent person."

"I wish I could dock your pay for every one of these that slips by," he muttered then resumed his perch on his elevated throne.

The morning passed *slowly*.

Over the lunch hour, my two fellow temp workers walked off and never came back. The Grand Poobah squealed with glee, "We don't pay for half-days so those guys just worked for free! HA!" He looked at me like this had personal meaning to me. I suppose that it did, since it left me one-on-one with the guy for the rest of the day.

"Since it's just you, I'll have you work the belt for another hour or two than you can push a broom 'til quitting time."

"Uh, thanks?"

True to his word, I unloaded empty bottles for another two hours then he shoved a broom in my hand. I reckon he did this more for his sake than mine—with only one person to crack the whip on, he struggled to stay awake on his perch. My guess is he excused himself to a bathroom stall with a girly magazine for the rest of the day.

Pushing a broom wasn't the sexiest job in the world, but it beat working the conveyor belt and gave me a chance to look around the large warehouse. The place was full of motion—forklifts zipped up and down aisles, machines washed empty bottles, machines filled clean bottles. The sweet smell of syrup hung in the air.

I watched a large piece of machinery—what I'd call an auto-stacker—stack pallets of freshly filled bottles vertically. When it hit three-stories high, and the spire began to lean, I turned and ran.

Behind me, the groan of stressed plywood gave way to the loudest explosion of glass I've ever heard. A wave of Pepsi, three inches deep, rushed past my feet in every direction.

When I turned around, the scene was total chaos.

Hundreds of bottles had crashed to the floor. All machinery ground to a halt as workers rushed to the scene. Now I'm not a mathematician, but here's a good exercise: If a warehouse is three hundred feet long and three hundred feet wide (just my wild guess) and a bottle of soda is sixteen ounces, how many broken bottles does it take to cover the floor of the warehouse in three inches of soda? (I guess that's impossible to solve without knowing how many pallets are on the floor, displacing the soda. For sake of this exercise, let's pretend there were twenty five pallets with a footprint of 48" by 40." If you're smart enough to figure this out, please e-mail the answer. I'm dying to know.)

Now I've smelled some nasty things in my day (the mix of a petroleum plant amidst pineapple fields in Hawaii, my brother Lorne's belches, are two examples), but there's nothing like the sickening-sweet smell of Pepsi syrup and forklift exhaust. The combination, in the sweltering heat, makes me want to puke to this very day.

My supervisor-for-the-day splashed through the soda and screamed, "Well, don't just stand there! Start sweeping up this glass!" And there was glass *everywhere*.

After a long, dissatisfying day of conveyor belt work and one near death experience,[21] Fat Boy had the nerve to ask, "So, you coming back tomorrow?"

Snatching my signed timesheet, I replied, "Not hardly."

• • •

Throughout the summer, I made the four-hour drive south to Porterville. One regular stop was Nina's house even though we were no longer dating. Much to her frustration, her parents and I enjoyed a mutual adoration. On one such visit, Ray asked me how I liked going to school in Los Angeles.

"I like it a lot," I said matter-of-factly, "but I'm pretty much broke all the time."

"How would you like a job at the hospital next summer?"

My pulse quickened. I hadn't even thought of hitting him up for a job.

"That would be great! But . . . what would I do?"

He took a drink of St. Pauli Girl and thought for a moment.

"The highest paying department you could work in would be the maintenance department. You'd make more than most of the nurses."

"I . . . I don't know what to say!"

"Say 'Yes'"!

"Yes!"

This seemingly innocent conversation turned out to be a pivotal point in my life. I've worked in healthcare ever since.

• • •

After a long night of partying, I found myself in the backseat of Joe's brother's Mustang. Joe and Ted cleaned houses in their spare time and thought nothing of driving the two and a half hours from Porterville to northern Los Angeles County for a

---

21   How many people's death certificates read, "Death by falling Pepsi?"

day's work. Having nothing else to do and always in need of extra money, I went along as a hired hand. We left Porterville at 4 a.m. with Joe behind the wheel and his brother in the passenger seat.

In no time, Ted and I dozed off. Not long after that, I awoke to the world in a slow spin, my ears filled with the shriek of squealing tires and Ted screaming at the top of his lungs.

" AHHHHHHHHHHHHHHHHHHHHHHHHHHH!"

I believe that no one can truly predict how a person will behave under extreme, life threatening stress and I was surprised at my response.

"It's cool! It's cool! It's cool! It's cool!" I spit out these two words, in rapid fire sequence, over and over again.

Joe had fallen asleep on a steep downhill grade midway through the Tehachapi Mountains (better known as The Grapevine), and the car had drifted into the shallow ravine separating north- and southbound I-5. As the car dipped and slid into the ditch at eighty miles an hour, Joe awoke and jerked the wheel to the right, severely overcorrecting our trajectory.

Thus, the spin.

On a dry road, the Mustang would have rolled with nothing but a two-foot-high barrier separating us from Pyramid Lake some 1,500 feet below. If the tumble down the mountain wouldn't have killed us (though it *surely* would have), splashing into the lake and drowning with massive internal injuries would have been just as effective.

As the world spun, and Ted shrieked, and I patted Joe on the shoulder repeating my two words (*"It's cool! It's cool! It's cool!"*), Joe sat with both hands gripped on the wheel. An odd sense of serenity emanated from his glazed-over eyes and goofy grin.

I remember these finite details because I am convinced that the brain microprocesses moments such as these. Death had a grip on our car and I watched the barrier, and the blackness beyond it, come closer and closer . . .

WHAM!

The passenger side door smacked the barrier and we spun in the opposite direction.

The guardian angel looking down on us saw the car do a three sixty spin then a five forty (another three hundred and sixty degrees then a one eighty) so that when the car finally came to a rest and stalled, we were looking up at the darkened freeway pointed in the wrong direction.

The sound of light rain against the windshield was broken by Joe's utterance. "Whoa."

Ted, having fallen silent, looked at his brother then looked back at me. Seconds passed as we wrapped our minds around what had just happened. Joe looked back at me and said in perfect monotone, "Well, that was fun."

A thousand yards up the hill, headlights appeared. I jammed my finger into Joe's shoulder and screamed, "Start the car right now! Start the car! Start the car!" The brothers turned and realized that, while we may have just escaped death thanks to a stubborn guardrail, we were moments away from getting creamed by a big rig bearing down on us.

Joe turned the key.

The car refused to start.

In a blur of words I screamed, "If the car doesn't start get ready to jump out!" With that, Ted grabbed his door handle and pulled. The passenger side door, with a fresh imprint of the guard rail crushed into it, didn't budge.

The lights racing down the hill grew brighter.

"Start the car! Start the car!" Ted and I cried in unison.

The engine started on the second try (thank you Ford Motor Corporation) and Joe flipped the car around into the slow lane. Five seconds later, the big rig zoomed by a foot away in the fast lane.

Ted's Mustang was totaled by State Farm's definition, having suffered a bent frame (along with a crushed door and cracked windshield).

I have never slept in a moving car again.

In November, the barrier separating East and West Germany–the "Berlin Wall"–came crashing down. German reunification formally concluded less than a year later. Prior to this, communist East German guards shot anyone, including women and children, attempting to "defect" to democratic West Germany.

CHAPTER 19

I returned to my job as clerk at the video store. Joe and I, having earned our yellow belt in karate the semester before, decided to continue on in Karate 2. This was a fortunate thing.

Video stores in the eighties retained personal checks to serve as collateral for damaged or lost videos. We kept these uncashed checks in a metallic box behind the counter. Before I go any further, you need to understand the layout of the store.

The business was set up with empty boxes lining the shelves around the store. This prevented people from grabbing a movie off the shelf and fleeing into the Chatsworth night. Customers exchanged the empty box (stuffed with fitted styrofoam and shrink-wrapped with plastic) for the movie located on shelves behind the linoleum counter separating the public area from the employee-only area. The counter was open on one end and bisected in the middle for easy employee access. Two monochrome monitors sat on the counter–serving as both cash registers and inventory control. Customers were not allowed behind the counter.

The twenty-year-old black dude started out respectfully with my boss as I watched a few feet away. Their conversation grew heated.

"I am not paying a late fee!" the guy yelled. "You were closed yesterday!"

My boss, a foot shorter and forty pounds lighter than the Skeezer responded, "We're open every day of the week and *yes, you will pay a late fee!*"

"I don't have to pay *nothing*, man!"

I looked around the store and the dozen people milling around had stopped browsing the shelves–this argument was much more interesting than hunting for New Release stickers.

My boss reached down and thumbed through the box of personal checks. With a look of triumph, the former high school principal produced the guy's security deposit and waved it in the air.

"Well," he grinned, "I guess I'll just have to cash *this*, huh?"

The guy snatched at it from across the counter just as John whipped it back.

I looked at the Skillet for a long second then instinctively strode forward. As I closed the gap between me and my boss, the Homey stepped through the opening in the counter and there we were–the enraged customer in front of me, John behind me. For another long second, nothing happened.

The guy lunged his hand past my left ear, another attempt at recovering his check, just as *John hopped and threw a punch over my right ear.* It happened so fast, but I remember thinking, *My little boss sure is brave with me sandwiched between him and this big mofo.*

I shoved the guy backward, thinking he'd step back to his side of the counter, and shoved John backward thinking he'd retreat as well.

In what felt like slow motion, Kareem Abdul Ja-Wannabe, who thought he was above the law, trying to return *Above The Law* without the $2.49 penalty, threw a roundhouse kick. It was so slow and awkward that I laughed at the absurdity of it. He took two steps forward to my one as I grabbed him by the throat with my left hand and reared back with my right.

My brain kicked in, *If you punch this guy in the face the cops will definitely have to be called. Do NOT throw the first punch.*

I waited for Homey D. Clown, who was six inches taller than I was, to smack me upside the head but he just stood there, flailing and confused.

My left hand squeezed tighter and I pulled his face down to mine. What I whispered surprises me to this day.

"Well, *c'mon motherfucker.*"

We were nose to nose and his eyes shifted to my right fist, cocked and ready to crash into his face. I gripped my left hand tighter around his larynx and his face turned bright red. Both his hands locked onto my left arm. I backed him through the opening in the counter and shoved. He fell, hard, on his back and began gasping and coughing for air.

Every customer in the store stood transfixed. I looked around thinking, *Not a single person stepped in to help me.* The guy glared up at me, clutching his throat, coughing and spitting.

"Get out of here!" I yelled, and, for the first time, felt my heart crashing in my chest. "If you come back again, I'm calling the cops!" With that, John flung the check in the air. It fluttered and landed at the guy's feet. He scooped it off the floor and ran out the front door.

In comical fashion, the business of video renting resumed without pause. A lady stepped forward with her video. I dropped the box on the floor, shaking all over. John picked it up and patted me on the shoulder. "I'll handle this," he said quietly. I stumbled down the narrow hall leading to the rear exit and bathroom, stepped into the bathroom and splashed cold water on my face. My body shook uncontrollably.

Even though the virtual fight card read: Harvey 10, Above-The-Law-Late-Fee-Dude 8, I fought back the urge to burst into tears. I sat down on the floor trying to regain control of my breathing. Five minutes passed. Then another five minutes.

By the time I walked back down the hall, the store was empty of customers. John stood behind the counter with a blank expression on his face. We were both in shock. It was 8 p.m., an hour before closing, and he said, "I'm going home." All I could do was nod. For the next customer-less hour, I looked out into the night and thought, *If that guy comes back with a gun and shoots me, at least they'll have a pretty good idea who did it.*

After locking up the store at 9 p.m. I noticed, taped to my timecard, a ten dollar bill with a Post-It note with two words, *Thank you.* I skewered the bill on the spike file (the six inch nail used for filing paid bills) with my own Post-It, *Just doing my job, boss.*

• • •

My college experience did not include living in a dorm at any point along the way and I sometimes wonder if I short-changed myself. Nevertheless, one constant in the years attending Cal State Northridge was our apartment in Canoga Park, eight miles from campus.

Another constant was the rotating turnstile of roommates.

There was Jennifer, Steve, Rhonda, Sunil, Karen, Jamieanne, Nadir and, oh, let's not forget the three roommates that lasted less than a month. An incident I call the Roommate Revolt.

Joe took a semester off and stayed on at his California Department of Forestry (CDF) job—the guy had serious cooking skills so I can't blame the CDF for wanting to keep him—so we vacated the master bedroom. Ted also bailed for dwellings closer to UCLA, leaving me, the solitary man, in our three-bedroom apartment. The rent, a daunting $850 a month, would have been an impossibility for me, so we devised a plan.

We posted a Roommates Wanted ad on campus with the intent of renting two of the three bedrooms, including the spacious master bedroom. Just before the fall semester began, the phone rang off the hook with students looking for housing. We decided on two pretty girls and one hulking surfer dude. The girls, strangers to each other, agreed to share the master bedroom for $250 each per month. The surfer, a massive Italian guy (I'll call him "Frank") paid $300 for his own room.

Do the math. Joe and I shared rent of $50 a month. *Brilliant!*

It only took the three strangers a week to discover the inequity—to them, the *injustice*—of the arrangement. Their reaction, one of *extreme* displeasure, surprised us. We felt a certain ownership of the place since every scrap of furniture belonged to Joe, Ted, or me, and we kept the apartment year-round, even though none of us were there during the summer months. For this, we felt entitled to charge whatever we liked.

I returned one afternoon after class to find the three conspiring on the couch. The moment I walked in the door, their conversation stopped and they glared up at me.

"What's going on?" I asked.

"That's what we'd like to know," Frank snarled. The girls nodded in unison. He continued.

"How much rent do *you* pay?"

Survival mode kicked in. When in doubt, throw the absent guy under the bus. "Joe sets the rent around here. He's the boss." My heart pounded wildly.

"When will he be back?" Mr. Six-Foot-Five-Two-Hundred-and-Forty-Pounds snapped.

Sweat popped up on my forehead.

"He'll be back this weekend. Let's talk to him then!" I answered cheerfully then ducked into my bedroom. Behind me the grumbling continued.

I called Joe from work that evening and told him we may have a full scale riot on our hands. He answered calmly, "Hey, we never said everyone paid equal rent."

"I can tell you one thing. Frank is *pissed!*"

"I can handle Frank," Joe said calmly. "What's he gonna do? Hit me?"

I hung up the phone and took another swig of Maalox, compliments of Dr. Brautman at the campus health center.

For the next few days, my three new companions didn't say a word to me. I've never felt such tension.

When Friday came and Joe walked through the door, the *Showdown in Apartment 801* was on. Joe and I sat on one couch, our three tenants sat on the other. Frank took the offensive.

"I want to talk about the rent arrangement," he snapped.

"Yeah," Joe said calmly. "I'm listening."

Frank's huge arms and shoulders began quivering and the volume of his voice doubled with each spoken word.

"I THINK IT'S REALLY FUCKED!"

I shrank into the cushions, hoping the couch would swallow me whole. Joe rose to his feet as Frank rose to his. The two stood with nothing but the small coffee table between them. Frank towered over Joe.

The girls, as wide-eyed as I was, sat motionless.

"We never said we'd pay equal rent," Joe snapped. "You're living in a fully equipped apartment. If you don't like the arrangements, you can find somewhere else to live!"

Frank's face distorted in rage, but all he could manage was a loud, low growl. The guy was the human equivalent of a severely pissed off Pit Bull. He sat back down and slammed his fist on the coffee table. Finally, he said, "You . . . you . . . you're nothing but a couple of greedy bastards!"

I blurted out laughing. Nervous energy picks some sucky times to manifest itself.

Frank looked at us and shook his clenched fist.

Joe, still at his defiant best, said, "You must be a real tough guy, huh? Putting on a big show for these two girls! Why don't you just hit me? Hit the little guy! Bet it would make you feel better, seeing how tough you are! Better yet, go ahead and hit both of us! I dare ya!"

I tugged at Joe's pants to *sit the hell back down*. I couldn't believe he was instigating the guy. My immediate thought was, *I still have to live with these people*.

Frank sprang to his feet again, spittle flying from his mouth, "I ought to just beat the living hell out of both of you, right here, right now! Yeah, I would feel better you little fucking worm!"

"Go for it Tough Guy!" Joe barked. "Show us all how tough you are! Got a little steroid rage going on, huh?"

Frank let out another loud growl and raised his fist to the huge pulsating vein bisecting his massive forehead. After the eternity that was three seconds, he stormed out the front door, slamming it so hard that the entire building shook. The girls turned and marched down the hall to the master bedroom without saying a word.

We adjourned ourselves to Malibu Grand Prix and a night of pinball.

The reason the trio didn't pack up their stuff and walk out at the end of the month was that one of the girls had given us a deposit *and* paid two month's rent in advance. Despite the fact that we were unable to get a deposit out of Frank or the other girl–and the two of them could have easily left at any time–they were now a unified threesome.

The next day Frank growled, "The girls and I are going to get a place together. How do you like that, you little fucking turds?"

"Fine by me," Joe replied. "The sooner the better."

"You need to give back the deposit and rent money you're holding!"

"Not until you find replacements that are acceptable."

Thus began another Roommates Wanted posting. With Joe gone during the week, I spent my evenings at work or the college library. Anything to stay away from the apartment.

We called the phone company and cut off outgoing call capability–afraid that our disgruntled threesome would leave us with an enormous long-distance phone bill. Frank was none too pleased. Cowering in my bedroom one night, I heard him scream into the phone, *"No, I can't call you back! My asshole roommates turned the outgoing phone off!"*

I installed a lock on my bedroom door and survived on Maalox, nonstop, for two weeks.

The nightmare ended when we accepted the first two applicants who came to look at the place. It was an absurd scene as the five of us sat on the couch with plastered on smiles. One big happy family.

We learned that, true to his word, Frank and the girls found an unfurnished two bedroom apartment nearby. At $300 each, the big roided out surfer paid more for less. I suppose they figured it was all a matter of principle. Then again, what do I know? I never understood stupid people very well.

● ● ●

1989 Fun Fact #2:

Nintendo releases the Game Boy and Sega releases the Sega Genesis (Sonic the Hedgehog is born)–gamers rejoice!

CHAPTER 20

When Ray sat the Maintenance Supervisor down–a short, balding man named Paul–and informed him that he'd have a new man on the dayshift with weekends off, Paul was none too happy.

"I don't have an opening at this time, Mr. Grant," Paul said blankly, looking down at the floor. Paul's hands were clasped together as he nervously twirled his thumbs.

Ray looked across his desk, unwavering.

"Tom's a college student. Perhaps you have some paperwork he can help you with." With that, he waved us out the door. The walk through the hallways from Ray's office to the HR department was tense. The only noise from Paul was a low growl.

And paperwork was most of what the summer entailed–sitting at an industrial shredding machine eight hours a day destroying outdated classified information. I admit, reading all the old personnel files–who had slept with whom and which doctors had paid out million dollar malpractice settlements–was fascinating. Occasionally, Paul would swing the door open and bark, "Less reading and more shredding!"

It was mundane and miserable. He knew it. I knew it. Everyone knew it. But since I was supposedly Ray's nephew–a rumor I chose to keep mum about–I was untouchable. The only way Paul was going to get rid of me was if I quit.

My only reprieve came doing other menial tasks: washing and sterilizing gurneys covered with blood and guts from the ER, collecting heavy bags of soiled linen[22]

---

22 And I mean *soiled* in the truest sense–linens saturated in human waste of all kinds: feces, blood, urine, infectious ooze.

scattered up and down the hallways, autoclaving surgical waste into trash appropriate for the landfill.[23]

One day, the shop phone rang from the surgery department. They needed someone to adjust the thermostat and I jumped at the chance to get out of the warehouse. After donning a disposable, white, Tyvek suit,[24] and disposable shoe covers, I walked into the surgical suite.

Five people–the surgeon, his assistant, the anesthesiologist, and two nurses–screamed in unison: "WHAT DO YOU THINK YOU'RE DOING?"

Shocked, I stammered, "Uh, I'm here to turn down the thermostat?"

"WHERE'S YOUR SURGICAL MASK?"

I hastily retreated, found a surgical mask on a hallway supply cart, and re-entered the room.

"Now, where's the thermostat, hmmm?"

The orthopedic surgeon, covered in blood and tissue as he worked to replace the ball of a broken femur, looked up and said, "This one's not too bright, huh?"

I stood, mesmerized by the sight of a human hip filleted to the bone. For a moment I was transfixed. *The barbarity of it all!*

A nurse pointed to the thermostat. "Turn it down already then get lost!"

I did as I was told then fled to the solitude of the warehouse. Back to reading seven-year-old personnel files.

• • •

Today, I occasionally receive two-word emails from a few of my female friends on Facebook: *Elephant trunk.*

The summer started innocently enough. Not a lot of pressure working at the hospital while living on Mike's living room couch. Joe's mom hadn't invited me back to the garage.

In August, Joe informed me of a one-night-only job.

"My sister's having a lingerie party and we're going to be the bartenders."

"I've never mixed a drink in my life."

---

23   The autoclave was an oven-like contraption that, literally, baked blood, tissue, and everything else from red surgical bags into a steaming, ill-smelling, brown sludge.

24   Think of the scene from *Willy Wonka and the Chocolate Factory* when Mike Teevee shrinks himself.

"That's beside the point. We'll be the only guys there. It's going to be wild. *Trust me.*"

On the appointed night, as promised, Joe and I were the only two guys among twenty riotous girls. As Joe's sister, Anna, displayed various lubes, oils, and obnoxious latex appendages, Joe and I kept the drinks flowing.

One drink for this girl, one drink for us.

One drink for that girl, one drink for us.

Repeat twenty times.

Joe and I drank whatever nasty concoction we could come up with ("Here, drink *this*, I dare ya!") until I couldn't taste anything. Anna walked into the kitchen in a panic.

"My entertainment's not here yet and the girls are getting restless!"

Joe and I burst out laughing.

"Hey, we just pour the drinks," I slurred. I could barely stand, and Joe's face was as red as Tina Turner's flaming-red wig.

Anna grabbed my unsteady shoulders, locked eyes and said, "I need you . . . and . . . I said you'd fill in!"

"Fill in? Fill in what?"

The mob in the other room began to chant.

"Tom, Tom, Tom, TOM, TOM, TOM!"

"You've got to do it," Joe agreed.

"We want Tom! We want Tom! We want Tom!"

"I've got just the thing," Anna said and held up the most absurd piece of polyester I'd ever seen. Even in my drunken stupor I had enough sense to say, "You don't have *anything* else?"

"Oh, no," Anna grinned. "This is the ticket."

Joe followed me in the bathroom with a drink in each hand. "Give us two minutes then blast the music," he told his sister.

"WE WANT TOM! WE WANT TOM! WE WANT TOM!" The natives were restless.

There we stood in Joe's small bathroom looking at a g-string in the form of a black elephant trunk. It had plastic beady eyes the size of quarters with *nothing but a string in the back*.

"This is insane, Joe!"

"I know! Hahahaha!"

To say that I stripped would imply that I started fully clothed and worked my way to the g-string. That's not what happened. As the music blared from the living room, and the chanting continued, I stepped into the ridiculous scrap of clothing wearing nothing but . . . the ridiculous scrap of clothing.

Joe opened the door, slapped me on the bare ass and said, "Go get 'em tiger!"

I'm not above saying that the eight-inch trunk afforded *puh-lenty* of room. I went out with trunk-a-bobbing, hips-a-gyrating, and head-a-spinning.

After twenty minutes of dancing around, I earned exactly *one dollar*.

The doorbell rang and I dashed into the bathroom. The "hired professional" had arrived. He looked like a blonde bodybuilder.

I re-emerged in my waiter apparel to enthusiastic applause.

I had another tasteless drink in the kitchen and started mashing my face with my fingers. "I can't feel my face."

The music started and the chants began anew. *"We want Tom! We want Tom! We want Tom!"*

"You have *got* to be kidding," I said to Joe.

Anna strode back in the kitchen. "I need you back out there. The girls like you better!"

The girls got a 2-for-1 that night. And, still, the night's income stayed at *one dollar*.

After the party, I spent the rest of the night sleeping on the bathroom floor with my head *literally* in the toilet. The next morning, Joe's mom lifted my head out of the toilet bowl cheerfully. "I'll feed you breakfast!" *Where did she come from?*

It didn't take long for word to spread that, in addition to my job masquerading as a hospital maintenance man, I was a self-employed exotic dancer. As I walked down the hospital hallways, nurses clustered together, giggling and pointing. Seemed everyone had heard about the elephant trunk. Great.

Nurses aren't shy creatures and one of Mom's friends, Sarah Myers, paged me to her nursing station.

"Tom, I hear you're available for hire."

I didn't know whether to be flattered, embarrassed, or angry.

She continued. "My niece's thirtieth birthday party is coming up and I'd like to hire you." A small group of nurses leaned into the conversation. It was just like that old EF Hutton commercial, *When EF Hutton talks, people listen*.

I raised my eyebrows.

Dressed to make $50 plus tips . . . the hard way!

"How much do you charge?" She pressed on.

My mind raced. Do I tell her she was mistaken? Do I accept the invitation calmly and coolly? Do I have to report self-employed income on my taxes?

"I charge . . . "

Hell, I didn't know what I charged.

"I charge . . . fifty dollars plus tips. How does that sound?"

"Done." Every nurse within earshot broke into a smile.

What have I just done? I wobbled off down the hall.

My mix-tape consisted of *Good Thing* by The Fine Young Cannibals, *You're So Fine* by The Egyptian Lover, *I Want Your Sex* by George Michael, *You Shook Me All Night Long* by AC/DC, *Going Back to Cali* by LL Cool J, and the live version of *I Just Can't Get Enough* by Depeche Mode. The mix of pop, funk, and rock, as I discovered, worked well.

The image in my mind of a male stripper came from the Chippendale's scene out of the Tom Hanks comedy, *Bachelor Party*, so that's what I went with: black slacks, long sleeve white shirt, and black bowtie. At the time I was, arguably, in the best shape of my life–able to bench-press 225 pounds weighing a trim 170 pounds. I also had enough hair to pull back in a pony tail which further added to *the look*.

I called David to tell him of my new business venture.

"What the hell are you thinking?" he asked.

"I figure I'll be the only sober person in the room. That should make it easier."

I showed up at that very first "gig" excited, nervous, and confident. I met Sarah at our agreed upon time outside her house–the party's finale was a surprise. She ushered me to a back bedroom and I handed over my ghetto blaster.

"Give me five minutes," I said.

"You got it."

"Hit play on the tape and crank it."

"You got it."

"Oh, and you'll have to point out your niece to me. It looks like you've got a house full of women."

"I will. And I do." She looked me up and down and laughed, "Oh, if your mother could see you now."

"Oh, and here's my camera. Would you mind taking pictures until it runs out of film?" With slightly shaking hand, I handed her my small, point-and-shoot camera.

"You got it, Tom! Five minutes!"

She closed the door leaving me to my pounding heartbeat. I dropped to the floor. One, two, three, four, five.

The pushups came easy as adrenalin surged through my body.

Ninety seven, ninety eight, ninety nine, one hundred.

The guitar riff of The Fine Young Cannibals hit song blasted through the living room. I flung the door open and swaggered down the short hallway.

The house was alive with energy from two dozen women ranging in age from 18 to 80 scattered all over the place. Parting the sea of giggling women, fingers pointed to the guest of honor.

Oh, she was pretty!

Taking your clothes off for a room full of enthusiastic women requires a bit of mathematics and the equation goes like this: Divide the number of items to be removed by the total music time. Too fast and the last song isn't climactic–too slow and the last song is rushed. Without a practice run (an embarrassing notion even in the privacy of Mike's living room), I figured I had twenty minutes to achieve the following, in this order: 1) remove shoes and socks, 2) remove long sleeve shirt, 3) release ponytail,[25] 4) remove pants,[26] 5) remove satin black shorts, to 6) ultimately arrive at a pair of bikini briefs.

I strolled around the room, music cranking, girls clapping, camera bulbs flashing. Any aspirations of becoming an elected official permanently flew out the door after that first picture.

This is unbelievable. All this energy is for me. Hell, this is easy!

And, it *was* easy.

I pointed at a girl–a dozen girls shrieked–and she removed my shoes and socks. The first song ended.

I chose another girl to dance with as she unbuttoned my shirt. The second song ended.

Girls pointed at the guest of honor and I pranced around her–yeah, her time was coming. She and I danced the entire last song. When the music ended, I bolted from the room amid rip-roaring applause. Now that was fun *and* I made a total of $89 ($50 "fee" and $39 in tips) in twenty minutes!

Talk of the party spread like wildfire around the hospital and Sylvia from the pharmacy hired me a few weeks later for her sister's *divorce* party. I want to say her sister's name was Sheila.

This one was just plain crazy.

"I'd like you to show up at dinner dressed as a UPS guy. I'll get you the uniform. How does that sound?"

"Sounds good!"

What I didn't immediately realize was that dinner was at China's Alley (pronounced CHEE-NA), a Mexican restaurant in Lindsay, filled to capacity for this private party. When I pulled into the overflowing parking lot the night of the deed, I immediately thought, *This is a bad idea. There are tons of guys*

---

25   Not an article of clothing, obviously, but I needed as many moves as I could get.

26   ALWAYS a crowd pleaser–not to be removed until at least the fourth song.

here and riotous girls turn husbands and boyfriends into jealous husbands and boyfriends.

I walked into the restaurant wearing jeans and a brown UPS shirt carrying my mix tape and an empty box. The place was packed with people eating, drinking, and standing around the bar. The middle of the room had a linoleum dance floor. My heart pounded as I looked at the mass of people.

"You the stripper?" a guy yelled over the roar of conversation.

"Uh, yeah."

"I'm the DJ. I'll let Sylvia know you're here. "

I handed him my cassette tape.

Sylvia came over grinning.

"Sheila is completely oblivious! How do you want to do this?"

Sweat poured down my face as groups of people watched our huddle by the front door. Sylvia, her sister, and their dates sat in a booth at the far end of the room. I was to burst into the room calling Sheila's name, holding the empty box. When I said the magic words–"absolutely nothing"–the music and lights were to start.

With Sylvia satisfied with the plan, she announced, "Twenty minutes."

I walked back out the front door as people streamed in. Just around the corner, I began my push-up routine . . . one, two, three . . . ninety eight, ninety nine, one hundred.

You're out of your mind on this one.

Mexican guys dressed in their best cowboy attire filed in. I looked at their dangerously pointed boots.

You are going to get your ass kicked. That's what going to happen here. These guys are going to be pissed by the time this thing is over.

My heart slammed in my chest.

Five minutes passed.

Ten minutes passed.

I paced around in the cool night air, sweat pouring down my face. Even from the parking lot, the place was loud and riotous.

I did *another* hundred pushups. My arms and chest ached in pain but my biceps bulged, full of blood and adrenalin. Despite the cool night air, the brown UPS shirt was drenched in sweat.

The door swung open and the DJ shouted, "You're on!"

Dizzy from two hundred pushups and thoughts of getting a steak knife in the back, I squeezed through the throng of people. There they sat, thirty feet and a hundred people away. Sheila sat at the end of the booth, oblivious to the plan, talking with her date.

I held up the box and yelled, "Is there a Sheila here?" Half the restaurant didn't hear the question.

A spotlight came on, blinding me.

My heart still crashing in my chest, I repeated the question. "Is there a Sheila here? Special delivery for Sheila!"

A hush fell over the crowd.

Fingers pointed to Sheila. People had confused looks on their faces. This was a surprise to all but a few.

When I reached Sheila, I looked the pretty Hispanic girl in the eyes and asked, "Are you Sheila?"

"Yes."

"I have a special delivery for you." I held up the box.

"What's in the box?"

I looked around the room, my face quivering in nervous energy. *"Absolutely nothing!"*

On cue, the beginning of The Fine Young Cannibals' *Good Thing* came on and I led Sheila out onto the dance floor. Sylvia followed behind us pushing a chair. A rainbow of pulsating lights lit up the floor and there we were: the bogus UPS delivery guy and the new divorcee. I threw the empty box over my shoulder and began circling the now seated guest of honor.

A fitting picture. The fake UPS guy praying not to die in the packed Mexican restaurant. I mean, look at the dude to my left. He already looks pissed!

As my eyes adjusted to the array of lights and the bright spotlight, I scanned the room. *Yep, this is a very bad idea.* My initial thoughts of pulling various women into the act, working my way up to Sheila for the finale, quickly went out the window. Every woman on the perimeter had a fierce looking guy sitting next to her and they (the women, that is) looked at me with wide, pleading eyes. Eyes that said, *"Please, please, please don't come near me . . .for both our sakes!"* Every guy in the room had his arms crossed with a glare that said *carne muerta!*

Sheila, on the other hand, enjoyed every moment of it. She shaked, rattled, and rolled with me. It was, after all, her coming out party. After posing for pictures with her afterward, I fled the premises.

I did six gigs that summer before calling it quits. The upside was a glove-compartment overflowing with cash–a hundred dollars in ones and fives tumbled to the floorboard whenever I needed gas money. The downside was coming home bruised, scratched, and bleeding. B.B. King said it best after I dug a ten dollar bill out of the crack of my ass: the thrill was gone.

• • •

Toward the end of the summer, it occurred to me that I could make more money working sixteen hours a week at the hospital than twenty hours at the video store–even with the two and a half hour drive. This was ideal for studying as I no longer had to work weekday evenings. Ray was kind enough to honor my request, and I spent the next year driving up and over the Grapevine, back and forth, every Friday evening to Porterville and every Monday morning back to Northridge. In no time, the paint on the hood and roof of my VW Sirocco blew off by the Santa Ana wind that rattled through the Grapevine.

CHAPTER 21

The date was October 29, a Sunday. It was 3 p.m. and we were congregated in the maintenance shop–just fifteen minutes before punching out for the day. One of the swing shift guys burst through the door and said, "Oh, there's a fresh one in the ER! You guys gotta check this out!"

My pulse quickened. I looked around, hoping the regular guys found no interest in the news.

My coworker and confidante, Odie, bounded up and grabbed me by the arm. "Well," he said, "what are we waiting for?"

Knowing that a dead body is less than a hundred feet away, and that you have unfettered access to an upfront peek, is *surreal*. As we approached the locked side door to the Emergency Room, I felt dizzy.

All six treatment rooms swarmed with doctors and nurses working on multiple car accident victims. With all rooms occupied, "expired patients" (that's the politically correct lingo) were temporarily moved to side hallways and hidden behind accordion style olive green screens. This afternoon, the guy on the hallway gurney was in no longer need of–well–anything.

Odie opened the locked door and walked up to the body. I stood outside for a moment, my balance not quite steady.

"Oh, c'mon," he said. "It's not like the guy's gonna jump up and bite you. Besides, the cops will be here any second!"

I approached the corpse with a mix of horror and fascination. The guy was black–which was a bit odd since there weren't that many African Americans in Porterville (like less than ten in my high school of fifteen hundred). His short sleeve white T-shirt was saturated dark red. He wore baggy camouflage pants and grungy white Nike high-tops.

His shoes hung over the edge of the gurney.

His arms were draped over his chest.

His hands were rugged–fingernails, dirty.

And . . .

His face was *gone*.

Where his eyes, nose, and mouth were supposed to be, a thick pool of congealed blood lay. His face was completely crushed in.

It's probably silly to say, but when a person is lifeless, the air is *still*.

A bead of cold sweat ran down my face.

Other than the guy's missing face, everything looked normal–his arms and legs were perfectly intact, not a scratch on them.

We stood there for a long minute in silence. This was no joke.

His face was so mangled–so traumatized–that I stared at his shoes.

"Look at his shoelaces," I whispered. "He laced up those high-tops this morning thinking today was like any other day."

Odie said nothing.

"Someone else will unlace those shoes now."

At that moment, two young California Highway Patrol officers swung around the corner, startling me out of my trance.

Odie tipped his baseball hat, "Officers."

The officers nodded at us and we stepped back in unison. One held a camera, the other a binder with a pad of paper. They casually began taking notes and photographing the body showing no reaction whatsoever. I turned and walked out the door into the hot, bright day. *That poor guy had no idea today was his last.*

I didn't sleep that night. Every time I closed my eyes, I saw those shoelaces tied all the way up those dirty white Nike high-tops.

Sidebar #7:

AIDS in 1989

One class that sounded like fun was entitled "Communication and the Sexes." Joe and I enrolled thinking it would be a good opportunity to meet girls. The fact that the class was in the largest classroom on campus sealed the deal for this, and it would be our last common General Education class together.

From his place at the base of the semi-circular auditorium, our professor looked up at two hundred students and lectured on gender related communication behavior in a variety of settings.

Sound riveting?

Actually, it wasn't.

The day Professor "Smith" (that's what I'll call him for his sake) announced he had a guest speaker was memorable.

Dressed in brown corduroy pants, a long sleeve shirt and a vest, our guest lecturer looked the part of a young academic. He appeared to be in his early thirties, wore round glasses, had short brown hair, and smiled up at the full auditorium. Students murmured among themselves. With three words, two hundred students fell silent.

"I have AIDS."

It was as if everyone stopped breathing–the air hung in perfect stillness.

I had never seen anyone with AIDS and, based on the instant reaction, neither had anyone else. He spoke for half an hour about the virus then opened it up for questions.

I looked around the auditorium waiting for the obvious one.

I whispered to Joe, "I can't believe no one is going to ask him how he contracted AIDS."

Joe replied, "Ask him."

"You ask him."

"I'm not going to ask him. There's two hundred people in here. It's your question, you ask him."

My heart pounded. The thought of asking this very personal question–the question that hung over the room like a fog–was too intimidating.

I chickened out.

No one asked the question and our speaker never volunteered the answer.

What he did say, with conviction, was this:

"You can put your cut-up hands in a bucket of AIDS-infected blood and still not contract the virus!"

A girl close to the front asked if he was sure about that. The impassioned speaker repeated the statement, louder and with even more conviction. He added, "The only way you can contract AIDS is through unprotected sexual intercourse! That is the *only* way!"

We walked out of class in the fall of 1989 with that visual–hands in a bucket of blood–and this misinformation provided to us by a major university in the greater Los Angeles area. Even in 1989, AIDS was greatly misunderstood.

Upon returning for the winter 1990 semester, our guest speaker's obituary was in The Daily Sundial. As it turned out, the man left behind a male partner so our assumptions regarding how he contracted AIDS (through unprotected sexual contact) seemed to be confirmed. It saddened me to read of his death simply because a few short months earlier the man looked perfectly healthy. Vibrant, confident, *defiant*.

• • •

Tuesday, October 17, was a warm evening—one of the rare instances when I had the apartment to myself. I welcomed the quiet solitude.

With the roommate fiasco still fresh in our minds, Joe and I reoccupied the master bedroom and our fair share of the rent.

I lounged on the king-size bed reading one of my Greek history textbooks straddling the thin line between consciousness and sleep.

Persephone really got the short end of the stick. Hades was such a prick for kidnapping her. Run, girl, run! Don't eat those pomegranate seeds . . .

My eyelids drooped shut . . .

The only noise came from the TV at the foot of the bed. The familiar voices of Al Michaels and Tim McCarver were reviewing highlights of Game Two of the World Series, minutes away from the start of Game Three. For all the hype of the unprecedented "Battle of the Bay," the Oakland Athletics hadn't had any trouble with the San Francisco Giants and were up 2-0 in the series.

Al Michaels' voice faded . . .

Wham!

The framed picture of Joe's girlfriend, Karen, fell over on the headboard. The bed suddenly transformed into one of those cheesy vibrating beds you see in the movies. It was an earthquake, no doubt. My instant thought, *People, somewhere, are dying at this very moment.*

Al and Tim were replaced with a fixed image that simply read, World Series.

Al Michaels' voice sounded like he was speaking into a walkie-talkie: "*I don't know if we're on the air. We're in commercial. I guess we're still here.*" As the vibrations continued, Al nervously chuckled, "*That's the greatest open in the history of television.*" The audio fell silent.

Three hundred and fifty miles to the north, the Loma Prieta earthquake, measuring 6.9 on the Richter Scale was no laughing matter. Within minutes, every TV channel began airing live feeds of the Bay Area's devastation.

Collapsed buildings.

Buckled streets.

Plumes of thick, black smoke rising through a dozen areas in the city.

Chaos.

Most channels cut to the most gruesome scene of all–a section of two-tier free-way known as the Cypress Street Viaduct: cars flattened under tons of steel and concrete on the lower deck, cars dangling on the edge of the twisted upper deck. Helicopters helplessly circled the scene. I watched wide-eyed and horrified.

When the stadium feed was restored, Al was no longer laughing and Game Three of the World Series was no longer of importance. Players from both teams milled around the field not knowing what to do. Some climbed into the stands looking for family members.

For days, San Francisco and the surrounding area slowly unburied itself from the carnage. In all, sixty three people died, thousands were injured, and thousands were left homeless.

When play resumed ten days later, ABC compiled footage of the grief, the rescues, the cleanup, and the rebuilding to Journey's *Lights*. It was a fitting, poignant tribute, and I fought back tears watching it in the living room with my roommates.

The A's went on to sweep the Giants in four.

• • •

The decade came to a close on a Sunday night. I talked Odie into going to the Visalia Holiday Inn–needing my married friend to provide an escape clause for a girl I agreed to meet there.

Did I ever.

The Holiday Inn's bar was rocking by the time we arrived at 9 p.m. The place was packed and in the middle of it all stood my date with a drink in each hand. With her long blonde hair, bright blue eyes, and tight black dress–a size or two too small by the looks of it–Odie patted me on the back and yelled, "Well, looks like I'll be finding my own way home tonight!"

She was a sight to behold dancing with no one in particular. On her head, a tiara. Around her bare shoulders, a bright pink feather boa.

I yelled back, "We came together. We'll leave together!"

The girl, I honestly don't remember her name, thrust a drink in my hand and pulled me onto the dance floor. Odie, in his Wranglers, cowboy boots, and cowboy shirt, made a beeline for the bar.

My date, we'll call her Linda, slurred, "I was supposed to meet a friend here . . . would have been great for your friend, but she flaked on me!"

I yelled back, "It's not a problem, he's mar . . ."

Before I could finish my sentence ("he's married anyway"), she planted a big, wet, drunk kiss on me. For a moment, we stayed there–frozen in time–then someone jostled us on the packed dance floor and the kiss was broken.

As the night wore on, Odie danced with every dateless girl in the place, oblivious to my growing concern around where and when the night would end for me. Every time I tried to steal a moment with him, a girl would grab him and he'd be back on the dance floor. His energy knew no bounds. A few times I heard him yell, *"Just so you know, I'm married!"* The girls just smiled and nodded.

It wasn't that the thought of a one-night stand was against my principles–but the thought of unprotected sex with an inebriated girl I barely knew posed too many variables. I had intentionally came *unprepared* (no pun intended), if you know what I mean.[27]

As the countdown to midnight began, the music stopped and I whispered in Odie's ear, *"Help me!"*

Odie giggled his boyish giggle and said nothing.

Five, four, three, two, one . . .

Happy New Year!

Everyone on the dance floor began kissing each other. While Linda locked lips with me again, Odie was getting peppered left and right, dodging the lips of his many dancing partners. The guy was a saint. I have to give him that.

A few seconds into the new decade, Linda grabbed my hand and said, "I have a room. Let's go!"

I called back to Odie, "Do *not* leave! I will be right back!" The pink feathered boa swirled behind her, blinding me in the process.

Within two minutes, we were in her quiet hotel room, the thumping music of the bar ringing in my ears.

"Want a drink?" she asked, motioning to an array of soda and hard liquor lined up on the nightstand. I eyed the bottle of Tanqueray and thought, *The girl's got good taste in gin.*

What happened next, I think, would have happened regardless of my answer.

"Um, no. I have to drive Odie home tonight and it's a thirty-mile drive."

---

27 All right, if you don't know what I mean, I wasn't packing condoms.

The black dress fell to the floor and there she stood in just the tiara and feather boa. To borrow an Odie-ism, she was *naked as a jaybird*.

She flung the tiara and boa across the room and jumped on the bed. Adding to the awkward moment, she grabbed a pillow and covered her face. Before I could say a word, there she lay: naked, headless, and quivering.

Which brings me to that classic scene in *Animal House*–Pinto's internal struggle with good and evil, complete with the manifestation of a sweet cherub and a crude demon.

My own debate began.

Demon: *Wow! This doesn't happen every day!*
Cherub: *Don't you dare!*

Demon: *Oh c'mon, don't be a wimp!*
Cherub: *You are NOT prepared for this!*

Demon: *What is your problem?*
Cherub: *Odie is downstairs waiting for you!*

There she lay, naked. Her sides heaved in nervous anticipation.

For the next long minute, my conscience debated the pros and cons. I sat on the bed, looking up and down the length of her pale skin. She was pretty. This was oh-so-tempting.

Finally I said, "Yep, you're not prepared for this." I was speaking to myself.

She replied, her voice muffled by the pillow, "The hell I'm not!"

I gently squeezed her calf and her entire body flinched.

"No, I meant *I'm* not prepared for this. I'm sorry but I have to go."

With that, I walked out the door and locked it behind me. My pace picked up with each long stride. Back in the bar, the party raged on. Odie leaned against the bar with a Coors Light longneck in his hand. His grin was a mile wide. Grabbing him by the shirt, I yelled, "*Let's get the hell out of here! And I mean, right now!*"

And that's how the eighties ended and the nineties began for me. Not with a bang, but with Odie laughing at me the entire way home.

CHAPTER 22

REFLECTION AND WRAP UP

March, 2011

I am in the airport on my way home to Seattle and wander into the duty-free store. On the shelves sit the usual assortment of hard alcohol, cigarettes, and fragrances. To my surprise, I notice the round, dimpled bottle in front of its bright pink box. By the look of the half empty sample bottle, the fragrance is still going strong.

After a full exhale, I bring the nozzle to my nose, close my eyes, and slowly inhale. It takes a moment for my nose to register the smell, then another moment for my brain to flip through twenty six years of memories. I crack open an eye to see if anyone finds this behavior odd–no one does–so I close my eyes and inhale again.

And, *there she is.*

Tiffany and I are eighteen again. We're at her dad's Portuguese club spaghetti dinner. Amidst the aroma of garlic bread and tomato sauce, I smell that smooth area of bare skin between her left ear and shoulder.

I breathe in again.

She's next to me and we're standing outside Ahhhs, a novelty store in Westwood Village. The night is cold and we're huddled together on the sidewalk. She says matter-of-factly, "I think I'll apply for a job here. This looks like a fun place to work." I say something disparaging.

"ALASKA AIRLINE FLIGHT SEVEN NOW IN FINAL BOARDING. PAGING MR. HARVEY TO GATE 41B."

I open my eyes and I'm forty three-years-old again, alone, in an airport store in Newark, New Jersey.

Without thinking, I mash on the plunger and *soak* my left hand with the fragrance.

"MR. HARVEY TO GATE 41B. THE GATE IS CLOSING IN SIXTY SEC-ONDS."

No time to run to the restroom. Damn.

The plane is full and I have an exit-row-aisle seat, 15C. I'm the last to board and the overpowering odor of sweet perfume swirls around me. The guy overflowing in 15B sniffs the air, confused. I *sit* on my left hand.

As soon as the plane is airborne and the seatbelt indicator chimes off, I rush to the lavatory and douse both hands with soap and water. Twice.

It's no use. My skin has absorbed the liquid and I've transferred the smell to both hands.

My brain is in total recall mode now: the white, ruffled dress she wore to the '85 Prom, the black and red dress she wore to the Christmas Ball, passionate kisses in her dark living room, that stupid Don Johnson poster in her bedroom (Don, in full white, leisure suit–soaked to the skin standing knee deep in the ocean. God, I hated that poster.), *Love Zone* by Billy Ocean, *I Send A Message* by INXS, the entire Tao cassette by Rick Springfield, the night I broke the heart of that pretty half-Portuguese girl.

Enya in my earphones, "*Sail away, sail away, sail away . . .*" Even the iPod gods are unrelenting. I hit the shuffle button. Metallica's *Broken, Beat and Scarred.* Better.

The drink cart is a welcome intrusion as the distinct smell of Yves Saint Laurent's *Paris* wafts unmercifully from the guy in 15C.

"Gin and tonic. Actually, make that two, please."

And that's kind of how it is, looking back at the past. We all have our *Paris* perfumes and *Back In Black's* and Star Wars action figures as reminders of our youth.

Our lost innocence.

Whether we're looking for the journey or not.

• • •

I graduated from Cal State Northridge in December 1990 with a BA in History but never made it to law school. The sudden death of my friend and benefactor, Ray, in October 1990, sent me careening down a different career path. Instead of law, I studied healthcare administration and graduated with a Master's Degree from Cal State Bakersfield. I've been in healthcare ever since.

• • •

Could I continue writing a book about the nineties? Not even to save my life and I'll tell you why. I don't have a diary of my teen years. Everything in this book came from vivid, colorfully clear memories. These memories come to me driving down the road, and walking the dogs, and sitting at my desk.

In contrast, the nineties are a blur of working for a paycheck, failed relationships, and mortgage payments. Not that the nineties were bad–they just weren't that memorable. There were no more first kisses and school rallies and college roommates.

On New Year's Day 1990, no one stood up and said, "HEY! The eighties are now officially over! Girls, turn in your legwarmers and Pat Benatar albums! Guys, the mullets have to go and, for Chrissake, throw out that Twisted Sister CD!" I certainly didn't pause to mourn the passing of the Decade of Decadence. Sometimes I wish I had.

It was, arguably, a simpler time.

We didn't have the internet or personal cell phones.

Mountain Dew was the only energy drink we knew.

Blackberries were fruit you hurled after drinking too much Jack and Coke.

Dennis Rodman had shock value.

The Commodore 64 was cool.

Someone knew someone who knew a victim of spontaneous human combustion.

You could get a raw egg in your large Orange Julius.

● ● ●

Which brings me full circle to my twelve-year-old niece, Chloe. Not long ago, we sat on her bed reading my favorite book–Maurice Sendak's *Where The Wild Things Are*. God bless that girl for indulging her uncle's simple pleasures.

She stops mid-sentence. "I'm thirsty."

I move to remedy this and she grabs my arm. "I'll call down to my dad for a drink."

"OK." I plug my ears. The girl has a piercing scream.

She picks up her cell phone (the bright pink one with sequins) and hits speed dial.

"Hello, Dad? Can you bring me a glass of water?" Surrounded by twenty posters of Justin Beiber smiling down at us, I can't help but laugh.

Times have changed.

• • •

In the dessert table of my life, the eighties is that seven-pound chocolate cake from Costco. You know the one: covered in a thick layer of frosting and shaved chocolate, that wondrous dessert is a sight to behold.

It is yummy.

It is memorable.

And, *it is decadent*.

Thank you for taking this journey with me. You're *bitchen* in my book!

Tom Harvey

April, 2011

Tom and Susan Harvey about to enjoy U2 rock the stadium in Seattle. June, 2011. The '80s are alive and well . . . how could anyone forget it?

APPENDIX I

I'm sure every decade has its share of one hit wonders, but, honestly, I never paid much attention before or after the eighties.

Music provides guideposts along the trip down memory lane and certain songs remind us of very specific moments. For example, I remember that the DJ played *Can't Live Without You* by the Scorpions at the 1985 Christmas Ball. Tiffany, much more into INXS than heavy metal, huffed off before I pulled her back on the dance floor.

I took a recent poll of Facebook friends and asked them to give me their favorite eighties one-hit wonder. In less than four hours, I had thirty comments. This is what we came up with, listed in chronological order:

- *Cars* by Gary Numan (1980)
- *Theme from Greatest American Hero (Believe It or Not)* by Joey Scarbury (1981)
- *Come On Eileen* by Dexys Midnight Runners (1982)
- *Mickey* by Toni Basil (1982)
- *The Safety Dance* by Men Without Hats (1982)
- *I Ran* by A Flock of Seagulls (1982)
- *Der Kommisar* by After The Fire (1982)
- *Something's Going On* by Frida (1982)
- *Electric Avenue* by Eddy Grant (1983)
- *True* by Spandau Ballet (1983)
- *Major Tom* by Peter Schilling (1983)
- *Too Shy* by Kajagoogoo (1983)

- *Rockit* by Herbie Hancock (1983)
- *Somebody's Watching Me* by Rockwell (1984)
- *99 Red Ballons* by Nena (1984)
- *Obsession* by Animotion (1984)
- *Take On Me* by A-Ha (1985)
- *Party All The Time* by Eddie Murphy (1985)
- *Voices Carry* by Til Tuesday (1985)
- *Let's Go All The Way* by Sly Fox (1986)
- *I Can't Wait* by Nu Shooz (1986)
- *The Rain* by Oran "Juice" Jones (1986)
- *Heart and Soul* by T'Pau (1987)
- *The Lady in Red* by Chris DeBurgh (1987)
- *Here I Go Again* by Whitesnake (1987)
- *I Need Love* by LL Cool J (1987)
- *The Promise* by When In Rome (1988)
- *Don't Worry, Be Happy* by Bobbie McFerrin (1988)
- *She's Like The Wind* by Patrick Swayze (1988)
- *Love Song* by The Cure (1989)

OK, so before you rush to your computer and fire off an email to me with the title, "You missed *this one* dumbass!" I offer a disclaimer. Though easy enough to do, I have not searched online for a listing of One Hit Wonders by the years 1980-1989 and relisted it here. And I have no doubt that entire books can be dedicated to a discussion of the One Hit Wonders of the Eighties.

A few comments:

Herbie Hancock is more than just a jazz musician, he's a jazz *genius*. I list his song, *Rockit* because it was *revolutionary* in 1983. A song with no words, for as good as it is to listen to, the music video is even better. Take a trip out to You-Tube and tell me if this isn't the coolest video of all time? Go ahead and see for yourself.

Admittedly, my Top Thirty has holes. There are *true* One Hit Wonders by definition–artists that had one hit on one album/cassette/CD then disappeared–and there are bands that kept at it.

A true one hitter is Frida with *Something's Going On*. In 1982, Jason Patterson cranked this song in his slammed-to-the-ground, ice-blue, late-70s, Lincoln Continental in the high school parking lot. An only child, Jason had the best of everything and the piercing, wailing voice of Frida cranking through his $5,000 car stereo,[28] was, in a word, memorable. Five thousand dollars was a *helluva lot of money* in 1985, especially to a high school kid. It was akin to something along the lines of the Pied Piper. People gravitated to the music and, soon, he had two dozen kids milling around. Jason was the conduit; Frida was the muse.

CDs were just beginning to make their appearance in late 1982. Up to that point, the latest and greatest was the cassette tape. And we went through a lot of them since they were constantly melting inside our locked cars on hundred degree Central California days.

The cassette tape *did* give way to the compact disk, and, eventually, everybody that was anybody bought the first ever CD player for the car: the Sony CDXR-77. The only problem with this first generation car CD player was that it didn't have buffer protection. The laser skipped with every bump and jolt. Something as small as the round white lane indicators in the road caused the music to stop for a second. When you had Madonna or Sammy Hagar or Van Halen cranked to the hilt, a skipping CD was unnerving.

Speaking of Madonna, the first CD I ever held in my hands was her self-titled CD released in July, 1983.

Falling in the dual Multiple Hit and Hairband Categories, Whitesnake came into the mainstream with *Here I Go Again* in 1987.

I remember sitting in Nina's white, convertible 1987 Mazda RX-7. Oh, that car was cool. She knew it and she loved it. The car looked like a Porsche 944—one of my all time favorite cars—straight out of the John Hughes movie, *Sixteen Candles*. As we sat in her car at Zalud Park in Porterville, I said, "Take a listen to *this*." I loaded the self titled Whitesnake cassette and turned up *Here I Go Again*. The song was climbing the charts at the time and ended up at #1. She listened intently. After a minute, she started the car.

"Where are we going?" I asked.

"You're going to buy me this cassette. Right now!"

It is a simple statement of fact that my Whitesnake cassette lasted longer than my relationship with Nina.

---

28   David lovingly remembers Jason's Blaunkpunkt cassette player, the Rockford Fosgate Power 1000 amp, the paragraphic ZAPCO equalizer, and the twin Fosgate Punch 18" sub-woofers. We could actually see the windshield pulsing outward against the rubber molding in time to the music when the thing was cranked. Eardrums? Who needs 'em?

Now if I had to choose just one song from my Top Thirty list–and here's where the pain comes in–I'd have to go with *I Ran* by The Flock of Seagulls. I think it has a lot to do with 1982. It was my first year of high school with newfound freedoms, new friends, and lots of pretty girls. Simply, the song sounds good cranked up loud and it was a departure from the pure rock sound I was accustomed to. Back then, we called it "new wave" and the "new wave" sound took a large place in the music that later defined the decade (with bands such as Depeche Mode, The Clash, The Cure, Adam and the Ants, and Oingo Boingo–to name a few–leading the way).

I have to mention one more one hit wonder because it was so unique: Paul Hardcastle's *19*. This unlikely song was a worldwide smash and peaked at #15 in the U.S. in 1985. What made it so bizarre was that Hardcastle sang about the atrocities of the Vietnam conflict with a beat that's almost impossible not to dance to. He even incorporates an interview with a soldier who talks about getting splattered with another guy's brains–and still we danced on![29] Truth be told, I still listen to this groovin' song–the stutter (nu-nu-nu-nu-nineteen, su-su-su-su-Saigon) and the flute solo are irresistible. Outside of Jethro Tull, when do you ever hear a flute solo?

OK, so now that we're knee-deep in talking about music, let's dive into the not-quite-as-obvious Two-Hit-Wonder list, in alphabetical order:

- Dead or Alive: *You Spin Me Round (Like a Record)* (1985) and *Brand New Lover* (1986)
- Falco: *Vienna Calling* (1985) and *Rock Me Amadeus* (1986)
- Golden Earring: *Radar Love* (1973) and *Twilight Zone* (1982)–technically an eighties one hit wonder, but the 1973 song is worth mentioning
- Information Society, The: *What's On Your Mind (Pure Energy)* (1988) and *Walking Away* (1988)
- Level 42: *Something About You* (1985) and *Lessons in Love* (1986)
- Naked Eyes: *Always Something There To Remind Me* (1983) and *Promises, Promises* (1983)
- Parr, John: *Naughty, Naughty* (1985) and *St. Elmo's Fire (Man In Motion)* (1985)

---

29 The soldier's interview within the song goes something like this: "You're walking around with some guy's brains on your shirt because he got his head blown off right next to you." My friend, Ed, came up with his own version that went: "You're walking around with some guy's load on your shirt because he was jerking off right next to you." No disrespect intended to our Vietnam Vets, but that Ed was a clever one.

- Planet P Project[30]: *I Won't Wake Up* (1983) and *Why Me?* (1983)
- Power Station, The: *Some Like It Hot* (1985) and *Get It On (Bang A Gong)* (1985)
- Romantics, The: *What I Like About You* (1980) and *Talking In Your Sleep* (1983)
- Scandal: *Goodbye To You* (1982) and *The Warrior* (1984)
- Slade: *My Oh My* (1983) and *Run, Run Away* (1984)
- Twisted Sister: *We're Not Gonna Take It* (1984) and *I Wanna Rock* (1984)

And, if that weren't enough, let's talk about Three-Hit Wonders.

- Human League, The: *Don't You Want Me* (1981), *(Keep Feeling) Fascination* (1983) and *Human* (1986)
- Klymaxx: *The Men All Pause* (1984), *Meeting in the Ladies Room* (1985) and *I Miss You* (1985).
- Midnight Star: *No Parking on the Dance Floor* (1983), *Freak-A-Zoid* (1983), and *Operator* (1985)
- Mr. Mister: *Broken Wings* (1985), *Is It Love* (1986), and *Kyrie* (1986)
- Quiet Riot: *Bang Your Head (Mental Health)* (1983), *Cum On Feel the Noise* (1983), and *Mama Weer All Crazee Now* (1984)
- Simple Minds: *Don't You Forget About Me* (1985), *Alive and Kicking* (1985), and *Sanctify Yourself* (1986)

I specifically mention the Three-Hit-Wonder category because my second favorite song of the decade is contained within the list: Simple Minds' *Don't You Forget About Me*. From the very first note–the sharp beat of a snare drum–the song just *feels* right.

It's happy.

It's joyous.

It makes me feel young.

It's also the theme song of, in my opinion, the best movie of the decade: *The Breakfast Club*.

---

30 I'm really going off on a tangent with this one. *Why Me?* peaked at #64 in 1983 which paved the way to me listening and loving, *I Won't Wake Up*. They're my own two-hit wonder, and I thank you for allowing me this indiscretion.

• • •

The glaring omissions from this music discussion are obvious: Michael Jackson, Madonna and Cyndi Lauper were *beyond* huge. Just a notch behind them were Billy Joel, Lionel Richie, and Bruce Springsteen. You'll have to wait for the revised version of this book when I dive deeper into the impact these superstars enjoyed. Fret not my friends! I've also neglected my favorite CD of the decade, Paul Simon's Graceland, so I feel your pain.

• • •

When Fab Morvan and Rob Pilatus, the duo better known as Milli Vanilli, released their album "Girl You Know It's True" in March 1989, there is no denying that they made a big splash.

Huge.

Their music, a mix of pop and funk sprinkled with a dose of rap, was a welcome alternative to their contemporaries—I'm thinking of Skid Row, specifically. After their self-titled song peaked at #2, three songs reached #1: *Baby Don't Forget My Number, Blame It On The Rain,* and *Girl I'm Gonna Miss You.*

I can hear Casey Kasem's giddy voice now. Seriously, I can.

What a debut! The CD went platinum six times over and they won the Grammy for Best New Artist in February 1990. Fab and Rob were on top of the world.

They were fit and trim; hell, they were *exotic.* They looked like professional athletes and, donned in their signature spandex, had the calves of Adonis.[31] Yeah, Fab and Rob were hitting on all cylinders during their brief rise to the top.

It's too bad, for them anyway that their recording skipped at the most inopportune time—in front of a live audience. And it's too bad that they freaked out and ran off stage, but what choice did they have?

There's no denying that Fab and Rob were lip-syncers extraordinaire. As quickly as their star rose, it plummeted back to earth in a God-awful thud of embarrassment and shame.

Stripped of their Grammy.

Purged by Arista Records of their very existence.

---

31   Adonis is that Greek stud who was the lover of Aphrodite—little Greek history lesson there people.

A class action lawsuit from "defrauded" fans.

Ridiculed.

So it wasn't them singing.

So what?

They were entertainers. They weren't selling the cure for cancer. So they couldn't sing. Homeboy's could dance, though. Why wasn't *that* good enough?

It wasn't good enough because they weren't truthful– OK, they *lied*–about their act. It's unlikely that the true singers–whomever they were (and, honest to God I don't care who they were)–would have enjoyed six *million* record sales with Fab and Rob acting as The Solid Gold Dancers.[32]

To be honest, I liked Milli Vanilli *even more* after the scandal. Did I feel duped? A little. What I felt even more, though, was *respect* for a couple of entertainers. What a couple of jokesters!

Were they phonies? Is that how you remember them?

In an informal office poll–the two girls on either side of my cubicle walls–I heard very different opinions. Brandy said they were "Sellouts. Lame, with a bad weave but pretty eyes," and Dawn said America was way too hard on them. Posing the question on Facebook ("What do you think of when you hear the words Milli Vanilli?"), almost all the responses were negative–i.e., "Fakers!" and "Guys with better hair than me who couldn't sing!" and "Losers with blue contacts!"

I'm not here to persuade you one way or the other but I will say this: I cherish my Milli Vanilli cassette tape and look for backups every time I peruse the Goodwill or a decent yardsale. Long live the lip-syncers of the world.

[March, 2012 update: Just scored the Milli Vanilli CD at the Bellevue Goodwill for $2.99! Mint condition! *Bitchen*, man!]

---

32   If you are a product of the eighties, there's no doubt you remember The Solid Gold Dancers–the TV show of spandex clad dancers gyrating to the Top 10 songs of the day. Much like Fab and Rob of Milli Vanilli.

APPENDIX 2

THOUGHTS ABOUT THE MOVIES

There were hundreds of movies that made up the decade and as far as bona fide *blockbusters* go, we'd have to include *ET–the Extraterrestrial*, *The Empire Strikes Back*, and the *Indiana Jones* movies. Commercially successful movies, aside, I'd rather mention the select few that were most memorable to me. In chronological order:

Perhaps the greatest sports related comedy of all time, *Caddyshack*, set the bar high in the wee days of the decade. With the all-star cast of Chevy Chase, Bill Murray, Ted Knight, and Rodney Dangerfield, *Caddyshack* is the classic story of underdog boy does good *and* gets the girl (more than one girl, at that). I (and, arguably forty million other guys) still have fantasies about Lacey Underall. Enough said.

A movie packed with one of the greatest eighties soundtracks ever is *The Last American Virgin*. With hits from Devo, Journey, REO Speedwagon, The Human League, The Cars (the list goes on), this 1982 movie centers around the age old, "Boy meets girl, other boy gets girl, first boy won't give up" storyline. Joe and I saw this in the theater and instantly loved it. With one of the best all-time lines (*"Come here my big burrrrrrito . . ."*), it's great fun–even if the movie ends with our hero driving off in tears. *Still a virgin. Still a loser!* The movie isn't well known because absolutely *no one* was a star (unless you count Steve Antin who is, perhaps, best known as "Jessie" in the Rick Springfield music video. Someone *had* to be Jessie. It may as well have been Steve Antin). Applying relational logic learned in my college philosophy class, Steve Antin is to Brad Pitt as *The Last American Virgin* is to *Fast Times At Ridgemont High*. Think about it.

I was sitting next to Joe in Algebra 2 our junior year and he could not stop laughing. "What?" I whispered loudly. Mrs. Cotta's Algebra 2 class was hard enough without his distraction.

"I just saw the funniest movie ever. You have *got* to see it." He began describing the hilarious scenes in *Top Secret!* That night, in 1984, we went to the Porter Theater and watched it. And laughed. And laughed. And laughed.

I don't know if *Top Secret!* was what launched Val Kilmer's career, but we became instant fans of this tall, blonde unknown actor. Slapstick humor, at that point was few and far between (the most notable being *Airplane!*).

One movie that I watch every time I come across it channel-surfing is the 1984 movie, *The Woman in Red*. I would test the unscientific theory that *every* American male in their early forties loves Gene Wilder. We grew up adoring him as Willy Wonka, The Waco Kid, and Dr. Fron-ken-steen. His collaborations with Richard Pryor (especially *Silver Streak* and *Stir Crazy*) are classic. Throw in Miss Kelly LeBrock, with her English accent and full, pouty lips, and any red-blooded, sixteen-year-old boy couldn't take his eyes off the screen. Watching our lovable underdog hero, goofy blonde perm and all, try to woo the prettiest thing of our generation is irresistible fun. An added bonus is that if you pause the movie at just the right moment, you can see Kelly LeBrock's bush. How cool is that?

Long before we knew him as Gil Grissom on *CSI*, William Peterson starred in the 1985 cult classic *To Live and Die in L.A.* The movie revolves around a rogue Secret Service agent hell bent on nailing a counterfeiter, played by the sinuous Willem Dafoe. Dafoe murders Peterson's partner and our hero stops at nothing in his quest for revenge. Wang Chung, of all guys (or is that a band?) provides a pounding soundtrack to the nonstop action.

Spoiler alert.

The thing that hooked me is the ending. How many heroes take a shotgun blast to the face? The day the movie came out on DVD many years later, I bought three copies: one for me, one for my brother, and one for my friend Mike. Turns out director William Friedkin didn't kill off our hero in one version. Unknown to us aficionados, but available to us on the DVD, Mike and I watched William Peterson take that same blast to the stomach then find him recuperating in a remote snow covered shack. Pale, sickly, and bored, but recuperating, nonetheless. Blasphemy I say! We preferred the shotgun blast to the face. So, too, did the director based on his final released version. Our hero lived fast, broke the rules, and ultimately crashed and burned–but what a ride!

The Breakfast Club deserves mention in everyone's short list of eighties movies. I am not alone since this 1985 movie is ranked No. 1 on *Entertainment Weekly's* list of the "Fifty Best High School Movies." That says a lot about a movie that takes place, in real time, inside a school library on a quiet Saturday. The cast includes members of the beloved "Brat Pack"–Molly Ringwald, Emilio Estevez, Ally Sheedy, Judd Nelson, and Anthony Michael Hall. It's a fun coincidence to me that, as different as *The Breakfast Club* is to *To Live and Die In L.A.*, both movies have Wang Chung music.

I had the pleasure of meeting Molly Ringwald when she came to Bellevue to sign her book, *Getting the Pretty Back: Friendship, Family, and Finding the Perfect Lipstick*. Does it count as meeting someone if you're a star struck guy in a line of all women waiting to have a book signed? She was very sweet and sincere with me. I made her laugh when I nervously blurted, "You are ten days younger than me and I just have to say, you look *absolutely fabulous*." I could almost hear Molly's French husband grinding his teeth, five feet away.

Another movie released at the same time as *The Breakfast Club* gained cult status as well: *Vision Quest*. This coming-of-age high school movie introduced us to Matthew Modine, Madonna, and the song *Lunatic Fringe*. It's your classic underdog story, complete with the tension of high school athletics, wooing a seemingly unimpressible older woman and beating the adversary.

Note: If actor Frank Jasper was 168 pounds in that movie, I will eat a whole cantaloupe–and I hate cantaloupe.

It's impossible not to love Matthew Modine. He's clumsy, thoughtful, happy and humble. We saw him later as Private Joker in Stanley Kubrick's 1987 Vietnam drama, *Full Metal Jacket*. I mention this not for his role, but for his line which was trail-blazingly sampled by The 2 Live Crew in the 1989 song, *Me So Horny*. The answer, if you don't know, to Modine's question is "every ting you want!"

One movie that is suitable for the whole family, save one word uttered by Mandy Patinkin toward the end, is the timeless classic, *The Princess Bride*. The story weaves its way along with much humor and love. Our hero does not die of a shotgun blast to the face. Oh, he dies but is brought back to life to save his true love. How charming is that?

One movie that pokes serious fun at the stereotypical casting of black actors–before the likes of Denzel Washington, Will Smith and Halle Berry gained super-stardom–is Robert Townsend's 1987 movie, *The Hollywood Shuffle*. Mr. Townsend funded the movie with his own credit cards. Despite this–or, maybe, because of it–the movie comes off as campy and hilarious. When actor Grand Bush (now *there's* a name), a graduate of "Black Acting School" rattles on about all the roles he's recently played (gangbangers, drug dealers, and convicts) art imitates art as he's all these things in the 1988 movie, *Colors*.

The last of the 1987 movies is Oliver Stone's *Wall Street*. Charlie Sheen is just plain cool. Not quite Steve McQueen cool, but cool none-the-less. Michael Douglas'

Gordon Gecko character is so over-the-top–how can anyone not love the slicked back hair and the shit-eating grin? What strikes me as funny is the scene with Michael Douglas watching the sunrise from his beachfront home. He's talking on the phone– but not just any phone–one of those *brick-sized* first generation cell phones. *Even then* they looked ridiculous. Gecko says that $800,000 is a day's pay–and there he is, speaking into the lamest phone known to mankind. My step-grandpa had that same phone and when he died in 1995, it was offered to me as a keepsake. I respectfully declined.

Speaking of slicked back hair, the Chuck Norris of the eighties has to be Steven Seagal. When the 1988 movie, *Above The Law*, hit the video shelves, we had six copies at National Home Video–which was a lot–and those VHS' rented nonstop for nearly a year. Mr. Seagal was a svelte, almost feminine, tough guy. With his jet black hair pulled back in a ponytail and scowl that looked like he had just stepped in pile of dog-shit, the guy was cool. I stopped watching his movies eventually. They were all pretty much the same story rehashed over and over and it worked when he was thin–not so much as the Pillsbury Doughboy.

The movie that was actually life threatening to see in the theater in 1988 was *Colors*. This movie introduced the world to the turf battles of the very real Bloods and Crips in Los Angeles. Real life fights and gunfire broke out in some L.A. theaters. When it came out on video, we had a serious discussion whether we should carry it. We didn't know if gangbangers in the San Fernando Valley rented movies and didn't really want to find out. (We did end up stocking it without incident.) Not that I like the movie for its glorification of violence. The brilliance is the real humanness of the characters. Some of the bad guys aren't that bad, and some of the good guys are far from good. Throw in a page from *To Live and Die In L.A.*,–namely, the good guy punching his ticket to the next life at the end–and the movie remains tragic and memorable. I also *love* the title song by Ice-T.

Honorable mentions:

- *The Shining* (1980 horror): From the mastermind Stephen King himself. Jack Nicholson at his best. To this day, I occasionally talk with my index finger.
- *Caveman* (1981 comedy): Really doesn't belong on this list but the fact it had all the junior high boys speaking caveman–specifically the word *zug-zug*–when looking at a pretty girl deserves some sort of recognition. It also

had a fart scene and, let's face it, in 1981 there weren't that many flatulent scenes (outside of *Blazing Saddles* I can't think of one).

- *Stripes* (1981 comedy): With the lovable Bill Murray and Harold Ramis–*Sergeant Hulka for President!*–who would team up again in Ghostbusters.

- *Poltergeist* (1982 horror): Movie where a piece of meat crawls across the table and bursts into a churning pile of maggots. That may have been the #1 topic of conversation during recess that year. That, and well-endowed seventh grader Wendy's boobs.

- *An Officer and a Gentleman* (1982 drama): Where a loser ultimately succeeds and gets the girl, despite getting kicked in the balls–literally–along the way. My favorite line is the whiny, "I've changed, sir! I've changed!"

- *All The Right Moves* (1983 drama): High school football and coming-of-age in a poor Pennsylvania steel town. Admittedly, I am a huge Tom Cruise fan and this isn't even his best eighties film by any stretch–*Risky Business* (any movie with Guido the Killer Pimp has to be good) and *Born On The Fourth of July* come to mind–but one scene in this movie steals the show. Tom's character is *so pissed off* that he can't even articulate words and takes his frustration out by sprinting away down the dark, wet street. Every seventeen-year-old guy can relate to this moment of ultimate frustration. If you pause the movie at just the right moment, it's rumored you can see Tom's johnson . . . not that I've ever tried.

- *Ghostbusters* (1984 comedy): This movie was so good it made the sequel look very, very bad. Saw it twice in the theater.

- *The Goonies* (1985 comedy/adventure): With names like Chunk, Sloth, the "*Where's The Beef?*" lady, the kid from *Rudy* and Steve Antin, this movie's a winner.

- *Weird Science* (1985 comedy): With the beautiful Kelly LeBrock, another John Hughes classic. Begged the question why anyone would be a wanker in front of her.

- *Fletch* (1985 comedy): With the bumbling, stumbling Chevy Chase. One of his best works.

- *Casual Sex?* (1988 comedy): One of the few Andrew "the Dice Man" Clay movies that exist. I saw this movie with my friend Katherine. We needed a laugh after I was on the receiving end of a traffic ticket from two motor-cycle cops–illegal u-turn–while she did everything in her power to hide the six pack of Lucky Lager on the floorboard. We did have casual sex that night so, all in all, the evening wasn't a total bust.

- *Dead Poet's Society* (1989 drama/feel good movie): Robin Williams' "carpe diem" speech still gives me goose bumps.

Ten more I love then I'll stop:

- *Stir Crazy (1980 comedy)*
- *History of the World, Part 1 (1981 comedy)*
- *Heavy Metal (1981 animated adult)*
- *Escape from New York (1981 action)*
- *The Dead Zone (1983 drama)*
- *A Christmas Story (1983 comedy)*
- *Mr. Mom (1983 comedy)*
- *Purple Rain (1984 drama)*
- *After Hours (1985 comedy)*
- *Say Anything (1989 comedy/romance)*

HOMAGE TO A FRIEND:

THE FIRST OF 290

It finally happened.

At work, the email subject line from Mike read: Sad News. Clicking on the link brought me to the *Visalia Times Delta* obituaries.

Ryan Bernasconi, a Visalia police officer who fought cancer since 2001, died Tuesday. He was 39.

This makes Ryan the first death out of the Monache High School graduating class of 1986. The first that I'm aware of and I've kept dibs on the local hometown of Porterville through the local newspaper's online obituary. Morbid checking the online obituaries on a daily basis? Perhaps, but somehow necessary.

As I sit here at my desk in Seattle, a thousand miles away from the Central Valley, I'm surprised at how sad this news makes me. I'm even more upset that my schedule won't allow me to attend his funeral two days from now. The funny thing is, I hadn't seen Ryan in twenty years. Funnier still, when we first met, we didn't even like each other.

My family moved to Porterville when I was twelve. Showing up ten days into the sixth grade year, unfortunately for me, made me the "new kid." The morning of the very first day, Ryan and a couple of guys asked if I could throw a football. I smiled and said nothing. I think a few of them felt threatened by me as an unknown factor and soon Ryan and I had tension between us. He made a crack about my long hair and name: "Tom-*Ass*." I made a remark about his last name and he invited me to *meet him after school to settle some things*. I wasn't much of a fighter and replied, "I ride the bus." Within days, we were friends.

In junior high, we played on the flag football team together (we went 5-1) but Ryan was much more competitive than I was and went on to play basketball and base-ball.

In high school, we tried out for the freshman football team. Tried out isn't exactly the truth, though, since everyone made the team. He quickly rose to quarter-back, Number 15, while I struggled at the thankless position of defensive cornerback, Number 21. It didn't matter that we only won one game out of ten that year. We were fourteen years old. Competing, checking out the cheerleaders, getting to know all the new kids in the universe known as high school. We were immortal.

I can't say that Ryan and I were the best of friends through school. That simply wouldn't be the truth. But we did share the formidable years of twelve to eighteen and there's a lot of growing up in those six irreplaceable, precious years. He dated and ended up marrying Deanna Hall, a girl that I'd also known since the sixth grade. Together they radiated a genuine bond of love. When two good people come together, well, that's a pretty special thing.

So I sit here at my desk in Seattle, twenty years removed from those times and I mourn the loss of someone I haven't seen or talked to in twenty years. He had been battling cancer for five years and I didn't even know he was sick. The paper says he has a son, Tyler, twelve, and a daughter, Krysta, eight. Synovial Cell Sarcoma took their daddy away and here I sit claiming to have a right to my grief.

What gives *me* the right to feel sad?

I'd say that a person is nothing more than a collection of the memories he makes. I lost a rare someone who goes back to my junior high and high school days. This feeling of sadness is that with his death a part of me has died as well. How many guys have I known since I was twelve? The list is short and now it's one gaping hole shorter. It's a feeling of helplessness, knowing that his death by this terrible, rare can-cer was nothing more than cruel randomness. Looking at his young, smiling face in our Senior Class yearbook, there was no way of knowing he wouldn't make it to our twenty-year reunion. It could have been any one of the two hundred ninety graduates of the class of 1986. For some reason, it was him.

I grieve for his children I've never met. I can't claim to know how they feel even though I lost my dad when I was ten. I had the luxury of distance and trauma–my dad lived a thousand miles away, and a single, accidental gunshot took his life. For me, he just wasn't there anymore. For Tyler and Krysta, they had to say their goodbyes and I'm sure that's infinitely worse. When my dad died, no one came forward to tell me what a great guy he was, that was left largely to my limited memories and imagination. For Tyler and Krysta Bernasconi, though, I have the ability–I have the obligation–to tell them about their dad.

When he was twelve.

When he was fifteen.

When he was eighteen.

Something tells me he was a topnotch police officer, a loving husband, a wonderful dad. Something in my soul knows these things as fact. He was on the Board of the Visalia *Wish Upon A Star* organization, a foundation sponsored by California Law Enforcement personnel dedicated to granting wishes to children with catastrophic illnesses. This makes me smile.

It will take time for me to get over Ryan's death, though I will always be sad knowing that he was the first of the Monache High School class of 1986 to leave us.

God speed Ryan Bernasconi.

May 10, 2006

Research Reading

20th Century Pop Culture: The 80s by Dan Epstein, Publisher: Chelsea House Publications

A Cultural History of the United State Through the Decades: The 1980s by Stuart A. Kallen, Publisher: Lucent Books

American Popular Culture Through History: The 1980s by Bob Batchelor and Scott Stoddart, Publisher: Greenwood

Generation of Swine–Tales of Shame and Degradation in the '80s by Hunter S. Thompson, Publisher: Simon & Schuster

Remember the 80s: Now That's What I Call Nostalgia! by Richard Evans, Publisher: Anova Books

Talking to Girls About Duran Duran: One Young Man's Quest for True Love and a Cooler Haircut by Rob Sheffield, Publisher: Dutton Adult

The Eighties: A Reader by Gilbert T. Sewall, Publisher: Da Capo Press

Totally Awesome 80s by Matthew Rettenmund, Publisher: St. Martin's Griffin

Books That Made Me a Better Writer

Tuesdays with Morrie by Mitch Albom, Publisher: Broadway

Just a Man: The Real Michael Hutchence by Tina Hutchence and Patricia Glassop, Publisher: Pan Books

Cash: The Autobiography by Johnny Cash, Publisher: HarperOne

Love Is a Mix Tape: Life and Loss, One Song at a Time by Rob Sheffield, Publisher: Three Rivers Press

The Life and Times of the Thunderbolt Kid: A Memoir by Bill Bryson, Publisher: Broadway

On Writing: A Memoir of the Craft by Stephen King, Publisher: Scribner

On Writing Well: An Informal Guide to Writing Nonfiction by William Zinsser, Publisher: Harper Paperbacks

Writing About Your Life: A Journey into the Past by William Zinsser, Publisher: Da Capo Press

Inventing the Truth: The Art and Craft of Memoir edited by William Zinsser, Publisher: Mariner Books

How To Write a Memoir by William Zinsser, Publisher: HarperAudio

Writing To Learn by William Zinsser, Publisher: Harper Paperbacks

In Cold Blood by Truman Capote, Publisher: Random House.

Breakfast at Tiffany's: A Short Novel and Three Stories by Truman Capote, Publisher: Modern Library

A Walk in the Woods: Rediscovering America on the Appalachian Trail by Bill Bryson, Publisher: Anchor

Into the Wild by Jon Krakauer, Publisher: Anchor

Honeymoon with My Brother by Franz Wisner, Publisher: St. Martin's Griffin

The Tender Bar: A Memoir by J.R. Moehringer, Publisher: Hyperion

How the World Makes Love . . . And What It Taught a Jilted Groom by Franz Wisner, Publisher: St. Martin's Press

Red: My Uncensored Life in Rock by Sammy Hagar, Publisher: It Books

Still Me by Christopher Reeve, Publisher: Ballantine Books

Nothing Is Impossible: Reflections on a New Life by Christopher Reeve, Publisher: Random House

Kiss Me Like A Stranger: My Search for Love and Art by Gene Wilder, Publisher: St. Martin's Griffin

Monster: The Autobiography of an L.A. Gang Member by Sanyika Shakur, Publisher: Grove Press

Good Rockin' Tonight: Twenty Years on the Road and on the Town With Elvis by Joe Esposito and Elena Oumano, Publisher: Avon Books

Still Life with Chickens: Starting Over in a House by the Sea by Catherine Goldhammer, Publisher: Plume

No Angel: My Harrowing Undercover Journey to the Inner Circle of the Hells Angels by Jay Dobyns and Nils Johnson-Shelton, Publisher: Broadway

Rawhide Down: The Near Assassination of Ronald Reagan by Del Quentin Wilber, Publisher: Henry Holt and Co.

Bossypants by Tina Fey, Publisher: Reagan Arthur Books

The Tylenol Mafia: Marketing, Murder, and Johnson & Johnson by Scott Bartz, Publisher: CreateSpace

ACKNOWLEDGEMENTS

First and foremost, I thank my wife, Susan, for her never ending love and support. Every night ends and every day begins with a kiss. Her almost childlike love and fascination with life is a daily inspiration to me.

To Margaret Land, my dear friend, former teacher, and mentor. Margaret taught me the comma rules in the tenth grade and, along the way, how to read and write critically.

My small circle of readers, turning the first-pass rock into a gem: Deanna Bernasconi, Chris Turner, and Chaz Serame. You guys will be thanked twice, incidentally.

My friends from the Good Old Days: John Flower (premierautovisalia.com), Mike Wells (the only guy I know who can do a back flip), Ed Hughes (the only guy I know who aced the SAT; also has impeccable taste in music and women), Alex Fermin (the greatest break dancer in a fifty-mile radius of Porterville back in the day), Tim "Bulldog" Miller (most talented sculptor in the world at tkmiller.com), Kellie Pengilly-Kroutil, Emerson Racca, Staci Noel, Deanna Bernasconi, the late Ryan Bernasconi, Donna Garrett-France, David Fine, David Facio, Leonard Pesta, Mike McMaster, Gina Pitigliano, the late Roxanne Ward, Richie Morris, Allen Raye, Sherman Smith, Bill Bushey, Eric Streiff, Don Johnson, Betsy Slattery, Ramiro Rodriguez, Cheryl Strong, Mari Deisman, Jennifer Sattler-Dalrymple, Kris Lambert, Brock Bovetti, Philip Gutzwiller, Frank Tate, Ruben Zamora, Ruben Castillo, Cruz Hernandez, Jaime Smith, Brendan Toney, Mike Watson, Ryan Todd, Bruce Havens, Hugh Callison, Mark Witcher, Mark Geistlinger, Jaime Chambers-Campbell, Brian Massey, Art Cain, Ken Cauwet, Robb Rugeroni, Wendy Ziebell, Linda Petrucelli-Swofford, Vicki Gentry, Mary Wobrock, Kelly Julian, Janette Waters, Kevin Barber, Mark Avila, James Avila, Russell Lentz, Melinda Horn, Jim "Big Blue" Lampman, Kevin "Snip Me Off" Moody, Richard Miguel, Keith "Stormin'" Norman, Jason Burns, Shawnie Gunn, Valerie Landsen-Duncan, Charlynn Weaver-Davidson, Stacy Tandy, Maureen Speakman-Waite, Chad Perigo, Phillip Smalley, Billy Thompson, Paula Zaninovich, Debbie Davila-O'Bosky, Darrell Latham, Crystal Claborn-Milinich, Kip Fallert, Shelley Furr, Diana ChaCha Oceguera, Serina Creekmore-Leslie, Katie Nutting-Moore, Tim

Paul, Melissa Gregg-Cabral, Val Cowan, Ted Burns, Jay Rice, Mike Sarr, Shannon Clement-Sexton, Pam Holt-White, Tracey Dudley-Wallette, Rhonda Stracener-Maine, Bryan Janeway, and Penny Locke. For those I haven't mentioned, I apologize for the oversight.

Former coworkers: Paul Moorhead and Alvis "Big Al"–"Alvis Has Left the Building"–Hodge. The late Steve Turner.

Former teachers: Erroll Vangsness, Paul "Skip" Sonksen, Bruce Lankford, Jane Smith, Hal Hevener, Carroll Land, Lisa Sampietro, Hans Budnarowski, Bob Briscoe, Randy Quiram, Travis Bierman, Charles Fishburn, Jim Crichlow, the late Carlos Valencia, and Rick Vafeades.

Former college professors: Melvin Weiss (CSUS), John Syer (CSUS), Morris Schonbach (CSUN), the late Helmut Haeussler (CSUN), Linda Kawaguchi (CSUN), Thomas Martinez (CSUB), Don "Do *Not* Call Me Doctor" Mason (CSUB), and "Multi-Employer Trust" Tim Brady (CSUB).

"Mr. Wonderful" Jim Holmes, Elissa Sime, Chaz "-a-Saurus" Serame and family, Chris Turner, the Wells family, the Abbott family, Kim K., Bill and Carol Klatt, Butch and AnneMarie Horn, William Bryan Nix, Derek Phillips, Don Ferguson, Paul Collard, John Lindsay, Paulie McKillop, Rob Spero, Gavin Anderson, Phil Christensen, LaMarcus Ford, Lee Fritz, Glen Gaz, Steve Hauser, Rick Henson, Gerry Horn, Matt McDaniel, Ron Robillard, Brooks Schomburg, Todd Stallworth, Kerry Steichen, Tim Stern, Tom Stice, Rick Wells, Michelle Kite, Suzanne Daly, Bob Strupp, Barb Mosley, Becky Bush, Bill Bauman, Brian "Uncle B" Morgans, Stephen and Sheryl Castro, Bob and Lance Beauchamp, Charles Price, Ed and Pam Santin, Bob and Mike Mars, Mark and Billy Hilton, Jill Patterson, Dr. Lee Herskowitz, Dr. Thomas Castle, Shawn Kemp, Eric Loverich, Lisa Story, Jake and Stephanie Miller, David Wanger, the Good family, Julia and Brenda Burke, Jennifer Vollmer, the Henrique family, Gary and Teresa Martin, Lorraine Smith, Maryellen Brady, Christian Haerle, Jaime "Anya Heels" Salazar (Rat City Rollergirl Sockit Wench Extraordinaire), Kris "Where No Sushi Is Safe" Uthaisilpa, Ken "Bald Is Beautiful" Moleski, and the North Carolina McCann Clan (Tom, Mary, Jason, Amy, Tommy, Chad, and Courtney). My in-laws Bud and Becca Barnett.

I'd like to thank the following musical artists for their inspiration:

First and foremost, the King of Rock and Roll, Elvis Presley. Elvis is alive and well in the hearts and souls of millions. He certainly lives on in mine.

Johnny Cash, Cash'd Out (the best Johnny Cash tribute band ever at cashdout. com), Marty Robbins, Loverboy, April Wine, Night Ranger, U2, Def Leppard, Led

Zeppelin, AC/DC, Ozzy Osbourne, Sammy Hagar, Pink Floyd, Depeche Mode, The Cars, Erasure, INXS, Poe, The Beastie Boys (rest in peace, Adam "MCA" Yauch), Chris Isaak, Israel Kamakawiwo'ole, Scorpions, Information Society, Roxette, Prince, Metallica, Alanis Morissette, Stabbing Westward, Seal, Nina Simone, Aaron Neville, Paul Simon, Rage Against The Machine, and Muse.

I'd like to thank the two greatest storytellers of our generation, Stephen King and Bill Bryson. Mr. King continues to entertain me-and millions of other Constant Readers–with his wicked storytelling ways. Mr. Bryson has, perhaps, written the best twenty four pages in existence (chapter twelve entitled "Out and About" in his book, *The Life and Times of the Thunderbolt Kid*).

I'd also like to thank author and fellow Generation Xer, Rob Sheffield, and his two marvelous books, *Love Is a Mix Tape: Life and Loss, One Song at a Time* and *Talking To Girls About Duran Duran: One Young Man's Quest for True Love and a Cooler Haircut*.

Author William Knowlton Zinsser and his phenomenally helpful books on writing.

To my co-workers and friends at Soundpath Health. OK, I'll list a few: Randee, Sadie, Diana, Bekka, Jeanette, Dawn, Vicki, and the rest of you! Need a Medicare Advantage product for your loved one? Check us out at soundpathhealth.com.

To Gloria Campbell of Sundial Press, LLC for her editing skills and Kirk Werner at itchydogproductions.com for his sound advice. Also, much thanks to Kris Dalbke Menneke, Davi Tavares and Kelly Gondek for their infectious enthusiasm.

Thank you to the gals at Bellevue Tropical Tan, both past and present (tropicaltan. net): Trish, Anna, Hayley, Brittini, and Nikki. I've been transformed from a whiter shade of pale to a golden god. (And thanks to Cameron Crowe for the "golden god" term.)

Thank you to my family–David, Lorne and Tricia–for letting me grow up into the person I am today. And the family that inherited the person I am now: nieces Hannah, Chloe, and Alli Kay, and nephew, Tommy. My father-in-law, Jerry Watkins. My sister-in-law and best mother I've ever known (outside of my own), Tamara.

To my mother, Patricia, who I miss with every breath I take.

To my uncle Harold, who was so full of passion–I wish I would have known him better during his lifetime.

To Grandma Bun and all the Walla Walla-based Harvey's.

To my best friend, Odie Dwayne Miller, who will forever be my inspiration. The night after Odie

died, he visited me in my dreams and said, "You should see what kind of deal I have now!" Thanks for checking in with me, my friend. If there's Coors Light in heaven, I hope God stocks it in longneck bottles–just how you like them.

Thanks to God, for the taste of passion fruit and the smell of brown sugar. For blue eyes. For puppy breath and puppy teeth. For little sisters and big brothers. For nieces and nephews. For grandmothers and step grandfathers. For a mom who called me "baby" for forty years.

Lastly, why support the Christopher and Dana Reeve Foundation? 1) Christopher Reeve was Mom's favorite actor and *Somewhere In Time* was her favorite movie, (and what kid doesn't love Superman?) 2) My brother, David, suffered a spinal cord injury and if it wasn't for a brilliant neurosurgeon by the name of Dr. Bahram Chehrazi he'd likely be in a wheelchair today, and 3) Odie wasn't so lucky and suffered a catastrophic spinal cord injury in an automobile accident. Paralyzed from the chest down, Odie died eight years to the day of his accident of multiple infections his body couldn't shake off. Research and advances in spinal cord injury treatments–I'm all for that!

Potential chapters for future versions:

- Death in the Ring
- Two Superstar Athletes That Weren't
- Purple Reign
- The Album of the Decade *was* a Thriller
- The Band With the Name We Couldn't Pronounce
- The Roots of Rap
- Hairbands!
- The Material Girl
- She *Was* So Unusual!

• • •

Look for my next book, currently in the works:

"Don't Fight With The Garden Hose
and Other Lessons I've Learned Along the Way"